Symbol, Myth, and Culture

Essays and Lectures of Ernst Cassirer
1935–1945

Edited by Donald Phillip Verene

New Haven and London   Yale University Press   1979

Published with assistance from the Ernst Cassirer Publication Fund.

Designed by John O. C. McCrillis and set in Baskerville type. Printed in the United States of America by The Murray Printing Company, Westford, Massachusetts.

Published in Great Britain, Europe, Africa, and Asia (except Japan) by Yale University Press, Ltd., London. Distributed in Australia and New Zealand by Book & Film Services, Artarmon, N.S.W., Australia; and in Japan by Harper & Row, Publishers, Tokyo Office.

Library of Congress Cataloging in Publication Data

Cassirer, Ernst, 1874–1945.
  Symbol, myth, and culture.

  Includes bibliographical references and index.
  CONTENTS: The concept of philosophy as a philosophical
problem.—Critical idealism as philosophy of culture.—Descartes, Leibniz, and
Vico. [etc.]
1. Philosophy—Addresses, essays, lectures.
2. Civilization—Philosophy—Addresses, essays, lectures.
3. Aesthetics—Addresses, essays, lectures.
4. Political science—Addresses, essays, lectures.
I. Verene, Donald Phillip, 1937– II. Title.
B3216.C31V47 1979   193   78-9887
ISBN 0-300-02306-5

Contents

Preface   vii

Introduction   1

PHILOSOPHY OF CULTURE

The Concept of Philosophy as a Philosophical Problem
(1935)   49
Critical Idealism as a Philosophy of Culture (1936)   64

PHILOSOPHY OF HISTORY

Descartes, Leibniz, and Vico (1941–42)   95
Hegel's Theory of the State (1942)   108
The Philosophy of History (1942)   121

LANGUAGE AND ART

Language and Art I (1942)   145
Language and Art II (1942)   166
The Educational Value of Art (1943)   196

THE MYTH OF THE STATE

Philosophy and Politics (1944)   219
Judaism and the Modern Political Myths (1944)   233
The Technique of Our Modern Political Myths (1945)   242

KNOWLEDGE AND PERCEPTION

Reflections on the Concept of Group and the Theory of
Perception (1945)   271

Appendix: A Description of Cassirer's Papers   293

Index   299

Preface

These writings are a selection from the unpublished papers of Ernst Cassirer which were acquired by Yale University Press in 1964 and are now housed in the Beinecke Rare Book and Manuscript Library at Yale. The papers range from a copy-book of notes from Cassirer's university studies, titled "Wundt, Psychologie I, Leipzig, Winter Semester 1892–93," to Cassirer's reflections on his essay "The Concept of Group and the Theory of Perception," including several pages of introduction written on the morning of his death, April 13, 1945. These reflections are the last selection in this volume.

I first came to know of Cassirer's papers through an exchange of letters with Charles Hendel in the spring of 1964, which quite by accident corresponded almost exactly with the time of the acquisition of the papers by the Press. It was not until May 1972 that I had the opportunity to see the papers. By that time they had gone from the offices of the Press to the Beinecke Library and a working list of them, totaling 219 items, had been prepared. It was at the time of this visit six years ago that my work on the papers began.

My work on them has been more than the scholarly task of handling unpublished manuscripts; it has been an opportunity for communication with Cassirer's spirit, for those experiences that come with seeing a thinker's work as it was written. To see the way in which various published works of Cassirer took shape, to observe how certain ideas were arrived at, to perceive the interconnections between projects, is to enter into a philosophical world in the making. This has had a considerable effect on my own interpretation of Cassirer and on my understanding of the significance of Cassirer's ideas themselves.

In selecting the papers for this volume I have centered on the last decade of Cassirer's life. This is the period in which most of Cassirer's unpublished work is concentrated. It is also a period of Cassirer's thought greatly in need of understanding, a period in which Cassirer was pointing to new directions in his thought which cannot be understood on the standard neo-Kantian interpretation—that is, the view that his thought is simply a development of the Marburg school of neo-Kantian epistemology. Cassirer appears here as a Kantian thinker, but one developing the basic insights of Kant in terms of the whole movement of modern philosophical idealism, including Hegel, and strongly concerned with the ethical understanding of freedom and humanity as the bases of culture. This is a point I have discussed in the introduction.

I have included in this volume only works which Cassirer himself prepared for oral presentation as lectures, either for graduate seminars, often with his philosophical colleagues in attendance, or for special occasions such as academic colloquia. The phrase "essays and lectures" in the subtitle of this volume indicates that Cassirer intended some of these writings to see print; for example, the lecture he gave at Princeton, "The Technique of Our Modern Political Myths," has indications of editorial preparation, and others show signs that he intended them for more than oral delivery. The fragment or draft of Cassirer's article "Judaism and the Modern Political Myths" is an exception to the principle that the papers of this volume were intended for public reception. It is included because it assists in understanding Cassirer's conception of political myths, an idea about which Cassirer's philosophy suggests so much, but is so briefly developed in his final chapter of *The Myth of the State*.

The reader will discover that some of the manuscripts overlap at points. Cassirer sometimes uses the same quotation or makes the same point. This is particularly true of the papers that comprise the section on Language and Art. I have not attempted to eliminate these repetitions. The papers were written by Cassirer as wholes, and the reader's patience at such points is rewarded by reading the whole rather than by perhaps wondering exactly what was left out by editorial attempt to streamline or otherwise condense papers. I believe this approach has special importance for the three papers on art, as they, together with his chapter on art in *An Essay on Man* and an earlier paper, "Mythic, Aesthetic, and Theoretical Space," are all that Cassirer wrote directly on the subject. They represent all that exists of Cassirer's plan, which I quote from one of his letters in the introduction, to include a volume on art in his theory of symbolic forms.

Eleven of the twelve manuscripts that comprise this volume are in English. The exception is the first, Cassirer's inaugural lecture at Göteborg, Sweden, which is in German. I have translated it here. The manuscripts, which are handwritten, were prepared for press by putting them into typescript and then checking the typescript word for word against the original. Manuscripts existing in both typescript and longhand were checked against each other. In preparing the manuscripts for press I have subjected them to principles of routine copyediting such as Cassirer himself, I believe, would have sought had he prepared them for publication.

No attempt has been made to reword Cassirer's thoughts or alter his style. Cassirer's style is not necessarily that of one whose native language is English, but his thoughts are always clearly expressed. I have indicated in a footnote where a break in the text occurs or there exists some matter of unclear order. The text of each of the selections follows the running text that appears in the original. The manuscripts frequently have lines, paragraphs, and sometimes whole pages crossed out; I have followed Cassirer's intentions and omitted them. Lest the reader feel that perhaps in this way important content is lost, let me point out that these deletions by Cassirer are made in almost all cases for stylistic reasons. Cassirer usually rewrote these passages and included them immediately or at a later point in the manuscript.

Cassirer, however, does not consistently supply bibliographic sources for his quotations and the works cited in the papers. I have in most instances supplied such references in the footnotes, with the designation "Ed." Those which were supplied by Cassirer or substantially supplied by him are designated by his name. In quotations Cassirer often seems to have inserted the passages from memory, resulting in some misplacement of phrases or ellipsis. Sentences are sometimes run together as a continuous quotation when in fact they are spread quite far apart in the work quoted. These are not cases where the meaning of the passage is distorted, and would be generally acceptable in oral presentation, but not in print. I have in most cases sought out the works and the passages from which Cassirer quotes and resolved his quotations with the original. I do not believe such editoral practices will meet with objection, but I feel a duty to convey to the reader how the manuscripts have been handled. Scholars with a deep interest in Cassirer can, of course, consult the manuscripts themselves.

It is my hope that this volume may introduce Cassirer's thought to those who do not know it or who know it only partially. It is my intention that it may be read by the specialist and the nonspecialist. Cassirer's approximately 125 published works comprise 11,380 pages. For comparison, this is very nearly the same number of pages as the Prussian Academy Edition of Kant's collected works. The introduction and the editorial footnotes throughout the papers are intended to direct the reader's attention to connections with these many published works. I wish to make clear that it is not my intention in the introduction and notes to present a critical interpretation of Cassirer's thought as such. Although I have approached Cassirer's work with definite interpretive views I intend these views to remain as open possibilities, as an invitation to readers to consider the papers from their own perspectives, as I have done from mine. The papers must ultimately be approached for what they are; that is, Cassirer speaking clearly and directly to an audience not familiar with his ideas, in most cases an American audience, to whom he wishes to make his thought understandable in a short space.

In preparing this volume I have had the help, encouragement, and patience of many people. The first agency to be thanked is Yale University Press itself. In 1948, in his preface to the Library of Living Philosophers volume on Cassirer, a volume which went to press even though Cassirer's sudden death occurred during its preparation, Paul Schilpp called attention to the need for some publisher to undertake English translations of Cassirer's major works. At that time only *Substance and Function* and *Einstein's Theory of Relativity,* bound in a single volume, and Cassirer's small study, *Language and Myth,* existed in translation. It was the Yale University Press that brought into English the three volumes of Cassirer's major work, *The Philosophy of Symbolic Forms,* and which continued to bring out other works in English translation. It was also the Yale University Press that published the two major works Cassirer wrote in English during his American years—*An Essay on Man* and *The Myth of the State.* What the Press meant to Cassirer can be seen from a sentence of his about it which Mrs. Cassirer quotes in her biography, "Es ist ein wirklicher Genuß, mit solchen Menschen zu tun zu haben." Gratitude is in order from all those interested in the ideas of Cassirer to the Yale University Press and to those, especially Charles Hendel, who have been associated with the editions and translations that have made Cassirer's thought available to the English-speaking world. It is hoped, of course, that translations will continue to appear, such as the first three volumes of Cassirer's monumental study of the history of the problem of knowledge which, although currently in print in German, remain inaccessible to the English reader.

This volume cannot go to press without my thanks to John Smith of the Department of Philosophy, Yale University, who in a conversation following my first visit to the papers suggested this volume and generously aided its launching. I also owe a debt of gratitude to the Yale University Press for its patience throughout the years that the preparation of this volume has stretched; I have always felt their support. I owe a particular debt, which cannot go unacknowledged, to Jane Isay of the Press, who in an early conversation suggested to me that the manuscripts be accompanied by footnotes indicating points of connection with other of Cassirer's works; had I not followed this procedure the volume would be quite different.

I wish also to thank Sir Ernst Gombrich of the Warburg Institute, London, who in reply to a letter sent at an early point of my interest in these papers requesting information concerning the date of Cassirer's lecture "Critical Idealism as a Philosophy of Culture," kindly supplied me with an original copy of the program of the institute titled *Lectures, Courses and Classes* for January–June 1936, along with his own remarks establishing the occasion of the lecture. Paul Schilpp, with whom I spent an afternoon in the archives of the library of Southern Illinois University, generously supplied me with copies of Cassirer's letters planning the Library of Living Philosophers volume, which provided the basis for understanding the sense in which art was part of Cassirer's original plan of *The Philosophy of Symbolic Forms.* I wish to thank Mrs. Elizabeth Bodenstein, formerly of the Department of German of The Pennsylvania State University, Hazleton Campus, for her technical linguistic assistance.

I wish especially to thank John Krois, who while completing his doctoral studies at Penn State and subsequently while teaching at the Technical University of Braunschweig, assisted with my work on these papers. The contributions to my thinking which Krois has made during our common study of Cassirer have strongly influenced this volume.

My wife, Molly Black Verene, has at times practically acted as coeditor of this volume, deciphering handwriting, searching for a source, and working long hours in verifying the accuracy of a typescript of a manuscript. Without such careful and sustained help this volume could hardly have been produced. I am deeply grateful.

Funds for the preparation of the manuscript have been provided from the "Cassirer account" at Yale University. In this regard I wish also to thank the Central Fund for Research of the College of Liberal Arts of The Pennsylvania State University.

University Park, Pennsylvania
March 8, 1978

Donald Phillip Verene

Introduction

1

The papers in this volume are part of the work of the last decade of Cassirer's life. They begin with his inaugural lecture at the University of Göteborg, Sweden, in the fall of 1935 and end with a lecture he was working on at the time of his death in the spring of 1945. It is not often that one encounters a thinker's unpublished papers and there is a tendency either to overrate or underrate their importance.

Two examples of unpublished papers in philosophy come to mind, those of the American philosopher Charles Sanders Peirce, and those of the founder of the phenomenological movement, Edmund Husserl. Cassirer's papers do not constitute the kind of corpus that gave rise to the Peirce Edition Project or the Husserl Archives of Louvain. However, they contain material of great interest to anyone concerned with the nature of the symbol, culture, history, art, and political myth and their significance for understanding humanity, freedom, and society. It is this range of topics, with the addition of Cassirer's theory of perception, which are treated in these papers. They are, of course, of considerable significance for persons with a special interest in Cassirer.

The papers are not only interesting in themselves, for the subjects they treat and the illumination they offer, but also for the picture of Cassirer they present. Anyone who comes to the works of this last decade with the view that Cassirer was a neo-Kantian primarily concerned with technical epistemological problems, perhaps mostly centering on the philosophy of science, who also turned his attention to the history of ideas and culture, will be greatly surprised. The interpretation of

Cassirer's thought has been dominated by the view that he followed the traditions of the Marburg neo-Kantian school of Cohen and Natorp and directed his attention to the application of Kantian philosophy to epistemology and the understanding of culture. The works of his American years that have been so widely read, that have gone through so many printings and been translated into nearly every major Western and Oriental language—*An Essay on Man* (1944) and *The Myth of the State* (1946)[1]—are regarded as exceptions involving no new direction in Cassirer's thought. They are seen as works of general interpretation written for his English-speaking audience. In a sense all this is true.

Short accounts of Cassirer's thought in histories of philosophy, encyclopedia articles, and passing references often follow this neo-Kantian approach. There is good reason for this, as all the evidence, in a sense, points in this direction. Cassirer's inaugural dissertation was written at Marburg at the turn of the century. His major professor was Hermann Cohen, the principal figure in a school of neo-Kantianism known for its emphasis on epistemology and science (though Cohen also published books on ethics, politics, religion, and aesthetics). Much of Cassirer's first work was in epistemology, philosophy of science, and logic.

Cassirer's monumental study of the problem of knowledge, *Das Erkenntnisproblem in der Philosophie und Wissenschaft der*

1. For full references to Cassirer's works see Carl H. Hamburg and Walter M. Solmitz, "Bibliography of the Writings of Ernst Cassirer to 1946," in *The Philosophy of Ernst Cassirer,* ed. Paul Arthur Schilpp (Evanston, Ill.: The Library of Living Philosophers, Inc., 1949), pp. 881–910 (chronologically arranged); and Raymond Klibansky and Walter Solmitz, "Bibliography of Ernst Cassirer's Writings," in *Philosophy and History: Essays Presented to Ernst Cassirer,* ed. Raymond Klibansky and H. J. Paton (New York: Harper Torchbooks, 1963), pp. 338–53 (arranged by subject matter). This is a revised bibliography of that which appeared in the first edition of this festschrift in 1936 and includes translations of Cassirer's works. Robert Nadeau, "Bibliographie des textes sur Ernst Cassirer," *Revue internationale de philosophie* 28 (1974), 492–93, notes several small items which these bibliographies omit. Not appearing in Nadeau's addendum is Cassirer's contribution to a collection of statements on chess by the chess master Edward Lasker, *Chess for Fun and Chess for Blood* (New York: David McKay, 1942), pp. 15–18. I am indebted to Professor David Lovekin, Sauk Valley College, Dixon, Illinois, for making me aware of this interesting statement. See also note 9 below.

neueren Zeit, originally published in two volumes between 1906 and 1907, was intended to show how the philosophical understanding of knowledge developed from the thought of Nicholas of Cusa and culminated in the philosophy of Kant. This study was later to be expanded to the period of Hegel and beyond in two more volumes. Cassirer was also the editor of a major edition of Kant's works which includes as the final volume his own book on Kant, *Kants Leben und Lehre* (1918). His first original work of systematic philosophy, *Substance and Function* (1910), was a theory of the interrelationship between logical theory and the formation of scientific concepts. This book was also the first to be translated into English (in 1923), and until the 1940s, when he began to write in English, it was the introduction of his thought for the English-speaking world. All of this lends weight to the neo-Kantian interpretation of Cassirer.

Cassirer's three-volume *Philosophy of Symbolic Forms* appeared in the 1920s and constitutes the basis of his original philosophy. Although Kant's influence is strongly felt in this work, Cassirer introduces the problem of a philosophy of symbolic forms as an outgrowth of the overall development of philosophical idealism, which he regards as a movement in modern philosophy from Descartes to Hegel whose roots lie in Plato's conception of idea and form. In his general introduction to *The Philosophy of Symbolic Forms,* Cassirer, in an often-quoted line, makes use of Kant to describe his project. Having indicated that each of Kant's three critiques takes up a different aspect of the human spirit, Cassirer speaks of extending the basic principles of idealism to other areas of human activity, and "thus," he says, "the critique of reason becomes the critique of culture."[2] *The Philosophy of Symbolic Forms* is a work of objective epistemology in which the forms of language and myth are treated as forms of knowledge in the first two volumes and, in the third, are conceived of as specific functions of consciousness, the *Ausdrucksfunktion* and *Darstellungsfunktion,*

2. *The Philosophy of Symbolic Forms,* trans. Ralph Manheim, 3 vols. (New Haven: Yale University Press, 1953–57), I, 80.

which become the bases for a developmental account of scientific-theoretical knowledge.

These volumes can be seen to employ the epistemological perspective for which Cassirer is known in the neo-Kantian interpretation of his work. This interpretation sees his historical works, *The Philosophy of the Enlightenment* and *The Individual and the Cosmos in Renaissance Philosophy*, both of which were written during the 1930s, as extensions of his scholarly interests, a widening of his neo-Kantian base but not a departure from it. It suggests that Cassirer's later American works, such as *An Essay on Man*, were undertaken at the urging of friends to present his ideas to his new American audience. In *An Essay on Man*, Cassirer himself refers the reader back to *The Philosophy of Symbolic Forms* for more detailed treatment of specific questions. According to this view *The Myth of the State* appears to take something of a new direction but it can be explained as Cassirer's response to the requests of American friends to tell them something of his understanding of the events that determined the life of the twentieth century during the Second World War. As a Jewish philosopher who had left Germany with the rise of the Nazi regime and as a scholar of culture, Cassirer could be expected to have views and reflections on the nature of the time.

All this, I think, contributes to the image of Cassirer as a neo-Kantian. In fact, the neo-Kantian interpretation seldom invokes such a full picture of Cassirer's thought and the course of his work. For the most part his thought is simply identified with its origins, with Kant and Marburg neo-Kantianism, and is thus classified and understood. Cassirer was quite aware of this problem and on two significant occasions he made his own views clear.

In his meeting with Heidegger at Davos, Switzerland, in 1929, Cassirer said in reply to an opening question by Heidegger about his neo-Kantianism: "One ought to think of neo-Kantianism in functional terms and not as a substantial entity. What matters is not philosophy as a doctrinal system but as a certain way of asking philosophical questions. . . . One understands Cohen aright only if one sees him historically, i.e., not merely as an epistemologist. I do not look upon my own development as a defection from Cohen. The status of the mathematical sciences of nature is only a paradigm for me and not the philosophical problem in its entirety."[3] Cassirer here explains his relationship to neo-Kantianism by using the distinction between substance-concepts and function-concepts which he had explained in *Substance and Function* nearly twenty years earlier, a work about whose fidelity to the neo-Kantian position Cohen himself had had some doubts. Cassirer claims that his position is to be understood in terms of his own notion of function, to be seen in terms of an original guiding principle that could enact a process of transformation and extension from a set of original elements.

On a second occasion Cassirer faces the question of his neo-Kantian origins in terms of the interpretation of science in his work *Determinism and Indeterminism in Modern Physics* (1936). His words show something of the tension evident in his earlier reply to Heidegger on the general relation of his philosophy to neo-Kantianism. As with his earlier essay, *Einstein's Theory of Relativity* (1921), he says that he expects the question whether his neo-Kantianism permits him to draw the conclusions he does. He points out that Cohen and Natorp saw Kant as the founder of a position, not as a "classical author" whose works contained the answers to all philosophical problems. Cassirer sees his relation to Cohen and Natorp in the same light. "So also," Cassirer says, "the ties which connect me with the founders of the Marburg School are not loosened and my debt of gratitude to them not diminished when in the following investigations it turns out that the epistemological examination of the principles of science leads me to results different from those set forth in Cohen's *Logik der reinen Erkenntnis* (1902) or in Natorp's *Die logischen Grundlagen der exakten Wissenschaften* (1910)."[4]

3. Carl H. Hamburg, "A Cassirer-Heidegger Seminar," *Philosophy and Phenomenological Research* 25 (1964), 213–14. See my discussion of Cassirer and Heidegger in the fourth section of this introduction.

4. *Determinism and Indeterminism in Modern Physics,* trans. O. Theodor Benfey (New Haven: Yale University Press, 1956), p. xxiv.

2

Cassirer owes much to Kant and Kantianism, but there is little question that he was also influenced by many other
thinkers, by Vico and Hegel as well as Descartes and Leibniz.
Hermann Cohen was probably quite right to say that even in
such an early work as *Substance and Function* (1910) Cassirer
had departed from the Marburg neo-Kantian position,
although Cohen was persuaded by his friends that this was not
the case.[5] Cassirer is more a Kantian than a neo-Kantian, and
he is more the creator of an original philosophy of the symbol, of culture and humanity, than he is the interpreter of
Kantian thought. Cassirer understood that to follow Kant was
not in the spirit of Kant himself, who said in the first *Critique:*
"We cannot learn philosophy; for where is it, who is in possession of it, and how shall we recognize it? We can only learn to
philosophise, that is, to exercise the talent of reason, in
accordance with its universal principles, on certain actually
existing attempts at philosophy, always, however, reserving the
right of reason to investigate, to confirm, or reject these principles in their very sources."[6]

Cassirer as a thinker became an embodiment of Kantian
principles, but also of much more, of an overall movement of
spirit stretching from the Renaissance to the Enlightenment,
and on to Herder's conception of history, Goethe's poetry,
Wilhelm von Humboldt's study of the Kavi language, Schelling's *Philosophie der Mythologie,* Hegel's *Phenomenology of Spirit,*
and Vischer's conception of the aesthetic symbol, among many
others. Cassirer's own position is born through a mastery of
the whole development of this world of the humanistic understanding, which included the rise of the scientific world view—
a mastery evident both in his historical works and in his
systematic philosophy.

Because Cassirer wrote so much—his published writings
comprise nearly 125 items, ranging from short articles to

5. *Philosophy of Ernst Cassirer,* pp. 20–21.

6. *Critique of Pure Reason,* trans. Norman Kemp Smith (London: Macmillan, 1933), A
838; B 866.

books of 800 pages—and because his writings range over a large number of subjects in history, linguistics, mythology, aesthetics, literary studies and science, in addition to his own original thought, it is very difficult to form an image of his philosophy as a whole. This is made even more difficult by the fact that Cassirer's academic "Odyssey," as he called it,[7] took him into different intellectual atmospheres just at the time when an interpretation of his ideas by other scholars might have arisen. Because of having to leave Germany with the rise of the Nazi regime in 1933 and the conditions of the Second World War, Cassirer was always on the move, always in a place where his basic works were unknown.

In addition, the understanding of Cassirer's philosophy is made difficult by Cassirer himself, by the way he presents his ideas. Cassirer is always thinking from the perspective of the world of humanistic thought and knowledge—the unity of spirit from the Renaissance to the nineteenth century—as well as from a contemporary point of view. His works of original philosophy are a continual series of quotations and references to supporting studies from other fields of knowledge. They are illustrations of his own doctrine that form cannot be understood apart from the content to be formed, and he sees this content as arrived at in a cooperative fashion by philosophy advancing its views in relation to other specialized fields.

Cassirer never argues his case. His case always arises out of what is there in human thought as it has actually developed. As he puts it in the preface to the third volume of *The Philosophy of Symbolic Forms,* in referring to his intention to relate his ideas to those of other philosophers: "The custom, which has once more become popular, of hurling one's ideas into empty space as it were, without inquiring into their relation to the general development of scientific philosophy, has never struck me as fruitful."[8] Although Cassirer's point concerns his relation to other philosophers, it is very close to a statement of his general intellectual method. One must always make Cassirer's

7. *Philosophy of Ernst Cassirer,* p. 56.
8. *Philosophy of Symbolic Forms,* III, xvi.

thought emerge for oneself. This is the case not only in the search for an overall understanding, where one must look to a very large number of works, many still in German, but even in the attempt to understand the individual works, for here Cassirer's own view often emerges indirectly, through his way of rendering his materials. All this must be done without the aid of any real tradition of commentary.

The interpretation of Cassirer that does exist is largely the work of individuals who have come to his philosophy on their own in the period after his death. The only work that comes close to providing a basis of interpretation is the volume on Cassirer's philosophy in the Library of Living Philosophers series published in 1948, which contains essays by some of Cassirer's former students, colleagues, and associates. Although these essays are quite helpful for understanding Cassirer's thought and have been widely read, they are not greatly critical in tone and very few of the twenty-three contributors published further work on Cassirer.[9]

Cassirer himself was not really a member of any philosophical movement, nor did he found one. The interpretation of his thought, what there is of it, has no one major focus, for it arises out of the power of his philosophy, or some aspect of it, to strike particular individuals. Given all of these difficulties, it is no wonder that the attempt to characterize Cassirer's work has followed the line of least resistance. His work has simply been classified according to its origins, in the light of his earliest reputation and work. The origin of his philosophy is important, but typifying it in this way provides less under-

9. The principal exception is Carl H. Hamburg, *Symbol and Reality: Studies in the Philosophy of Ernst Cassirer* (The Hague: Martinus Nijhoff, 1956). Also Susanne Langer's work must be considered, although not directly interpretive (see note 23). For a comprehensive bibliography of writings on Cassirer's philosophy see Donald Phillip Verene, "Ernst Cassirer: A Bibliography," *Bulletin of Bibliography* 24 (1964), 103, 104–06, and "Ernst Cassirer: Critical Work 1964–1970," *Bulletin of Bibliography* 29 (1972), 21–22, 24. These two bibliographies are joined and extended by Nadeau, "Bibliographie des textes sur Ernst Cassirer," *Revue internationale de philosophie*, 28 (1974) 492–510. As these bibliographies include writings on Cassirer's thought in all languages they demonstrate the quite limited amount of critical literature that exists on Cassirer (Nadeau's list shows a total of 288 items, including doctoral dissertations and all other types of publications).

standing of Cassirer than such guides to the nature of a philosophical position usually do. Such an immediate image is
always by nature misleading, but in Cassirer's case it seems to
have hampered understanding more than usual.

I hope to put aside or at least modify this view of Cassirer
as a neo-Kantian so that the papers of this volume can be
understood. In themselves they offer the reader the best reasons for modifying it or holding it in doubt. What they present goes against the picture of Cassirer as a neo-Kantian
viewing the problems of human culture and knowledge at a
distance and seeing philosophy as a self-contained intellectual
activity that can be pursued apart from the actual problems of
humanity.

In saying this I do not mean to deny the positive contributions
of the major works of the neo-Kantian movement nor to equate
neo-Kantianism with the wider landscape of post-Kantian philosophy in which Cassirer's thought finds its place. I want only to
encourage the reader to avoid placing Cassirer's thought in a
particular, neo-Kantian framework, and then interpreting it
from this point of reference. This is particularly dangerous
because the traditional Anglo-American interpretation of Kant
has tended to identify his thought with the problems of the early
parts of the first Critique. This tradition has recently begun to
change, but in the past it has, for example, neglected Kant's conception of form and the theory of "reflective judgment" in the
third Critique, as well as Kant's concern with history, the state,
and philosophical anthropology, all of which so greatly interested Cassirer.

The neo-Kantian image of Cassirer as an epistemologist unin-
terested in philosophy as a normative activity is overturned by
Cassirer himself in the first lecture of this volume, his inaugural
lecture at the University of Göteborg. Here he declares that
there are two concepts of philosophy, the *Schulbegriff* (the "scholastic" conception of philosophy) and the *Weltbegriff* or *conceptus
cosmicus* (philosophy as related to the world); he admits he has
been guilty of the former but goes on to endorse the latter. In
fact, he takes this distinction from Kant.

I believe that Cassirer's theory of culture after 1933 can be seen as an attempt to come to an understanding of what it means to be human, to work out concepts of human freedom and society. I do not mean to imply that there is no basis for this in his earlier philosophy. He showed something of this concern in his work *Freiheit und Form*, which appeared in 1916 during the First World War, and in essays on more specific topics. The groundwork for the openly normative turn in his thought is laid in his analyses of culture as freedom and knowledge in his work during the first three decades of his career. In 1929 his primary question to Heidegger was about the place of human freedom in the latter's theory of being, a question that is taken up in relation to Spengler's conception of history in the essay "Philosophy and Politics" (1944, herein) and in *The Myth of the State* (1946).

3

Cassirer's philosophy always moves by a shifting of emphasis. Thus he does not make a sharp break to take up normative questions but instead bends his philosophy slowly in this direction. He does not become a political activist nor a follower of *Lebensphilosophie*, or "life-philosophy," a position he was always concerned to distinguish from his own and which he thought was opposed to a philosophy of spirit. He begins at this time to make the question of freedom central to his philosophy. He makes clear his view of the relation philosophy can have to society in the final chapter of *The Myth of the State* and in his analysis of political myths in the papers that follow. Philosophy can allow us to understand events and to formulate human ideals, but it is not a direct agent of change.

Cassirer's thought always involves a kind of objective vision, and he never forgets the value and power of this standpoint. Yet it is not that of pure epistemology. In Cassirer's view philosophy has a duty to society, the duty to preserve and further general understanding of the ideals on which social life and civilization are based. During this period Cassirer never gives up his interest in technical problems in philosophy. The last two lectures of this volume reveal these two aspects, one concerning the social and political dimensions of myth and the other the technical problems of the concept of group and perception, and it is typical that the two together should have occupied Cassirer during the last months of his life. He understood throughout this period of his devotion to philosophy as *Weltbegriff* that philosophy has duties to man as a knower as well as to man as a social animal, that investigation into technical problems of knowledge and perception must be carried on side by side with philosophical investigation of social life. He understood that philosophy must be able to deal with the problems of theoretical inquiry if it hopes to understand the social actions of man. What I think shocks Cassirer about the attitude of the German philosopher Lotze toward non-Euclidean geometry (which Cassirer mentions in his essay on the concept of group herein) is Lotze's willingness to dismiss such technical change in conceptual knowledge, as if philosophy had the power to do so. It shocks Cassirer, even though in this case a technical development is dismissed not to have a more "vital" grasp of existence but to pursue metaphysical logic.

In his work in the last decade of his life Cassirer is always attempting to bring his philosophy to grips with culture as something alive and concrete. This can be seen even in the historical investigations he published in Sweden. In his work on Descartes and Queen Christina *(Descartes,* 1939), he no longer looks at Descartes's philosophy purely in terms of the meaning of his philosophical principles, as he had earlier in the introduction to *Leibniz' System* (1902) and in the first volume of *Das Erkenntnisproblem* (1906), but instead turns to a consideration of the concrete conditions of its enactment and effect. Cassirer's original works of philosophy also involve a shift to a consideration of culture as a concrete process and normative activity. This can be seen in his distinction between naturalistic and humanistic theories of culture in his essay "Naturalistische und humanistische Begründung der Kultur-Philosophie" ("Naturalistic and Humanistic Foundation of the Philosophy of Culture") (1939), appearing the same year as his new Descartes study.

The Logic of the Humanities (1942) ends with the essay "The Tragedy of Culture," which discusses human creativity and the relation of the individual to culture. Culture is seen as the man-

ifestation of the individual's freedom as creative agent.[10] Behind
this is Cassirer's concern, which goes back as far as his essay
" 'Spirit' and 'Life' in Contemporary Philosophy" (1930), with
seeing culture as a transformation of life. Cassirer understands
culture as the fulfillment of life, not as an alienation from its
concreteness. This normative understanding of culture, this conception of culture as freedom, as an activity of "progressive self-
liberation," forms the basis of *An Essay on Man*.

An Essay on Man is not just a summary with some new reflections on old material, although it is this too. It begins with the
ethical problem of the "crisis in man's knowledge of himself"—
the problem of the fragmentation of contemporary life into the
various regions of human thought and culture. Man cannot
grasp himself and his world as a unity. He is faced with as many
views of man as there are fields that study man and areas of
human activity. Cassirer offers his answer to this fragmentation
in his definition of man as the symbolizing animal, the *animal
symbolicum*. It is the symbol that pervades all the activities of man
and on which all of culture depends. He takes up again the
problem of the connection between life and spirit. But now he
sees it in terms of the relation of biological interpretations of the
world to cultural ones. Here the symbolic function of man is por-
trayed as related to but distinct from the sign-activity of animal
mentality. He calls attention here, as in the papers of this volume, to the biologist J. von Uexküll's idea that every organic
being lives within its own specific world: "In the world of a fly,"
says Uexküll, "we find only 'fly things'; in the world of a sea
urchin we find only 'sea urchin things.' "[11] For Cassirer the
power of the symbol makes possible the world of "human
things," but it is not presented simply in terms of the epistemological problem of the relation of life to spirit or culture. For Cassirer the symbolizing power of the human world makes possible
the ethical, the movement from "facts to ideals" that is found
only in the human realm.

10. See Donald Phillip Verene, "Cassirer's Concept of Symbolic Form and Human Creativity," *Idealistic Studies* 8 (1978), 14–32.

11. *An Essay on Man* (New Haven: Yale University Press, 1944), p. 23.

The ethical is not possible apart from the ability to create the world of the ideal. This ability depends on the power of the symbol to transform the immediately given into the mediated objects of culture. This transformation brought about by the symbol is the distinctive mark of the human world. *An Essay on Man* is guided by a normative concern, by an attempt to make use of philosophy to make sense of the world of culture as a coherent project of human reason and imagination and, simultaneously, as a process of freedom, of "progressive self-liberation," as Cassirer calls it in the last paragraph of the work. It is an attempt to help us find our way within the social fragmentation of twentieth-century life. Cassirer is here performing, in his own way, the act of duty Schweitzer enjoins and for whose neglect he blames philosophy in his analysis of contemporary civilization (Cassirer refers to Schweitzer's ethical conception of philosophy in his lecture, "The Concept of Philosophy as a Philosophical Problem," and elsewhere in the essays herein).

Although it arose out of suggestions made by friends that he convey his views of the contemporary period, *The Myth of the State* must, more importantly, be understood as an extension of the project begun in *An Essay on Man,* the normative project involving the duty of philosophy. In *The Myth of the State* Cassirer takes the most important and original part of his philosophy of symbolic forms, his theory of myth, and shows how it provides the necessary basis for understanding the social life of the twentieth century.[12] Cassirer is the only major philosopher of the twentieth century to have developed a theory of myth. It grew out of his understanding of the philosophies of myth in the eighteenth and nineteenth centuries, notably his reading of Vico and Schelling.

In *The Myth of the State* he takes up human culture, not as a general enterprise, but as a historical and social structure, not culture as such, but society, the state, and political life. Specifically his goal is to understand our own time, the political life of the twentieth century. All of the power of his analysis of myth

12. See Donald Phillip Verene, "Cassirer's View of Myth and Symbol," *Monist* 50 (1966), 553–64.

and his historical perspective are brought to bear on a specific problem. He presents the nature of mythical mentality in the first part of the work and in the second traces the development of the notion of the state. In the third he generates an original but all too brief insight into how the logic of myth has come to constitute the basis of twentieth-century life. This brief vision was not to be developed, for he died before the manuscript was through press. But his essay "Judaism and the Modern Political Myths" (1944), together with the essays on political myth in this volume, offer some expansion of his views.

4

The course of Cassirer's thought in the last decade of his life, at least in its broad outlines, can, I hope, be seen from these remarks on his published works. But what do the unpublished works add to this? What do they contain? They do not contain discussions of topics and ideas that Cassirer never put in some way into print. The unpublished works, like the published works, overlap and flow into each other. Often the same quotations, sources, and authors are used from work to work. Cassirér, however, never truly repeats himself. What recurs is always seen in a new light. It is always shifting, much in the way that he claims categories shift their specific "tonality" (*Tönung*) from one symbolic form to another.[13]

The papers often reflect the ideas that formed the basis for the works Cassirer published at the time. For example, there are many instances of use of the same or nearly the same passages that find their way into *An Essay on Man* or *The Myth of the State*. However, what we find here is not the Cassirer of the published work. We find something—and as much as we ever can or will find—of Cassirer speaking directly, doing what we so often wish he would do in his published works. We want Cassirer to appear and speak concisely, to present his case. This is what he does in the papers. On each occasion Cassirer is explaining in a short space the nature of his ideas, and explaining them to an audience to whom he must immediately relate and for whom he must

13. *Philosophy of Symbolic Forms*, II, 60–61.

make his thought understandable. He cannot presuppose knowledge of his other works, as the audiences to which he is speaking generally had little.

The occasional overlap between parts of these papers and *An Essay on Man* or *The Myth of the State* should not be allowed to detract from the awareness that Cassirer is speaking more fully on a number of subjects than he ever did in his published works. The first essay concerns the nature of philosophy, a topic that Cassirer never takes up directly in his published works. His discussion in "Language and Art" is of sufficient length and substance to constitute a companion to his little volume *Language and Myth*, which has so often served as an introduction to Cassirer's philosophy. "The Technique of Our Modern Political Myths" was written as a summary and introduction to *The Myth of the State*.

In these papers Cassirer deals with various problems crucial to his philosophy—the sense in which culture is the empirical given necessary to make philosophical idealism work, the superiority of the Vichian to the Cartesian theory of truth, the validity of Hegel's conception of right, the problem of causality in historical explanation, the relation of morality and art, the view that the concept of group is not simply mathematical and physical but applies to all areas of thought.

The reader of these papers will see that Cassirer always keeps Kant present in his thoughts. Kant occupies much the same position here as in Cassirer's published works; he is a permanent point of reference. Cassirer's Kantianism is wider than the neo-Kantian movement of the turn of the century as it is generally understood (though neo-Kantianism is in need of creative reinterpretation and has positive philosophical ideas to offer which Cassirer himself never forgot). His Kantianism is based on a view of Kant much wider than the one that dominated Anglo-American philosophy up to the middle of the twentieth century. This approach tended to limit its interest to the "Aesthetic" and "Analytic" sections of the first Critique, with some attention to problems of Kant's "formalism" in ethics. It is this rather narrow approach to Kant's philosophy as an epistemology of theoretical reason from which I have attempted to free Cassirer's image as a thinker, rather than from the multifaceted dimensions of Kant's thought itself.

CASSIRER'S BIOGRAPHY

It will be helpful in approaching these papers if the pattern of Cassirer's intellectual life is kept in mind, what he referred to in his closing remarks to the Yale Philosophical Club as the "Odyssey" of his academic life. What is commonly known of Cassirer's intellectual career is that he received his degree from Marburg, wrote and taught in Germany, left Germany in the early period of Nazism, and spent his last years in America, having been for a short period in Sweden. This gives the basic facts. What I wish to do is to give a fuller picture so that the background events of the last decade of his life can be clearly seen. This temporal framework will not provide a biography of Cassirer, but only a kind of schema within which the general character of Cassirer's work can be seen.[14]

Cassirer was born on July 28, 1874, in Breslau, Silesia, and died suddenly on April 13, 1945, on the Columbia University campus. The events of his life can be seen in terms of the universities at which he taught. As a student he studied at Berlin, Leipzig, Heidelberg, and Marburg, completing his inaugural dissertation on "Descartes' Kritik der mathematischen und naturwissenschaften Erkenntnis" ("Descartes' Critique of Mathematical and Natural Scientific Knowledge") in 1899. This was printed as the introduction to his first work, *Leibniz' System* (1902). His major professor at Marburg was Hermann Cohen. After a short residence in Munich, Cassirer, his wife, and the first of their three children moved to Berlin.

Upon the publication of the second volume of his study of the problem of knowledge, *Das Erkenntnisproblem in der Philosophie und Wissenschaft der neueren Zeit* (1907), Cassirer submitted the

---

14. My remarks are dependent on the two biographies of Cassirer: Dimitry Gawronsky, "Ernst Cassirer: His Life and Work" in *The Philosophy of Ernst Cassirer,* pp. 1–37; and Toni Cassirer, *Aus meinem Leben mit Ernst Cassirer* (New York, privately issued, 1950). For a study of Cassirer's intellectual development in relation to his times see David R. Lipton, "Ernst Cassirer: The Dilemma of a Liberal Intellectual in Germany 1914–1933," Ph.D. dissertation, University of Toronto, 1975.

work as part of his credentials in applying for the position of *Privatdozent* at the University of Berlin. The first two volumes of *Das Erkenntnisproblem,* as mentioned earlier, trace the development of the theory of knowledge from Nicholas of Cusa to its culmination in Kant. In the final chapter Cassirer advances an interpretation of Kant's theory of the *Ding-an-sich,* and this he presented in his lecture as a candidate for the position at the University of Berlin. Following the lecture, Gawronsky reports, it was Wilhelm Dilthey who provided the crucial support for Cassirer's appointment.

Cassirer lived in Berlin between October 1903 and October 1919. During this period, besides numerous articles, he produced a three-volume edition of the philosophical writings of Leibniz and his ten-volume edition of Kant's works. Besides the first two volumes of *Das Erkenntnisproblem,* he published three major books: *Substance and Function* (1910), his theory of science; *Freiheit und Form* (1916), a study of German *Geistesgeschichte* which explores the humanistic ideals of German culture; and *Kants Leben und Lehre* (1918), the final volume of his edition of Kant's works. As Gawronsky reports, Cassirer was drafted for civil service during the First World War and was assigned work reading foreign newspapers. He also wrote the third volume of *Das Erkenntnisproblem,* which extended the discussion beyond Kant to Hegel and the post-Kantian systems of idealism. This was published in 1920.

In October 1919 Cassirer assumed the chair of philosophy at the newly founded University of Hamburg, where he remained until May 1933. He was elected rector of the university in 1930. During this fourteen-year period Cassirer published his major work of systematic philosophy, the three volumes of *The Philosophy of Symbolic Forms: Language* (1923), *Mythical Thought* (1925), and *The Phenomenology of Knowledge* (1929). Gawronsky remarks that Cassirer once related that his conception of the symbolic forms occurred to him when he was on a streetcar in Berlin in 1917. In the preface to the first volume Cassirer states that this conception goes back to his views in *Substance and Function* (1910), which is no doubt the systematic beginning point, the psychological beginning point being in the year 1917. It should be noted in reference to Cassirer's neo-Kantianism that he refers to Hegel at the beginning of each volume of *The Philosophy of Symbolic Forms,* at points where he describes the nature of his task, and in fact he identifies his conception of phenomenology in the third volume, *The Phenomenology of Knowledge,* with Hegel's sense of phenomenology.[15]

Shortly after coming to Hamburg, Cassirer visited the Warburg Institute. The institute became a major part of his sphere of activity while in Hamburg, and he became one of the central figures in its life.[16] Although Cassirer states in the preface to the second volume of *The Philosophy of Symbolic Forms* that the initial drafts of his study of myth were already completed when he first visited the institute, it is clear from what he says both here and in the preface to the first volume, that the Warburg Institute library, with its unique arrangement of materials, influenced his theory of culture and the symbol. The Warburg Institute published Cassirer's *Language and Myth* (1925), *The Individual and the Cosmos in Renaissance Philosophy* (1927), and *The Platonic Renaissance in England* (1932). At this time Cassirer also published *The Philosophy of the Enlightenment* (1932).

During this period Cassirer published two collections of literary essays, *Idee und Gestalt (Idea and Form)* (1921) and *Goethe und die Geschichtliche Welt (Goethe and the Historical World)* (1932). The first of these contains essays on Goethe as well as on Schiller, Hölderlin, and Kleist. Cassirer's interest in literature was considerable, centering on Goethe, who was a major influence on his thought and a frequent source. Mrs. Cassirer reports that Cassirer had received the Weimar edition of Goethe's works as a wedding gift and used its 135 volumes continuously throughout his life, keeping them with him through all their moves, including the final move to the United States. His interest in Goethe stretches from his discussions in *Freiheit und Form* (1916) and Goethe's "Pandora" (1918) to his lecture "Thomas Manns Goethebild" during the last year of his life (1945).

15. See Donald Phillip Verene, "Kant, Hegel, and Cassirer: The Origins of the Philosophy of Symbolic Forms," *Journal of the History of Ideas* 30 (1969), 33–46.

16. See "Critical Idealism as a Philosophy of Culture," herein, notes 14, 16, and 26 for explanation of Cassirer's relationship to the Warburg Institute.

The sixteen years of the Berlin period Cassirer devoted to work on the major figures of modern philosophy and on the theory of scientific and theoretical thought that became *Substance and Function*. During the fourteen-year Hamburg period he expanded his theory of knowledge to a philosophy of culture and symbol and developed an account of the spirit of modern philosophy. There are considerable differences between the account of modern philosophy given in *Das Erkenntnisproblem* and the one given in *The Individual and the Cosmos in Renaissance Philosophy, The Platonic Renaissance in England,* and *The Philosophy of the Enlightenment.*

In Cassirer's earlier accounts we see each doctrine treated purely in terms of its philosophical principles and concepts; the motion is that of the logical development of one idea to another. Philosophy is understood as an activity of pure thought with primary connections to other structures and problems of theoretical knowledge. In the three later works much of the same historical ground is gone over but here philosophy is understood in its connection with culture, and the culture of philosophy—the philosophical spirit of the modern world—is Cassirer's main concern. Here the movement does not follow the intellectual connections between principles but philosophical ideas as historically active and self-developing. Cassirer says, in the preface to his work on the Enlightenment, that he has tried to present, in this and the two works before it, a "phenomenology of the philosophic spirit." Thus, as he expands his theory of knowledge to a theory of culture, he also goes back over the history of modern philosophy and presents it as a dimension of the overall movement of culture.

This is not, however, to say that Cassirer loses his interest in the philosophy of science. Just as he continued throughout his life to write on literature and aesthetics, a series of works that passes from *Freiheit und Form* in 1916, through the literary essays of this period, to articles of the last decade, so his writings on particular problems in the philosophy of science span his entire career. These move from *Substance and Function* in 1910, to his essay on Einstein in 1921, to his work on *Determinism and Indeterminism in Modern Physics* in 1936, and on to several articles relating to science and the history of science in the last five years of his life.

On January 30, 1933, Hitler became chancellor of Germany. On May 2, 1933, Cassirer left his position at Hamburg. He accepted an invitation for a one-year visiting appointment at All Souls College, Oxford. The Cassirers arrived in Oxford in September 1933, after a summer trip to Vienna. It was at Oxford that Cassirer briefly met Schweitzer. Cassirer had to learn to speak English and to teach in English, although the first term he taught in German. His courses were on Kant, Hegel's *Philosophy of Right,* Leibniz, and Plato. He maintained his connection with the Warburg Institute, which had been moved to London in 1933. Cassirer's position at Oxford was renewed for a second year, until the spring of 1935. During this time his son, H. W. Cassirer, whose studies were broken off in Switzerland, took a position at the University of Glasgow, becoming a colleague of H. J. Paton. H. W. Cassirer was later to publish his study of Kant's third Critique in 1938 and one of Kant's first Critique in 1955.[17]

During the period when Cassirer was in England the Festschrift titled *Philosophy and History* was prepared by Raymond Klibansky and H. J. Paton for his sixtieth birthday. It contained essays by many distinguished thinkers, including Samuel Alexander, Léon Brunschvicg, Étienne Gilson, Giovanni Gentile, Theodor Litt, Émile Bréhier, Lucien Lévy-Bruhl, and José Ortega y Gasset.

Cassirer next accepted a professorship at the University of Göteborg in Sweden and arrived there in September 1935. He remained until the summer of 1941. Cassirer published *Determinism and Indeterminism in Modern Physics* in the Swedish publication *Göteborgs Högskolas Arsskrift* and wrote several studies on Descartes, particularly on Descartes's dialogue *Recherche de la vérité.* These investigations were brought together in a volume on Descartes's thought, personality, and influence, which discusses

17. *A Commentary on Kant's Critique of Judgment* (London: Methuen, 1938) and *Kant's First Critique: An Appraisal of the Permanent Significance of Kant's Critique of Pure Reason* (London: Allen and Unwin, 1955).

at length the relationship between Descartes and Queen Christina of Sweden. Cassirer also wrote a study of the Swedish philosopher Axel Hägerström, the founder of the influential Uppsala School of philosophy in the 1920s and 1930s. This might be considered rather peripheral, and it is difficult to understand why Cassirer produced such a study except in the light of the contention that after 1933 his philosophy takes a normative turn that centers on a concern with how philosophy is to stand in relation to society.

One of the important shortcomings Cassirer pointed to in Hägerström's philosophy was a nihilistic theory of value according to which statements of value cannot be true or false and all values are emotive and subjective in character. These were views that Cassirer could not accept, as he could not accept Hägerström's negative approach to the *Geisteswissenschaften*. As Cassirer says in his preface, in words very typical of the way he approached such situations: "I have nowhere sought polemic for its own sake, indeed I have intentionally avoided it. But I have in the development of my thought and my scholarly work gone in a wholly different direction than Hägerström and I have had, in regard to many fundamental problems, to oppose results such as he arrives at."[18]

In 1940, as the war in Europe escalated, Cassirer wrote *The Logic of the Humanities* and the fourth volume of *Das Erkenntnisproblem* in rapid succession.[19] *The Logic of the Humanities* appeared in Sweden in 1942, after Cassirer had arrived in the United States, but the manuscript of the fourth volume of *Das Erkenntnisproblem* was left behind in Sweden and appeared after Cassirer's death, first in English translation as *The Problem of Knowledge* in 1950 and only later in German, in 1957. I have already remarked upon the normative approach to culture in *The Logic of the Humanities*, in particular in the essay "The Trag-

18. *Axel Hägerström, Eine Studie zur schwedischen Philosophie der Gegenwart* in *Göteborgs Högskolas Arsskrift* XLV (1939:1), 5.

19. See Hendel's comments in the preface to *The Problem of Knowledge: Philosophy, Science, and History Since Hegel*, trans. William H. Woglom and Charles W. Hendel (New Haven: Yale University Press, 1950) and Mrs. Cassirer's *Aus meinem Leben mit Ernst Cassirer*, pp. 250–51.

edy of Culture." In *The Problem of Knowledge* Cassirer says he will depart from the method of the previous three volumes and try to penetrate the motives that led to the discovery of the types of knowledge underlying the development of thought since Hegel. *The Problem of Knowledge* may be seen as background, systematic review *(systematische Überblick)*[20] of the movement of thought whose historical development must be understood before the crisis of man's knowledge of himself can be treated as a systematic problem, as it later was in *An Essay on Man*. An extension of this approach to history is present in Cassirer's studies during his Hamburg and Göteborg periods.

In the summer of 1941 Cassirer left Sweden for the United States, having accepted an invitation to teach at Yale University. Cassirer taught both undergraduate and graduate courses for three years. He is listed in the Yale catalogue for the first two years as visiting professor and for the third year as research associate. Each year Cassirer taught a seminar jointly with his colleagues, and these he regarded as high points in his academic career. The subjects were the philosophy of history, the philosophy of science, and the theory of knowledge, in that order. Altogether, Cassirer taught three graduate seminars each year, in addition to some undergraduate courses in ancient and modern history of philosophy. His courses included the philosophy of Kant, language and principles of symbolism, a two-part seminar on aesthetics, the development of Plato's dialectic, and a seminar in the theoretical foundations of culture.

In Sweden Cassirer had taught in German, although he had learned Swedish for his own use. In the United States he taught and wrote in English. During these three years Cassirer wrote *An Essay on Man* and began writing *The Myth of the State*. He also published a considerable number of articles. From these facts it can be seen that this was a period of especially intense activity for Cassirer. In the United States he met Charles Hendel, his friend and colleague at Yale, who assisted him with the publication of *An Essay on Man* and who, after Cassirer's death, was to see *The Myth of the State* to press, introduce the English edition of *The*

20. *Problem of Knowledge*, p. 19.

Philosophy of Symbolic Forms, and co-translate *The Problem of Knowledge.*

In the fall of 1944 Cassirer moved from New Haven to New York to assume the position of visiting professor at Columbia University, where he remained until his death. At Columbia he taught a graduate course on the origin and nature of political myth during the winter session and, at his death during the spring session, was teaching a course on "philosophical anthropology—an introduction to the philosophy of culture," as well as directing reading in German philosophy and advanced work in medieval and Renaissance philosophy. He died unexpectedly on the afternoon of April 13, 1945, the day following President Roosevelt's death.

Cassirer's grave is in the Cedar Park Beth-El Cemeteries, Westwood, New Jersey, in the Congregation Habonim, and is marked by a simple stone. One hundred years after his birth, on October 20–22, 1974, a conference involving the presentation of several papers was held in Cassirer's honor under the title "Symbolische Formen."[21] A small bust of Cassirer was placed in the University of Hamburg.

Cassirer's intellectual odyssey, this odyssey of "the Olympian," as he was called in his student days, can be divided into three major phases. The first is that of the Berlin years, 1903–19. Following his doctoral thesis on Descartes and his work on Leibniz, Cassirer worked out his Kantian approach to scientific epistemology and was concerned with the history of the problem of knowledge. Even in these years, in *Substance and Function,* Cassirer went beyond the epistemological standpoint and formulated the

---

21. This meeting was sponsored by the Philosophisches Seminar der Universität Hamburg, the Joachim Jungius-Gesellschaft der Wissenschaften e. V., and the Warburg Institute of the University of London. The major papers for this meeting were Hermann Lübbe, "Cassirer und die Mythen des 20. Jahrhunderts" and two colloquia, *Symboltheorie als Kunsttheorie,* with major presentations by Sir Ernst Gombrich, "Zeit, Zahl und Zeichen," and Nelson Goodman, "Words, Works, Worlds"; and *Zur Logik der Sprechhandlungen,* with major presentations by Karl-Otto Apel, "Zur Idee einer transzendentalen Sprachgrammatik," and John R. Searle, "Meaning, Communication, and Representation." I wish to thank Klaus Oehler, the director of the Philosophisches Seminar at the University of Hamburg, for so kindly supplying me with a copy of the program and information on it.

groundwork for the theory of functional concepts that provides the basis for his later philosophy of the symbol. Also, his interest during this period in the study of *Geistesgeschichte,* as practiced in Germany, can be seen as providing a basis for his notion of freedom and his own theory of the history of the spirit.

It was during the Hamburg years of the 1920s through 1933 that Cassirer moved decisively beyond the neo-Kantian position, both in the expansion of his perspective from epistemology to the philosophy of culture and in his dramatic new approach to the historical understanding of the philosophical spirit and its development. The third period is that of Cassirer's Swedish and American years, with his brief time at Oxford as a transition. In the 1935–45 period his attention turned to the theory of culture as a theory of humanity and freedom and, finally, to a theory of man and contemporary social life, in *An Essay on Man* and *The Myth of the State.* Here Cassirer goes back over the philosophical ground he had established in the Hamburg years, asking of it not strictly epistemological questions but questions concerning the fragmentation of cultural life.

In each of these three stages Cassirer went over the material he had mastered from a more developed viewpoint. He asked new questions of it; often the same material appears but in a new light. Cassirer's own notion of the symbol's fundamental power of "finding again" *(Wiederfinden)*[22] can be seen to apply to his own thought, for he always found again in the given what was not given. In each instance he established new meanings and new fixed points from which to carry the spirit of understanding further. This "finding again" never reestablishes a truth known as a simple "substance," as a thing existing and asserted. It is always something that "functions," a truth subject to development and reestablishment on the basis of new meanings.

THE ROLE OF ART IN CASSIRER'S SYMBOLIC FORM

Cassirer's name is frequently associated with aesthetics and the philosophy of art. Yet he wrote no single work on art or aesthetics. The association is probably made because he based his philosophy on the notion of the symbol, a concept that brings

22. *Philosophy of Symbolic Forms,* III, 108.

aesthetics to mind. It is also because the thinker who has done most to carry on the ideas of Cassirer and whose work has served for many as an indirect introduction to his thought is the aesthetician Susanne Langer.[23] In American philosophical circles their names are often joined. Although Cassirer wrote little on art, he makes reference to it throughout his works and it frequently appears in his list of symbolic forms, in the complex of language, art, and myth. But what, really, is the place of a theory of art in Cassirer's thought?

In a letter of May 13, 1942, to Paul Schilpp, written in connection with the planning of the Library of Living Philosophers volume, Cassirer remarks that friends and colleagues have urged him to prepare an English edition of *The Philosophy of Symbolic Forms*. He also says that he has decided against this and instead plans to present his thought in a new volume, to be written in English. These remarks follow in content the opening lines of his preface to *An Essay on Man* (1944), and it seems clear that Cassirer is here, at the end of his first academic year in the United States, referring to the project that was to become this book. However, in the letter Cassirer goes on to say something quite noteworthy for the understanding of the relationship of art to his conception of symbolic forms. He states: "With regard to content it would be new, as I would give here for the first time a thorough [*eingehend*] presentation of my theory of aesthetics. Already in the first sketch [*Entwurf*] of *The Philosophy of Symbolic Forms* a particular volume on art was considered but the disfavor of the times postponed its working out again and again."[24]

It is sometimes said that Cassirer planned to write a volume on

23. Susanne Langer's translation of Cassirer's study of *Language and Myth* (New York: Harper and Brothers, 1946) has served as a valuable introduction for many readers to Cassirer. Her *Philosophy in a New Key*, 2d ed. (Cambridge, Mass.: Harvard University Press, 1942, 1951) has served for many as an introduction to philosophy itself and is in many ways an extension of Cassirer's philosophy of the symbol. Her book on aesthetics, *Feeling and Form* (New York: Charles Scribner's, 1953), which is a development of the ideas of *Philosophy in a New Key*, is dedicated to Ernst Cassirer and also involves his ideas and perspectives. See also Mrs. Cassirer's *Aus meinem Leben mit Ernst Cassirer*, p. 292.

24. "Inhaltlich würde sie insofern neu sein, als ich heir zum ersten Mal eine eingehende Darstellung meiner aesthetischen Theorie geben würde. Schon im ersten Entwurf der Phil. d. s. F. war ein besonderer Band über Kunst vorgesehen—die Ungust der Zeiten hat aber seine Ausarbeitung immer wieder hinausgeschoben." This letter is in the special collections section of the library of Southern Illinois University, Carbondale.

art. From this letter there can be no doubt of his intention. To my knowledge this letter is the only hard evidence we have. It is plain that his plan goes back to the original sketch of *The Philosophy of Symbolic Forms* and thus to his work and interests in the 1920s. Moreover, it is here made clear that this new work was seen by him primarily as an opportunity to present his views on art fully. Although *An Essay on Man* contains a chapter on art, it is not longer or different in character than the other chapters on myth and religion, language, history, and science. It is difficult to think that Cassirer's chapter in this work is the thorough presentation that he proposes in the letter to Schilpp. Cassirer no doubt changed his conception as he worked on *An Essay on Man,* and in fact the unpublished papers show evidence of different conceptions and drafts of this volume (not, however, showing that Cassirer ever wrote it out as a volume on art). It seems most likely that the chapter on art (which together with his essay "Mythic, Aesthetic, and Theoretical Space," 1931, are the only discussions of art as such in his published works[25]) was meant as a first step in the direction of finally carrying out his original plan.

Art and aesthetics, I think, have an even deeper connection with Cassirer's conception of symbolic forms than is revealed by the fact that a volume on art was part of his original *Entwurf.* Art and aesthetics have a tie with the origin of the term *symbolic form* itself. *Symbolische Form* is the one special term in Cassirer's philosophy. In "Der Begriff der symbolischen Form im Aufbau der Geisteswissenschaften" ("The Concept of Symbolic Form in the Structure of the Humanities"), his contribution to *Vorträge der Bibliothek Warburg,* 1921–22, Cassirer uses the term *symbolic form* for the first time in a title (the first volume of *The Philosophy of Symbolic Forms* appeared in 1923). In this lecture he explains that the concept had its origins in Goethe's interest in the symbolic. Thereafter the notion of the *Symbolbegriff* passed through the philosophies of Schelling and Hegel into aesthetic theory, and from this base the aesthetician Friedrich Theodor Vischer argues that it is the foundation of the aesthetic itself. It is from

25. Trans. Donald Phillip Verene and Lerke Holzwarth Foster, *Man and World* 2 (1969) 3–17.

the essay "Das Symbol" by the Hegelian Vischer, which appeared in a volume of essays honoring Eduard Zeller in 1887, that Cassirer claims to derive the conception of symbolic form (although Vischer does not use the term *symbolische form* as such). Cassirer says he wishes to expand Vischer's aesthetic conception of symbolic form to a wider notion that can cover each form of the human spirit, not only art but also language and the mythical-religious world.[26]

Cassirer first uses the term *symbolic form* in his essay *Einstein's Theory of Relativity*, published in 1921 but completed in the summer of 1920. In its final section he considers the general problem of the relation of the concept of relativity to the problem of reality. He says that philosophy must avoid the one-sidedness of considering the problem of knowledge only in terms of theoretical and scientific thought. Cassirer speaks of the concept of symbolic form in words reminiscent of his Warburg Institute lecture. He says that philosophy "has to grasp the *whole system* of symbolic forms [*das Ganze der symbolischen formen*], the application of which produces for us the concept of an ordered reality . . . and it must refer each individual in this totality to its fixed place. If we assume this problem solved, then the rights would be assured, and the limits fixed, of each of the particular forms of the concept and of knowledge as well as of the general forms of the theoretical, ethical, aesthetic and religious understanding of the world."[27]

Cassirer's conception of symbolic form and the system of symbolic forms goes back to the last years of his Berlin period but first appears in print during the early years of his Hamburg period. In his general introduction to *The Philosophy of Symbolic Forms* in volume 1 (1923), Cassirer grounds his conception of

26. See Cassirer, *Wesen und Wirkung der Symbolbegriffs* (Darmstadt: Wissenschaftliche Buchgesellschaft, 1956), p. 175. Also *Philosophische Aufsätze. Eduard Zeller, zu seinem fünfzigjährigen Doctor-Jubiläum gewidmet* (Leipzig: Fues's Verlag, 1887), esp. pp. 169–73, 192–93. Cassirer employs Vischer's essay as the beginning point of his lecture, "Das Symbolproblem und seine Stellung im System der Philosophie," *Zeitschrift für Aesthetik und allgemeine Kunstwissenschaft* 21 (1927), 295–312.

27. *Substance and Function and Einstein's Theory of Relativity*, authorized trans. William Curtis Swabey and Marie Collins Swabey (Chicago: Open Court Publishing Co., 1923), p. 447.

symbolic forms philosophically in the notion of form as it appears in Greek philosophy, particularly in the Platonic "idea," and also relates it to the development of modern philosophy since Descartes. But as the more immediate source he quotes Henrich Hertz's view in *Principles of Mechanics* (1894) that what the mind can know depends on the symbols it creates. Cassirer also refers the reader back to the discussion in his essay on Einstein.[28] He derives the concept of symbolic form both from science and from art. Moving toward the problem of the philosophy of symbolic forms from the side of traditional epistemology and science, he finds an origin point in the *Naturwissenschaften*, in Hertz's mechanics; approaching the concept from the side of the *Geisteswissenschaften* he finds the origin point in Vischer's aesthetics.[29]

These two sources of Cassirer's conception of symbolic form—the aesthetic and the scientific—are reflected in one of his most striking attempts to explain how symbolic form is directly grounded in the functioning of consciousness—his appeal to the notion of a simple, plotted line, a *Linienzug*, as an example of how consciousness functions in relation to its object. Cassirer makes use of this notion in two works of 1927—his lecture to the Congress of Aesthetics in Halle, titled "Das Symbolproblem und seine Stellung im System der Philosophie" ("The Problem of the Symbol and Its Place in the System of Philosophy"), which was published in 1927,[30] and the third volume of *The Philosophy of*

28. *Philosophy of Symbolic Forms,* I, 75 and n. 2. Cf. Cassirer's use of Hertz and Helmholtz in "Das Symbolproblem und seine Stellung im System der Philosophie," 297–98.

29. In *The Philosophy of Symbolic Forms* Cassirer says that his views go back to his researches in *Substance and Function* (1910), written during his Berlin years. Thus the concept of symbolic form has its origin in one sense in Cassirer's extension of traditional epistemological concerns that grow out of concern with the natural sciences, the *Naturwissenschaften*. If Cassirer's conception of the symbol as connected to art and the *Geisteswissenschaften* is traced back to his earlier writings, it can be seen as having roots in his study of the *Freiheitsprinzip* and *Formprinzip* in German cultural history and art in *Freiheit und Form* (1916).

30. I encourage the reader to consult this important lecture for Cassirer's most concise account of the perspective of his system and the epistemological principles of this concept of symbolic form; see *Zeitschrift für Äesthetik und allgemeine Kunstwissenschaft* 21 (1927), 295–312. For an English translation see John Michael Krois, "The Problem of the Symbol and Its Place in the System of Philosophy," *Man and World*, vol. II, no. 4 (1978).

Symbolic Forms, which, although published in 1929, was completed in manuscript at the end of 1927.[31] Cassirer intends the illustration of the line drawing or curve to be a kind of phenomenological demonstration that will make clear how symbolic form is rooted in the stances consciousness can assume in relation to an object. This example is the one point in the presentation of his philosophy of symbolic forms where he invites the reader to verify directly the sense in which the symbolic forms are grounded in the activity of consciousness. His account of this optical "experiment" revolves around the distinction between the aesthetic and the purely conceptual notions of symbolic form.

Cassirer asks the reader to consider his awareness of the *Linienzug* as a particular perceptual experience. He invites him to attend to the purely sensory qualities of the line, to follow its spatial character, its lightness and darkness, its movement up and down, its jerky and smooth character. Here we can see that the line expresses a particular mood, but it is not what it is simply as the arbitrary projection of our inner state onto the line and its space. Our mood is directed by our following of the line and as a result the line becomes present to us as an animated totality.

Cassirer then asks us to respond to the line in a fundamentally different sense, to apprehend it as a mathematical structure. In assuming this perspective we put aside the expressive dynamism of the former response. Now we apprehend it as a schema of a geometrical law. Its significance depends not on seeing its shadings and inner movements, but on the relations and proportions it represents. It is "the mere outward cloak of an essentially unintuitive mathematical idea."[32] He then asks us to shift perspective again and apprehend the line drawing as a mythical

31. *Philosophy of Symbolic Forms,* III, 200–02. Cassirer also cites the illustration of the *Linienzug* in "Zur Logik des Symbolbegriffs," in *Wesen und Wirkung des Symbolbegriffs,* pp. 211–12. This essay is a reply to criticisms of Cassirer's conception of the symbol made by Konrad Marc-Wogau. Cassirer's reply was originally published in *Theoria* 4 (1938), 145–75. When citing this example Cassirer states: "Ich habe dieses Beispiel angeführt, weil sich aus ihm vielleicht am einfachsten ergibt, in welchem Sinne ich den Begriff einer 'Materie' der Wahrnehmung annehme—und in welchem Sinne er mir unzulässig erscheint" (*Wesen und Wirkung,* p. 212).

32. *Philosophy of Symbolic Forms,* III, 200–01.

symbol marking the division between the sacred and the profane, as a symbol warning the uninitiated of the sacred. If we
then shift perspective from the mythical to the aesthetic, Cassirer
says, the line becomes an object of aesthetic contemplation, an
ornament structured by aesthetic vision.

This account follows the order of Cassirer's presentation of
the *Linienzug* example in the third volume of *The Philosophy of
Symbolic Forms*. In his lecture "Das Symbolproblem und seine
Stellung im System der Philosophie," Cassirer describes the
movement of consciousness as proceeding from its expressive
apprehension of the line directly to its aesthetic and mythical-
religious apprehension. Then follows its mathematical or con-
ceptual-logical apprehension. The way in which Cassirer here
presents the *Linienzug* example suggests the sense in which the
aesthetic and the mythical-religious have particular ties to the
world of pure expression. The order in *The Philosophy of Symbolic
Forms* (from pure expression to the mathematical perspective
and then to the mythical and the aesthetic) suggests a point similar to the one Cassirer makes at the end of *Language and Myth*,
where he conceives art and the aesthetic as the recapture of the
mythical-metaphorical power of language once consciousness has
freed itself from the world of the mythical.[33] This recapture is
not a return to the purely expressive powers of consciousness,
but rather the transformation of these powers into a new
perspective.

In his presentation of the *Linienzug* example in *The Philosophy
of Symbolic Forms* Cassirer offers the reader the basis for understanding the theory of perception that underlies his notion of
symbolic forms. The line, considered as a phenomenon apprehended by consciousness, shows that no matter what standpoint
consciousness takes toward the object, its sensory experience
leads directly to a determinate order of meaning. Thus Cassirer
claims that any perceptive act is "symbolically pregnant." The
Linienzug example shows how symbolic form is grounded in
"symbolic pregnance" *(symbolische Prägnanz)*. "By symbolic pregnance," Cassirer says, "we mean the way in which a perception as

33. *Language and Myth,* pp. 98–99.

a sensory experience contains at the same time a certain nonin-
tuitive meaning which it immediately and concretely represents
. . . the perception itself which by virtue of its own immanent
organization, takes on a kind of spiritual articulation—which,
being ordered in itself, also belongs to a determinate order of
meaning. . . . It is this ideal interwovenness, this relatedness of
the single perceptive phenomenon, given here and now, to a
characteristic total meaning that the term 'pregnance' is meant to
designate."[34]

Cassirer's discussion of *symbolische Prägnanz* suggests his idea
that the symbol is present in the most rudimentary workings of
consciousness and offers the reader an understanding of the
term *symbolic form* that goes beyond its broader use to designate a
series of cultural forms—myth and religion, language, art, history, and science—the chapter titles of the second part of *An
Essay on Man.*

Cassirer's placement of art and the aesthetic in relation to the
mythical and expressive determination of the object in the *Linienzug* example suggests the fundamental role art plays in his
philosophy of symbolic forms. Seen in this light his comment in
the letter to Schilpp—that a volume on art was part of the original plan of his theory of the symbol—is not surprising. Cassirer's
criticisms of "expression" theories of art in his published works,
and in the unpublished papers which follow, are intended to
show that art must be understood as a distinctive type of symbolism. It is developed from the symbolic pregnance of expression,
but the direct and immediate formation of the expressive functioning of consciousness, the *Ausdrucksfunktion,* is achieved
through the mythic symbol.[35] In his lecture "Das Symbolproblem
und seine Stellung im System der Philosophie," Cassirer indicates that each symbolic form, each area of symbolic determination, can be understood in terms of its development from the
expressive.[36] Cassirer's "phenomenology of knowledge"

34. *Philosophy of Symbolic Forms,* III, 202.

35. Ibid., III, 61–62.

36. "Das Symbolproblem und seine Stellung im System der Philosophie," 301, 303–04.
Cf. Heidegger's critical remark on this paper in the quotation from his 1928 review in the
Deutsche Literaturzeitung discussed in the following section.

(Erkenntnis), the subject of the third volume of *The Philosophy of Symbolic Forms*, demonstrates how consciousness passes from the world of expression to that of pure cognition or mathematical-logical thought. In Cassirer's work there is no similar account of the phenomenology of art, or *Ästhetik*.

The papers in this volume on language and art and the educational value of art, taken together with *An Essay on Man* and "Mythic, Aesthetic, and Theoretical Space," offer the fullest statement we can now have of that view of art which was part of the original plan of *The Philosophy of Symbolic Forms*, and which provided a source of Cassirer's conception of symbolic form and the term *symbolic form* itself.

CASSIRER AND ETHICS

1

A theme which runs throughout the last decade of Cassirer's life, as I have noted earlier, is the relationship of philosophy to society and the notion of freedom. Cassirer sees philosophy as having an ethical dimension and a role in the production of ideals of cultural life.[37] Culture, for Cassirer, is to be understood as a *Werk*, as a production in which man comes to know his own nature, his humanity. This problem of culture is seen by Cassirer in terms of the contrast between the views of Spengler in *The Decline of the West* and Heidegger in *Being and Time*, on the one hand, and the view of Schweitzer in *The Philosophy of Civilization* on the other. His specific concern is to analyze how the viewpoint that underlies Schweitzer's reaction to the crisis of Western culture between the two world wars differs fundamentally from the viewpoints involved in Spengler's conception of history and Heidegger's conception of being.

In this volume, these issues can be seen in the lecture "The Concept of Philosophy as a Philosophical Problem" (1935), which discusses all three of these men, and in "Philosophy and Politics" (1944), in which Cassirer charges that Spengler and Heidegger put philosophy in a position where it "can no longer do its duty,"

37. For an account of Cassirer's relationship to ethics and normative questions see John Michael Krois, "Ernst Cassirer's Philosophy of Symbolic Forms and the Problem of Value," Ph.D. dissertation, The Pennsylvania State University, 1975.

an expression of Schweitzer. In *The Myth of the State*, Spengler and Heidegger are criticized in a similar fashion, and Schweitzer is seen by Cassirer as the proper ethical voice in an essay he wrote during the same period for the Schweitzer Jubilee Book. Spengler is also discussed by Cassirer in "The Technique of Our Political Myths," herein. The issues involved in this complex can be seen most fully in the relationship between Cassirer and Heidegger.

It is generally thought that the relationship between the two was confined to their meeting in Davos, Switzerland, in 1929, usually understood as a debate over their interpretations of Kant. While it is true that their meeting concerned Kant, it also included other matters and must be understood in terms of several prior exchanges between Heidegger and Cassirer.

These begin with Heidegger's footnote to Cassirer in *Sein und Zeit,* originally published in 1927 in the *Jahrbuch für Phänomenologie und phänomenologische Forschung,* edited by Edmund Husserl. In this note Heidegger acknowledges the value of Cassirer's analysis of the *Dasein* of myth for ethnological research (in *Mythical Thought,* 1925, the second volume of *The Philosophy of Symbolic Forms*), but points to the need for a more phenomenological approach. Heidegger indicates that Cassirer appears to be open to such an approach. As evidence for this he points to the footnote in the second volume of *The Philosophy of Symbolic Forms* in which Cassirer says that it has become apparent that Husserl's phenomenology has not been exhausted in the analysis of cognition and leaves open the possibility of its extension to include the mythical world.

In this connection it should be noted that the Husserl Archives contain a letter from Husserl to Cassirer, dated April 3, 1925, in which Husserl expresses a sympathetic interest in Cassirer's enterprise and denounces Hartmann for misunderstanding phenomenology and seeing in it the foundation of a dogmatic metaphysics.[38] Although this is not mentioned in Heidegger's note it would seem to support the point he is making. Heidegger concludes: "In a discussion between the author and Cassirer on the occasion of a lecture before the Hamburg section of the

38. See Herbert Spiegelberg, *The Phenomenological Movement: A Historical Introduction* (The Hague: Martinus Nijhoff, 1960), p. 359.

Kantgesellschaft in December 1923 on 'Tasks and Pathways of Phenomenological Research,' it was already apparent that we agreed in demanding an existential analytic such as was sketched in that lecture."[39]

In 1928 a review by Heidegger of the second volume of *The Philosophy of Symbolic Forms* appeared in the *Deutsche Literaturzeitung*. Heidegger concludes this review:

> But with all that the fundamental philosophical problem of myth is not yet attained: in what way does myth belong to *Dasein* as such; in what respect, after all, is it an essential phenomenon within a universal interpretation of being *(Sein)* and its modifications? Whether a "philosophy of symbolic forms" reaches toward a solution or even a working out of these questions might remain undiscussed. An opinion on this can only be produced when not only all the symbolic forms are presented, but also only when above all the fundamental concepts of this *Systematik* are thoroughly worked out and are brought to their ultimate ground. (Cf. at this point the indeed still generally held and all too free-floating views ventilated by Cassirer in his lecture: "Das Symbolproblem und seine Stellung im System der Philosophie," *Zeitschr. f. Äesthetik und allgem. Kunstwiss.* XXI, 1927, S. 295 ff.)
>
> The critical questions raised cannot diminish Cassirer's service, as it lies precisely in the fact that for the first time since Schelling it has placed myth as a systematic problem on the philosophical horizon. The investigation stands even without its insertion into a "philosophy of symbolic forms" as a valuable departure point for a renewed philosophy of myth. But only then, when it is again more firmly understood than up to now that a presentation of the phenomena of spirit, however rich and obliging to the prevailing consciousness, is never philosophy itself, the pressing necessity of which only breaks open when its few elementary, fun-

39. *Being and Time*, trans. John Macquarrie and Edward Robinson (Oxford: Basil Blackwell, 1962), p. 490.

damental problems, unmastered since antiquity, are grasped anew.[40]

Cassirer's own response to the phenomenological issues underlying the analysis of myth and the noncognitive functionings of consciousness that make possible science and cognition proper is contained in his third volume of *The Philosophy of Symbolic Forms*. Although this volume did not appear in print until 1929,[41] the manuscript was completed in 1927, before Heidegger's analysis in *Being and Time* could be taken into account in the discussion, as Cassirer points out. Cassirer did include four footnotes in response to Heidegger's work and a number of references to Husserl, including a discussion of Brentano's and Husserl's views on the theory of perception, which Cassirer brings together under his notion of "symbolic pregnance" *(symbolische Prägnanz)*.[42]

Cassirer's remarks are quite appreciative of Heidegger's analysis and are directed to Heidegger's views of space and time. He explains that a full discussion of Heidegger's position cannot be accomplished until Heidegger's work as a whole is available. But he does express this difference: "The Philosophy of Symbolic Forms does not question this temporality which Heidegger discloses as the ultimate foundation of existentiality *(Existentialität des Daseins)* and attempts to explain its diverse factors. But our inquiry begins *beyond* this sphere, at precisely the point where a transition is effected from this existential temporality to the *form* of time. It aspires to show the conditions under which this form is possible, the conditions for the postulation of a 'being' *(Sein)* which goes beyond the existentiality of 'being-there' *(Dasein)*."[43]

In these exchanges it is clear that the primary concern is the phenomenology of *Dasein* and not as yet the normative discussion that emerges in their Davos meeting, although these two issues are not unconnected. In the preface to the third volume of

40. *Deutsche Literaturzeitung* 21 (1928), 1011–12 (trans. Verene).
41. *Philosophy of Symbolic Forms*, III, xvii.
42. Ibid., 149 n. 4, 163 n. 2, 173 n. 16, 189 n. 34 and part 2, ch. 5.
43. Ibid., 163 n. 2.

The Philosophy of Symbolic Forms Cassirer says that he had planned to have a final critical chapter comparing his views with other contemporary philosophical positions, and that this intention delayed the publication of the volume until 1929. He indicates he now plans to place these discussions in another publication, to be called *"Leben" und "Geist"—zur Kritik der Philosophie der Gegenwart* ("Life" and "Spirit"—Toward a Critique of Contemporary Philosophy). This volume never appeared as such, although an essay dealing with Scheler, which had originally been given as a special lecture at Davos, appeared in 1930. Parts of what Cassirer planned for this work on contemporary philosophy exist as MS #184 in the unpublished papers, and it is clear from this manuscript that he intended to include a discussion of Heidegger.[44]

Cassirer never published his critique of Heidegger's phenomenology, but neither did Heidegger ever publish his critique of Cassirer, even though the whole of the system, which Heidegger called for in his review of the volume on myth, was placed in his hands. Heidegger was to write a review of the third volume of *The Philosophy of Symbolic Forms,* Cassirer's *Phänomenologie der Erkenntnis,* but he never completed it. Mrs. Cassirer reports in *Aus meinem Leben mit Ernst Cassirer* that on the occasion of a lecture at Freiburg, following their 1929 meeting at Davos, Cassirer asked Heidegger about the progress of this review. She quotes a letter Cassirer wrote to her at this time. He says he met with Heidegger the day following the lecture and found him quite friendly: "He admitted to me that he had exerted himself for a long time with a review of my third volume, but for the present he did not yet know how he ought to come to grips with the thing."[45]

The meeting between Cassirer and Heidegger at Davos was part of their participation in the Second Davos University Courses of March 17–April 6, 1929. The basic account of this meeting is contained in the *Davoser Revue* (April 15, 1929), which reports the general activities of the meeting and briefly summa-

---

44. See appendix herein.

45. "Er gestand mir, daß er sich seit langem mit einer Rezension meines dritten Bandes abquält, einstweilen aber noch nicht wisse, wie er die Sache anpacken solle" (*Aus meinem Leben mit Ernst Cassirer,* p. 167).

rizes each participant's lectures, and in the *Protokoll* of O. F. Bollnow and J. Ritter on the *Arbeitsgemeinschaft Cassirer-Heidegger*.[46]
Cassirer and Heidegger were by no means the only professors
offering lectures as part of these courses, but they were the fea-
tured event. The *Abendblatt der Frankfurter Zeitung*, in a story on
Monday, April 22, 1929, reported that there were over 200 students at Davos and about 30 professors; most of the students
and faculty were German, French, and Swiss. This news report
also makes clear that the major issue of the conference was the
opposition between the views of Heidegger and Cassirer over
Dasein and over the possibilities and meaning of human
freedom.[47]

Cassirer and Heidegger each gave three lectures in their regular courses. According to the *Davoser Revue,* Heidegger's lectures
were titled: "Kants Kritik der reinen Vernunft und die Aufgabe
einer Grundlegung der Metaphysik." As this title indicates. Heidegger's lectures reflected his study of Kant, which appeared the
same year as *Kant und das Problem der Metaphysik (Kant and the
Problem of Metaphysics),* dedicated to the memory of Max Scheler.
Cassirer wrote a review of this book which appeared in the *Kant-
Studien* in 1931. In their subject matter Heidegger's lectures followed the first three main sections of his book on Kant,
concerning various stages of the laying of the foundations of
metaphysics. The *Davoser Revue* reports that Cassirer's subject
was not Kant but three problems of philosophical anthropology—space, language, and death—formulated with a view to
taking issue with Heidegger's ontology and *Existentialanalyse*. Cas-

---

46. *Davoser Revue. Zeitschrift für Literatur, Wissenschaft, Kunst und Sport,* IV Jahrgang,
Nummer 7, 15 April 1929. Bollnow and Ritter's report is in Guido Schneeberger,
Ergänzungen zu einer Heidegger-Bibliographie (Bern, 1960), pp. 17–27. For an English trans-
lation of this from Schneeberger's volume see Carl H. Hamburg, "A Cassirer-Heidegger
Seminar," *Philosophy and Phenomenological Research* 25 (1964), 213–22. The full text of
Bollnow and Ritter's report has more recently come to light in French translation, *Débat
sur le Kantisme et la Philosophie (Davos, mars 1929) et autres texts de 1929–1931,* trans. P.
Aubenque, J.-M. Fataud, P. Quillet (Paris: Beauchesne, 1972), pp. 28–51. For explanation of the relationship between this and the earlier somewhat shorter text in Schneeberger's volume see Aubenque's remarks, pp. 10–11. See also note 49 below.

47. "Denken dieser Zeit. Fakultäten und Nationen treffen sich in Davos," *Abendblatt der
Frankfurter Zeitung* (22 April 1922).

sirer also gave the special lecture on "spirit" and "life" in
Scheler's philosophy, as mentioned above.[48]

The report on the *Arbeitsgemeinschaft* given by Bollnow and Ritter shows that although the exchange between Heidegger and
Cassirer was not over the interpretation of Kant as such their
views of Kant became the vehicle of their differences in philosophical standpoint. Heidegger begins by questioning Cassirer
on his neo-Kantianism, and he tends always to bring the issue
back to Kant (Cassirer's own study of Kant, *Kants Leben und Lehre*
(1918), had appeared more than ten years earlier). Cassirer's
remarks, like the topics of his lectures (to which in fact Heidegger refers) tend to direct the discussion to the differences and
points of contact between himself and Heidegger rather than to
the problem of interpreting Kant.

In the meeting between Cassirer and Heidegger at Davos, the
issues that concerned them in their earlier published exchanges
over the proper methodology through which to approach *Dasein*
and the questions concerning their respective phenomenologies
shift to a new ground. At Davos the debate is no longer methodological and phenomenological, it is normative and ethical. It
concerns the nature of man and the sense in which he can be
understood as a creature capable of freedom and infinity. In
response to several questions by students about how infinity is
related to man, Cassirer states that infinity is open to man "only
through the medium of form."

> Just this is the function of form that, as existence takes on
> form, man can experience it as an objective *Gestalt*. Only
> thus does he radically liberate himself; not from his finite
> point of departure (which, after all, is still wrapped up with
> his own finitude) but, while his experience grows out of the
> finite, it also points beyond itself and towards something
> new. This is an immanent infinity. . . . It is only in the realm
> of such forms that man is infinite. (Goethe's *Aus dem Kelche
> dieses Geisterreiches stroemt ihm die Unendlichkeit*) This 'realm of
> the spirit' is not a metaphysical realm of spirits; it is but the

48. See *Davoser Revue*, pp. 194–98 and also my remarks on MS #94 in the appendix
herein.

spiritual world which he has created himself. It is the very
hallmark of his infinity that he could, and can, build it up.

Cassirer says in reply to another question: "The infinite is not
just negatively determined by the finite. It does have its own significance. But it does not signify a realm which can be reached
only after struggling with the world of finite things. Instead it is
just this totality, the perfect fulfillment of the finite itself. The
infinite is constituted by this fulfillment of the finite. In Goethe's
words: 'Is the infinite your aspiration? Traverse all the finite's
configurations! (Willst Du ins Unendliche schreiten? Geh' nur im
Endlichen nach allen Seiten!').'' Cassirer says, finally, in answer to
another question: "Philosophy can free man only in so far as he
can be freed. Thus, she surely frees him radically from fear as a
mere feeling-state. The ultimate aim, however, is freedom in
another sense, namely, to rid oneself of all fear of the actual
world (Goethe's: 'Werft die Angst des Irdischen von Euch!'). This is
the position of idealism from which I have never wavered."[49]

It is clear that for Cassirer the freedom of man resides in his
ability to give form to experience. Freedom is natural to man
and it is present when he is most fully himself, as symbolic animal, as "forming" animal. This process of forming moves man
out of his finitude toward infinitude, but not as an absolute
other; rather, the finite is transformed into a series of infinite
forms, and in this way the finite is overcome and the infinite is
made accessible within the finite. Heidegger's view is quite different. In reply to Cassirer he speaks of "our different concepts
of freedom:"

> What matters to Cassirer is, first of all, to discriminate the
> various modes of (cultural) forms, in order to push on from
> there (and *post factum*, so to speak) to determinate [*sic*]
> dimension of the various formative powers. Now, one might

49. Hamburg, "A Cassirer-Heidegger Seminar," 218. In the French edition of *Débat sur
le Kantisme* (note 46) these statements of Cassirer are followed by remarks by Hendrik Pos
of the University of Amsterdam, who raises the question of the difference between Cassirer and Heidegger in terms of Heidegger's concept of *Dasein*. See also Pos's sharply
stated recollections of this meeting and of Heidegger in *Philosophy of Ernst Cassirer*, pp.
63–72.

say that this dimension is basically the same as that which I call existence *(Dasein)*. This would be erroneous, however. Our different concepts of freedom make this quite clear. I have spoken earlier of "liberation," to the effect that liberation of the inner transcendence of existence constitutes the very character of philosophy. Here the proper meaning of liberation is exactly to become free for the finitude of existence and to enter into the *Geworfenheit* (thrown into existence). While I have not given this freedom to myself, I can become myself only because of it. This "myself" is not to be understood, to be sure, as an indifferent entity of explanation. Rather: it is existence, as the really basic fact, in which man's existence and all problems of his existence in turn become what they essentially are. I believe that what I call *Dasein* (existence) is not translatable into Cassirer's vocabulary. Instead of just being determined in its essence by what is called "spirit" and "life," it is the original unity and structure of the immanent commitment of man who, bound to his body, is thereby bound to "what there is" *(Seiendem)* in the sense that existence (being thrown into what there is) breaks through to it. Such breakthroughs, being ultimately contingent and accidental, it is only at rare moments during his existence between life and death that man can exist at the very heights of its own possibilities.[50]

As Heidegger puts it here, freedom is not something that can be a project of *Geist* in Cassirer's sense. It depends on the notion of a "breakthrough," an *Einbruch,* which is not necessary to the being of man but contingent, something *zufällig.* It is this sense of freedom as something man can break through to only from time to time, a view in which freedom is a contingency, that Cassirer cannot accept, and which led him, in later works, to charge Heidegger with placing philosophy in a position where it "can no longer do its duty." In Cassirer's view, when philosophy makes freedom a contingency, history and culture are no longer understood as activities of self-understanding and man is robbed of the basis for self-respect.

50. Hamburg, "A Cassirer-Heidegger Seminar," 219.

Cassirer never gives up this objection to Heidegger, and it becomes the basis of his criticism in later years, when he connects Heidegger's thought with the intellectual climate of National Socialism. Hitler became chancellor of Germany on January 30, 1933. It was in May 1933, four years almost to the month from the time of his meeting with Cassirer in Davos, that Heidegger was inaugurated rector of the University of Freiburg and delivered his notorious address endorsing the goals and outlook of the Nazi regime.[51] It was also in May 1933 that Cassirer left his position at the University of Hamburg, where he had held the position of rector since 1930. Heidegger stepped down as rector after ten months, but he continued to teach at Freiburg.

For a full understanding the reader must go directly to these materials on Heidegger and Cassirer and their relationship. But in any case the basic facts of their interchange and actions at this time must be kept in mind in approaching the lectures in this volume which deal with the nature of philosophy and with political myth. What Cassirer objects to in both Heidegger's and Spengler's thought is not something that can be answered by intellectual exchange in an ordinary sense, by the techniques of interpretation of texts. Cassirer's objections are to a tonality, to a whole direction of thought and way of approaching the world.

Whether Cassirer has rightly or wrongly placed the idea of *Geworfenheit* at the center of Heidegger's philosophy is not the issue; Cassirer's criticisms are directed to a philosophy in which such a concept of existence can even arise.[52] His objection to Spengler, which he sums up by saying that he had not written a

51. *Die Selbstbehauptung der deutschen Universität,* Freiburger Universitätsreden No. 11 (1933). See Heidegger's interview, originally done in September 1966, but at Heidegger's wish not published until his death, "Aufklärung meines Falles," *Der Spiegel* 30 Jahrgang, Nr. 23, 31 May 1976, pp. 193–219 and the "Hausmitteilung," p. 3.

52. Something of what Cassirer was aiming at in his own way can be seen in Peter Gay's remarks in his *Weimar Culture: The Outsider as Insider* (New York: Harper & Row, 1970): "Among these prophets, Heidegger was perhaps the most unlikely candidate to influence. But his influence was far-reaching, far wider than his philosophical seminar at the University of Marburg, far wider than might seem possible in light of his inordinately obscure book, *Sein und Zeit* of 1927, far wider than Heidegger himself, with his carefully cultivated solitude and unconcealed contempt for other philosophers, appeared to wish. Yet, as one of Heidegger's most perceptive critics, Paul Hühnerfeld, has said: 'These books, whose meaning was barely decipherable when they appeared, were devoured.

book on history but a "book on divination," is that history from
Spengler's perspective is no longer seen as a process of self-liberation, as a story of human ideals sought; it is instead a framework within which humanity can only attempt to divine its place
in the total scheme at any given moment. Cassirer makes clear
that he does not see Spengler's and Heidegger's thought as
responsible for the events of the 1930s and the Second World
War. However, he sees philosophy as failing in the primary duty
Schweitzer claimed it must have: the duty to watch over and
inform humanity of its cultural ideals. For Cassirer it is not only
that "the watchman slept, who should have kept watch over us,"
as Schweitzer claims, but that the watchman assisted, as an interested and supporting bystander, in the robbery of Western
culture.

2

In order to construct cultural ideals and to place philosophy in
a position where it can do its duty, Cassirer, in the period after
leaving Germany, sees the need to reinterpret that development
of philosophical idealism that runs from Descartes to Hegel. In
his earlier introduction to *The Philosophy of Symbolic Forms,* he discusses this development in purely epistemological terms, in
terms of the concept and the symbol as the medium of the concept. In *The Logic of the Humanities* and the fourth volume of *The
Problem of Knowledge,* written so close together in 1940, and most
specifically in "Descartes, Leibniz, and Vico" herein (which goes
back to his Warburg Institute seminar of 1935, his second year

And the young German soldiers in the Second World War who died somewhere in Rus-
sia or Africa with the writings of Hölderlin and Heidegger in their knapsacks can never
be counted.' The key terms of Heidegger's philosophy were, after all, anything but
remote; more than one critic has noted that words like '*Angst*,' 'care,' 'nothingness,' 'existence,' 'decision,' and (perhaps most weighty) 'death' were terms that the Expressionist
poets and playwrights had made thoroughly familiar even to those who had never read a
line of Kierkegaard. What Heidegger did was to give philosophical seriousness, profes-
sorial respectability, to the love affair with unreason and death that dominated so many
Germans in this hard time" (pp. 81–82). For a philosophical analysis of Heidegger's relation to Nazism and its relation to the concepts of his thought see Stanley Rosen, *Nihilism:
A Philosophical Essay* (New Haven and London: Yale University Press, 1969), ch. 4, esp.
pp. 119–36.

in England, and is also part of the seminar he gave on the philosophy of history during his first year at Yale University, 1941–42), Cassirer argues for a theory of knowledge that rejects Descartes's conception of truth, according to which the humanities are excluded from any claim to knowledge.

Cassirer explores a development of thought that moves through Leibniz to Vico, whom he looks on as the founder of a theory of knowledge based on a philosophy of the humanities and cultural ideals. Vico emerges as the "discoverer of the myth" and the founder of the *Geisteswissenschaften*.[53] In so doing, Cassirer is not advocating something new, but bending his philosophy in a certain direction more strongly than before. The roots of this view go back to the origins of his thought. For Cassirer identifies Vico as the founder of the *Geisteswissenschaften* in his study *Leibniz' System* (1902), his first published work, and later in his study for the Warburg Institute at the beginning of the period during which he was writing *The Philosophy of Symbolic Forms* (1922), in *Die Begriffsform im mythischen Denken (The Form of the Concept in Mythical Thought)*.[54]

But his emphasis on Vico's conception of truth, which derives from the humanities and forms of society and history, over that of Descartes, which derives from the *Naturwissenschaften*, from scientific and mathematical thought, is crucial not simply because of its importance for the theory of knowledge, but because of its value for the normative task of philosophy in the understanding of ethical and cultural ideals. This ethical dimension comes directly to the forefront in his concern in this period with Hegel's *Philosophy of Right* (1821) and the famous dictum of the preface: "When philosophy paints its grey in grey, then has a shape of life grown old. By philosophy's grey in grey it cannot be rejuvenated but only understood. The owl of Minerva spreads its wings only with the falling of the dusk."[55]

In the introduction to *The Philosophy of Symbolic Forms* Cassirer is concerned simply with the tendency in Hegel's system toward

53. *Problem of Knowledge*, p. 296, and *Logic of the Humanities*, trans. Clarence Smith Howe (New Haven: Yale University Press, 1961), pp. 52–55.

54. *Wesen und Wirkung des Symbolbegriffs*, p. 5.

55. Trans. T. M. Knox (Oxford: Clarendon Press, 1942), p. 13.

a logic that reduces cultural forms to the form of the logical idea.
Here Cassirer's interest is focused on Hegel's *Phenomenology of
Spirit* and the problem he sees in the fact that his phenomenology of consciousness terminates in the *Science of Logic*. He says
that this tendency to the "ultimate reduction of all cultural forms
to the *one* form of logic seems to be implied by the concept of
philosophy itself and particularly by the fundamental principle
of philosophical idealism."[56] Thus Cassirer's thought of the
1920s is concerned with the beginning point of modern idealism
and with its end point. He wishes to expand Descartes's view of
the concept in the direction of the symbol, and he is concerned
with Hegel as the end point, to preserve the autonomy of cultural forms from the natural tendency in philosophical idealism
that Hegel's system manifests—the reduction of experience to
the logical idea.

In the 1940s Cassirer feels the need, in pursuing the ideals of
humanism, to move from Descartes to Vico, and from the problem of Hegel's theory of knowledge to his philosophy of right.
Here he finds the same tendency of philosophical idealism to
confine itself to the idea, to conceive of philosophy as simply a
reflection on experience. This is why Cassirer struggles in particular with Hegel's owl of Minerva statement, which taken in its
most literal sense and apart from his thought as a whole would
seem to deny philosophy any role in the production of cultural
ideals. Cassirer took up the question of Hegel's *Philosophy of Right*
in a seminar he taught at Oxford and, as with Vico's notion of
truth, he returned to it during his first year of teaching at Yale
University.

Hegel's view of the state, for Cassirer, represents both the positive and negative possibilities of the idealist conception—negative if seen in terms of the apparent literal meaning of the owl of
Minerva statement, but positive if taken in relation to Hegel's
notion of world history at the end of the *Philosophy of Right* and
his conception of the threefold activities of absolute spirit in the
last chapter of the *Encyclopaedia*. Cassirer maintains that Hegel's
idealist conception of the state is not the *Machtstaat*. He points to

---

56. *Philosophy of Symbolic Forms*, I, 84.

the fact that for Hegel the state is not ultimate, but is subject to the course of world history, and that above the state are the forms of art, religion, and philosophy, which comprise absolute spirit. Thus Hegel's philosophy provides a ground for the formation of cultural ideals which goes beyond the form of the state. It is the tension between the form of the cultural ideal and the form of the social fact that a philosophy of civilization must attempt to understand and reinterpret for man. The difference between these two dimensions of experience is effaced in the twentieth-century myth of the state.

In the myth of the state two forces are introduced into modern social life—technique and myth—neither of which maintains the tension between facts and ideals; instead they remove this tension at its roots. Technique becomes the basis of the state. It provides the state with a means of achieving definition and unity that makes it self-sufficient and independent of any ethos or need for cultural ideals. The need for a "spiritual" dimension to the state or social life is taken over by the joining of technique with the life forms and life images of myth. The forms of mythical consciousness are placed at the center of social life and are manipulated by the instrumentalities of technique, by the technologies of communication, the technologies of the word and the picture. Thus the state becomes a single self-reifying process in which there are no oppositions between facts and ideals, reason and emotion, the sciences and the humanities, nature and culture, spirit and life, the social and the individual.

Philosophy of Culture

The Concept of Philosophy as a Philosophical Problem

(1935)

This is Cassirer's inaugural lecture at the University of Göteborg, Sweden, in 1935, delivered on the occasion of the official assumption of his teaching post. The text is derived from two manuscripts in German—one a handwritten draft which is preceded by a number of sheets of rough notes (MS #53) and the other a typescript, mostly in carbon (MS #174). The version here is taken from the typescript except for the material between pages 5 and 7. This material, which is missing from the typescript, has been supplied from the handwritten copy. The title is taken from the first sheet of the notes of MS #53, which states: "Der Begriff der Philosophie als Problem der Philosophie." MS #174 indicates the specific date of the lecture as October 1935. The translation is mine.—Ed.

I wish to speak to you here on the concept, the nature, and the task of philosophy, a theme which is questionable, which indeed could appear presumptuous, when one considers the occasion of this ceremony and the narrow limits of time that are set here. The representative of a particular field, at the beginning of a new academic post, will hardly choose this way of introduction. He will try to lead his listeners *in medias res;* he will select a particular concrete problem which he can illuminate from the present position of his discipline. But it seems to be the fate of philosophy that it is denied this form of concreteness, this particularity. In all the directionalities of particular philosophical questions, in their unlimited abundance and differentiations, philosophy appears ultimately over and over again to return to the principal and original question, to the question of what philosophy is and what it is about.

Before this general question is elucidated philosophy can go nowhere in particular; if it has not laid out its goal for itself clearly and certainly, it cannot make its way. For it is this that distinguishes the intellectual position of philosophy from that of the special disciplines, namely that in the latter ones the respective themes which they treat are prescribed clearly and plainly by the object. The object of physics, the object of biology, the object of history or the special humanistic disciplines requires for each a definite treatment and, in a certain sense, forces on each a particular method. Philosophy, however, possesses no such simple object in terms of which it directly orients itself and to which it could point as a certain and positive possession. The great systematic thinkers in philosophy and in the particular philosophical schools separate themselves from each other not merely in the course they follow, but in the starting point which they choose, and it is in this choice that the deep problematical character of philosophy today comes to light.

The concept of philosophy shows itself again and again as a problem of philosophy, as a problem which in itself never comes to rest, but which must always be undertaken anew in a continual dialectical movement of thought. We stand yet today in the midst of this movement after classical Greek philosophy more than two thousand years ago recognized this question and put it clearly and sharply. I cannot attempt here to sketch a complete picture of it; I can only indicate some phases of this path, and try to show in what light the task of philosophy appears to me, and by what means, according to my conception and conviction, this task is to be undertaken.

There are two fundamental directions of philosophical searching and questioning which clearly oppose each other from the beginning. One cannot more sharply denote them and more impressively describe them than Goethe has done in that magnificent characterization of Plato and Aristotle that he gives in *Materialien zur Geschichte der Farbenlehre (Materials on the History of the Doctrine of Colors)*. Goethe says:

> Plato relates himself to the world as a blessed spirit, whom it
> pleases sometimes to stay for a while in the world; he is not

so much concerned to come to know the world, because he already presupposes it, as to communicate to it in a friendly way what he brings along with him and what it needs. He penetrates into the depths more in order to fill them with his being than in order to investigate them. He moves longingly to the heights in order to become again a part of his origin. . . . Aristotle, on the contrary, stands to the world as a man, an architect. He is only here once and must here make and create. He inquires about the earth, but not farther than to find a ground. . . . He draws a huge circumference for his building, procures materials from all sides, arranges them, piles them up, and climbs thus in regular form, pyramid fashion to the top; whereas Plato, like an obelisk, indeed like a pointed flame, seeks heaven. When two such men appear, who as it were share humanity as separate representatives of splendid but not easily reconcilable properties . . . then it follows naturally that the world . . . was compelled to surrender itself to one or the other, to recognize one or the other as master, teacher, and leader.[1]

This division, which found its first classical expression in Plato and Aristotle, henceforth runs throughout the whole history of philosophy. It defines and accounts for in large part those typical basic oppositions which we are accustomed to designate in traditional academic language as the oppositions of idealism and realism, of rationalism and empiricism. Again and again we become aware of these two opposed tendencies in the systematic development and expansion of philosophical thought. Philosophy claims to be the real, the true unified science; the whole of its striving and its conceptual longing appears to be aimed at absolute unity, at the unity of being as well as the unity of knowledge. But this unity of its goal in no way corresponds to an immediate unity of itself, its intellectual structure. It experiences itself as constantly governed by two opposed natural impulses. Both of these souls

1. See Goethe, *Gedenkausgabe der Werke, Briefe und Gespräche*, 24 vols., ed. Ernst Beutler, *Naturwissenschaftliche Schriften, Erster Teil* (Zürich: Artemis-Verlag, 1949), XVI, 346–47.—Ed.

abide in almost all great thinkers, the workings of which Faust perceives in himself:

> The one clings with a dogged love and lust
> With clutching parts unto this present world,
> The other surges fiercely from the dust
> Unto sublime ancestral fields.[2]

A significant moment, however, exists in the history of philosophy in which this antagonism seems to be appeased, in which both fundamental powers are no more opposed, but operate jointly and are placed in pure balance to one another. This is the moment in which the Kantian, the critical philosophy, appears, which also, in this respect, signifies a genuine "revolution in thought." Kant's system has been characterized by his interpreters just as often as a system of pure metaphysics as a theory of pure experience, as a system of critical empiricism, indeed positivism. But both characterizations do not express the kernel and the essential, fundamental intention of the Kantian position. For it is just this that is new in Kant's formulation of the problem, namely that it assumes a different *relationship* between the two opposed poles of experience and thought. A pure correlation takes the place of the opposition.

In his logical theory, in the theory of the a priori basis of knowledge, Kant follows the Platonic doctrine. But he sets a different and new goal for this doctrine. The revolution concerns the truly fundamental concept of Platonic idealism—the concept of a *mundus intelligibilis,* of a supersensible world. Kant does not entrust human reason with the power, nor does he grant it the right to build up such a supersensible world on the strength of the pure concept. On the contrary, according to him, all power of the pure concept should and must serve the opposite problem. It must not lead us outside the empirical world, but must lead us deeper within it; it should make experience itself understandable and transparent to us, its logical structure and its logical laws, its general principles and conditions.

2. *Faust,* trans. Charles E. Passage (Indianapolis, New York, Kansas City: Library of Liberal Arts, 1965), part 1, scene 2, lines 114–17.—Ed.

Kant thus denies to the human spirit a flight into the realm of pure ideas—the flight to that "place beyond the heavens" of which Plato speaks in the *Phaedrus*.[3] "The light dove," as it is called in the introduction to the *Critique of Pure Reason*, "cleaving the air in her free flight, and feeling its resistance, might imagine that its flight would be still easier in empty space. It was thus that Plato left the world of the senses, as setting too narrow limits to the understanding, and ventured out beyond it on the wings of the ideas, in the empty space of the pure understanding. He did not observe that with all his efforts he made no advance—meeting no resistance that might, as it were, serve as a support upon which he could take a stand, to which he could apply his powers, and so set his understanding in motion."[4] Kant demands at all times for his own efforts, for his critical analysis of knowledge, such a firm ground and support. He does not wish to raise himself above scientific knowledge and its range of validity in order to discover new unknown worlds beyond this range.

He stands firmly on the well-grounded earth, on the certain ground of science, but at the same time he wishes to lay bare the last supporting layer on which this foundation of the edifice of science rests. He is not satisfied, however, with the factum of science as such; he inquires into the presuppositions of this factum, into the conditions of its possibility. The general question concerning the validity of pure a priori knowledge resolves and divides itself for him into the subquestions: How is pure mathematics, how is pure natural science, how is metaphysics in general possible? And the answer goes that the last question can be answered and resolved only with the help of the first two. In the vacuum, in the space of a bare metaphysical transcendent world, reason can take no step forward. It must make itself at home in its own sphere; it must learn to understand and know itself before it can possibly make a declaration concerning the nature of its object, concerning the reality of things.

With this the interpretation of the concept, the meaning, and

3. See 247c–d.—Ed.

4. *Critique of Pure Reason*, trans. Norman Kemp Smith (London: Macmillan, 1933), A 5–6; B 8–9.—Ed.

the performance of philosophy experiences a decisive change. For philosophy now no longer claims to increase the substance of knowledge as such and to widen through dogmatic insights the sphere which the special fields of knowledge describe. It is satisfied to inquire into the function of knowledge and to understand and establish this function. This requires that it know the powers that build up knowledge not merely separately, but that it command a view of them in their inner association, in their order and systematic interdependence. This command of its own area, this knowledge of its own function, is the necessary condition for every expansion of our philosophical knowledge.

I cannot here go into this particular relationship; I am content to quote, by way of elucidation and illustration, a particular expression of Kant in which this is immediately brought to light. It is to be found in a note of Kant which Benno Erdmann published under the title *Reflexionen Kants zu Kritik der reinen Vernunft (Reflections of Kant on the Critique of Pure Reason)*. "The mathematician, the beautiful spirit, the natural scientist," Kant says, "what do they accomplish when they arrogantly mock metaphysics? Within themselves lies the call which demands that they make an attempt in the selfsame field. They cannot resist asking: From whence do I come? Whence is the whole? The astronomer is even more challenged by these questions. He cannot forebear searching for something which satisfies him therein. What takes him by surprise here is that from the first judgment he is in the area of metaphysics. Does he want here to rely merely on the convictions which arise within him without any direction, since he has no map of the field through which he wants to pass? In this darkness the *Critique of Pure Reason* lights a torch, but does not point out the regions unknown to us beyond the sensible world, but instead lights the dark space of our own understanding."[5] This is the new method which Kant desires in the critical philosophy, namely, a method to which he himself gave the name, the transcendental method. It does not extend to the tran-

---

5. Benno Erdmann, ed. *Reflexionen Kants zur kritischen Philosophie*, Bd. II, *Reflexionen zur Kritik der reinen Vernunft* (Leipzig, 1884), no. 128. Cf. Cassirer, *Kants Leben und Lehre* (Darmstadt: Wissenschaftliche Buchgesellschaft, 1974), p. 155.—Ed.

scendent, to the supersensible; it wants to lead us back into the depths of our own reason and wants to teach us to know and to grasp its presuppositions and its basic strengths.

In this critical endeavor Kant remains a child of his time, the thinker of the eighteenth century, that century which has its highest intellectual triumph in the areas of mathematics, mechanics, and astronomy. And so the question concentrates itself instinctively in him on this point. He inquires into the conditions of the possibility of Newtonian science, the mathematical principles of the doctrine of nature. But the one hundred and fifty years since the origin of the *Critique of Pure Reason* have broadened the problem considerably for us. The eighteenth century is the century of mathematical natural science, classical physics; the problems of biology, and even more the problems of historical science and the disciplines which we bring together under the concept of the humanities are also recognizable here in their outlines and methodological beginnings. Since then the scientific picture of the world and the general system of concepts of classical physics has not only been fundamentally altered through relativity theory and quantum theory, but also an abundance of new problems has been put before us through the founding of a scientific doctrine of life, the question of evolutionary theory and genetic history, through ethnology, linguistics, the comparative study of mythology, and the comparative study of religion, which philosophy cannot avoid if it desires to remain faithful to its pursuit and its vocation.

But however much the type of problems may have changed, and its circumference may have been widened and lost sight of, I still believe that we need not give up the basic critical problem as Kant saw it and as he first established it with great clarity. We must now direct the critical question to a completely new material, but we can and should maintain the form of this question. We must question not only how pure mathematics and pure natural science are possible, we must ask about the totality and about the systematic whole of each basic function, only by means of which do we have the power to sketch a picture of the cosmos, a picture of the universe and the human world. Nature alone does not belong in this sphere; rather, we must assign to it everything which we tend to think of and bring together under the broad general concept of culture. The historian, philologist, linguist, ethnologist, and the investigator of myth and history of religion are involved with the forms of culture. But here philosophy must go a step further back and, as it were, push forward into a new and deeper layer of questioning. Starting with such forms it must go back and ask about the formative powers, about the type of spiritual functions and energies which have produced and made possible these shapes of the human spirit.

It was Wilhelm von Humboldt who, in the area of linguistics, first raised this question, in the introduction to his great work on the Kavi language, and who through it raised the study of language to a new scientific and philosophical level. The examination of language, Humboldt makes clear, if it is not to become chimerical and lose itself in arbitary speculation, must begin with the quite dry, even mechanical dissection of the physical and structural, with that which we today call phonetics, with sound and form patterns. But it can and should not stop here; for language is rooted in the ultimate depths of humanity and, when properly considered and handled, leads back to it. Language, as Humboldt puts it, is not to be viewed simply as a lifeless product, but as a production. It is not simply an act *(Ergon)*, but an activity *(Energeia)*, and thus its true definition can only be genetic. It can only present itself to us as the continual recurring work of spirit, not as a finished and final product.

This expression of Wilhelm von Humboldt does not simply apply to language alone; it applies, with the same right and ground, to all productions of our spiritual culture, to all that I have tried to bring together under the general concept of "symbolic formation." Philosophical thought cannot be content to acquaint itself with these productions in their simple existence, simply to receive and accept them. It must attempt to comprehend this existence as soon as it becomes present in the special disciplines in their richest abundance; but this attempt is just the beginning of philosophical understanding, understanding that is not satisfied with the product but wishes to understand the specific manner of production out of which the product originates. Such productive activity, such continually recurring workings of spirit, are that on which not only language, but also myth, religion, and art are ultimately based. It is for each of them to grasp and to illuminate this in their individuality and peculiarity, in their particular form and mode of operation.

From this follows the prospect of an abundance of fruitful and significant analytical investigations which certainly can never be accomplished through the work of philosophical thought alone, but which can only be accomplished in close collaboration and cooperation with the special sciences. But even if all these particular investigations were successful in leading to a definite end, philosophy would still not be at the end of its problem. For a final, decisive question still remains, which lies beyond all these particular theoretical analyses, which arises at their limit and which, as soon as it has once been clearly and sharply put, necessarily goes beyond this limit. Philosophy cannot be satisfied to ask about the form and structure of particular cultural regions, about the structure of language, art, law, myth, and religion. The deeper it penetrates into this structure the more clear and the more urgent becomes the problem of the whole for it.

What is this whole of spiritual culture? What is its end, its goal, its meaning? Whenever this question of goal and meaning is put to the whole of culture, we stand at a decisive turning point of philosophical self-reflection. In the eighteenth century it was Jean-Jacques Rousseau who raised the question and who defended it with inner personal passion. Through him a new powerful force breaks into the solidly fixed and apparently so entrenched circle of thought of the eighteenth century, a force which appears for a long time as if it should explode all the solid forms of Enlightenment culture. Rousseau becomes the ethical critic of the Age of Enlightenment long before Kant becomes its theoretical critic, and Kant in his theoretical work never ignored or forgot the warning of the ethicist Rousseau.

"I am by inclination an investigator," he says in one of the notes in his journal. "I feel the whole thirst for knowledge and the greedy restlessness to get further, the satisfaction in each step forward. There was a time when I believed that all this could effect the glory of humanity and I despised the mob, which knows nothing. Rousseau has set me right. This deluded superiority is disappearing; I am learning to respect human beings, and would find myself more useless than the common worker if I did not believe that this observation is able to give a value to all the others in establishing the rights of humanity."[6] For Kant all philosophy is henceforth inextricably allied with that basic question which stirred the eighteenth century so deeply and passionately, with the question concerning the eternal, immutable, and inalienable rights of man. In just this question, in the question concerning the merit and the basic value of the moral law, Kant finds the closing and the true completion of philosophicial thought and inquiry. Only through regard for this goal, according to him, can the scholastic conception of philosophy pass over into a conception of philosophy as related to the world.

In the last part of the *Critique of Pure Reason* is a section which Kant titled "The Architectonic of Pure Reason." Here it is made clear that there exists a twofold employment and a twofold conception of philosophy—one of which can be designated as its scholastic conception and the other as a conception of its relation to the world. Kant thinks of the scholastic conception of philosophy as not at all unimportant; he is furthermore convinced that all solidity and all actual certainty of philosophical knowledge depend on it; that they depend on the lawful arrangement of principles, the essential determination of concepts, and on the attempted rigor of proof. And yet he is not satisfied with understanding philosophy according to this pure scholastic conception of it, and accordingly to seek in it nothing more than the logical perfection of knowledge and the systematic unity of knowing. "But there is," as he says, "likewise another concept of philosophy, a *conceptus cosmicus*, which has always formed the real basis of the term 'philosophy,' especially when it has been as it were personified and its archetype represented in the ideal *philosopher*. On this view, philosophy is the science of the relation of all

6. See *Kants Leben und Lehre*, pp. 93–94.—Ed.

knowledge to the essential ends of human reason *(teleologia rationis humanae)*, and the philosopher is not an artificer in the field of reason, but himself the lawgiver of human reason. In this sense of the term it would be very vainglorious to entitle oneself a philosopher, and to pretend to have equalled the pattern which exists in the idea alone."[7]

Does this ideal of a concept of philosophy as "related to the world," which Kant presents here in a sphere of ideas that we have long since left behind us, does it belong to those ideals for which we pardon the eighteenth century, on which we may look down from our own standpoint indulgently, as on an infancy and a youthful dream of human reason? I believe not. I am much more convinced that the question which is put here, the question of the connection of all knowledge to the essential aim of human reason itself, arises today more urgently and imperatively than ever before, not only for the philosopher, but for all of us who partake in the life of knowledge and the life of spiritual culture. One of the true cultural philosophers of our time, Albert Schweitzer, a man who is respected as much as a man as he is a thinker, has put to our whole present culture once again this basic question, this essential moral issue. And he has answered it clearly and fearlessly. Schweitzer recognizes in our culture serious spiritual and ethical wrongs and he reproaches contemporary philosophy that it has not seen this damage early enough and has not promptly warned us of them.

"Now it is evident for all," so Albert Schweitzer has said in the lectures which he delivered here in Sweden, in Uppsala, over twelve years ago,[8] "now it is evident for all that the self-annihila-

---

7. *Critique of Pure Reason*, A 838–39; B 866–67.—Ed.

8. Cassirer's reference is to Schweitzer's Olaus-Petri Lectures, delivered at the University of Uppsala in 1922. See also Cassirer's essay, "Albert Schweitzer as Critic of Nineteenth-Century Ethics," in *The Albert Schweitzer Jubilee Book*, ed. A. A. Roback (Cambridge, Mass.: Sci-Art Publishers, 1946), pp. 241–57. Mrs. Cassirer describes returning to their boarding house in Oxford in 1933 and finding in their mail a simple white card with only the words "Ich wollte Ihnen nur die Hand drücken, Albert Schweitzer." For a description of Cassirer's meeting with Schweitzer see Toni Cassirer, *Aus meinem Leben mit Ernst Cassirer* (New York: Privately issued, 1950), pp. 216–20. Schweitzer always was for Cassirer the primary and proper embodiment of the *Ethiker* in contemporary society. See also "Philosophy and Politics" herein.—Ed.

tion of culture is in process. Also what remains of it is no longer
certain. This still stands because it was not exposed to the
destructive thrust to which the other part fell victim. But it too is
built on rubble. The next landslide can take it with it." That it
could come to this disintegration, to this crumbling of our spiritual and ethical ideals of culture was, according to Schweitzer,
not the fault of philosophy, but a fact which appeared out of
other conditions in the development of thought. "But,"
Schweitzer explains, "philosophy is to be blamed for our world
in that it did not admit the fact. . . . In accordance with its ultimate vocation philosophy is the guide and the caretaker of reason in general. Its duty would have been to admit to our world
that the ethical ideals of reason would no longer find support, as
earlier, in a total world view, but would be for the present
dependent on themselves and would have to assert themselves in
the world by their own inner force. It should have shown us that
we have to struggle for the ideals on which our culture rests. . . .
Every effort should have been made to direct the attention of
the educated and the uneducated to the problem of cultural
ideals. . . . But in the hour of peril the watchman slept, who
should have kept watch over us. So it happened that we did not
struggle for our culture." I believe that all of us who have
worked in the area of theoretical philosophy in the last decades
deserve in a certain sense this reproach of Schweitzer; I do not
exclude myself and I do not absolve myself. While endeavoring
on behalf of the scholastic conception of philosophy, immersed
in its difficulties as if caught in its subtle problems, we have all
too frequently lost sight of the true connection of philosophy
with the world.

But today we can no longer keep our eyes closed to the menacing danger.[9] Today the urgency of the time warns us more

9. It should be kept in mind here that Cassirer is speaking in the fall of 1935, having left
his position at the University of Hamburg in the spring of 1933 after Hitler became
chancellor of Germany on January 30, 1933. He most specifically would seem to have in
mind the "menacing danger" of nazism, but this concern also involves the wider concern
with the fragmentation of culture which he discusses in later works, for example, "The
Crisis of Man's Knowledge of Himself" in the first chapter of An Essay on Man (New
Haven: Yale University Press, 1944).—Ed.

strongly and more imperatively than ever that there is once again a question for philosophy which involves its ultimate and highest decisions. Is there really something like an objective theoretical truth, and is there something like that which earlier generations have understood as the ideal of morality, of humanity? Are there general binding supra-individual, supra-state, supra-national ethical claims? In a time in which such questions can be raised, philosophy cannot stand aside, mute and idle. If ever, now is the time for it again to reflect on itself, on that which it is and what it has been, on its systematic, fundamental purpose, and on its spiritual-historical past. This is not the first time that the claim of philosophy to take hold of real events has been disputed, that its claims and ideals have been derided as empty dreams and utopias. But its inner power, its ideational power is not diminished or weakened through such derision and through such scepticism. And only in that it preserves this ideational achievement clearly and certainly and purely can it hope by means of it once again to have an effect on outside existence and events.

If philosophy should feel too weak for this struggle which is again today imposed on it, then it may serve as a comfort and strength that it no longer stands alone in this, that it does not have to appear for and advocate its own cause, but the cause of knowledge in general. Without the claim to an independent, objective, and autonomous truth, not only philosophy, but also each particular field of knowledge, natural science as well as the humanities, would lose their stability and their sense. Thus, in our time, it is not only a general methodological demand, but a general cultural fate that couples philosophy with the special disciplines of knowledge, and which binds them closely to each other. To the pessimism which believes that the hour of destiny for our culture has struck, that the "decline of the West" is inescapable,[10] that we can do nothing else than to observe this decline calmly and collectedly, to this pessimism and fatalism we

10. Cassirer's reference is to Oswald Spengler's *Der Untergang des Abendlandes*, published in 1918. Cf. Cassirer's remarks in *The Myth of the State* (New Haven: Yale University Press, 1946), pp. 289–92; see also "Philosophy and Politics" and "The Technique of Our Modern Political Myths" herein.—Ed.

do not wish to resign ourselves. On the other hand we can give ourselves over today less than ever before to that optimism which Hegel's famous words express: "What is rational is real; what is real is rational."[11]

Here we must take the same step as before; we must replace with a functional conception the substantive conception of reason with which Hegel's system is governed and permeated. Hegel declares reason as the substance which is immanent, and as the eternal which is present. But reason is never a mere present; it is not so much an *actual*, as it is a constant and ever *actualizing*, not a *given* but a *task*. Yet, far more than in the sphere of theoretical reason, it holds good for the sphere of practical reason, that we can never grasp the true nature of reason in bare existence, in the finished and extant. Instead, we must seek it in the continual self-renewing work of spirit. This work is not one of a substantial, metaphysical world spirit which peacefully completes its immanent work and transcends all individual desires and plans. It is the question of a problem which is placed before us and for which we must struggle, with the pledge of all our powers, with the exertion of rigorous investigation uncorrupted by prejudice, and with the whole weight of our will and our personality.

[*The philosophical content of Cassirer's discussion ends at this point. There follows a rather long set of ceremonial remarks in which Cassirer thanks the University of Göteborg for the invitation to his new teaching position. These remarks close as follows. They offer a sense of Cassirer's spirit as an academic thinker.–Ed.*[12]]

11. Cf. *Myth of the State*, pp. 295–96, and also "Hegel's Theory of the State," herein. In Hegel see the preface to the *Philosophy of Right*.—Ed.

12.   For a further portrait of Cassirer as colleague and thinker these comments may be compared with Cassirer's remarks to the Yale Philosophical Club in the spring of 1944 before leaving that post for Columbia. See Charles Hendel's address at the memorial services given for Cassirer at Columbia University on June 1, 1945, in *The Philosophy of Ernst Cassirer*, ed. P. A. Schilpp (Evanston, Ill.: The Library of Living Philosophers, 1949), pp. 56–57.—Ed.

I will not conceal from you that decision of acceptance of this, my new appointment, was not easy and that I have taken it only after long and careful reflection. For as I have felt the conferring of this position not only a high personal honor, I have also felt the whole burden of the responsibility which is therewith imposed upon me. Today, however, this burden also seems to me no longer as heavy as it seemed several months ago. If a short while ago I still approached my new task with a certain anxiety, and if some worries and doubts stirred in me as to whether I would be able to fulfill it in the way I would wish, these thoughts are today, I admit, in no way fully silenced. But they have become lightened and stilled through the reception which I have found here in Göteborg. Everywhere among you I have encountered, especially in the circle of colleagues, a personal confidence and genuine good will which has made me happy; everywhere a willingness was present to advise me, to encourage me in my activity, and to help me over the first difficulties. I know now that I will not stand alone here in my work and I can hope thus to carry it on, as any philosophical work must be carried on and as it only can succeed in closest connection with the particular disciplines, in lively community, in close personal touch with their representatives. In this expectation, in this pleasant hope and trust, I enter my position today, and I express once again my heartfelt thanks to all those who have helped to open up to me this new and wonderful sphere of activity.

Critical Idealism as a Philosophy of Culture

(1936)

This lecture was given at the Warburg Institute, 3 Thames House, Mill-bank, London, on May 26, 1936. It was a part of the institute's program titled Lectures, Courses and Classes for January–June 1936, and it was the last of five lectures given between February and May that year. The first lecture in the series was by Niels Bohr, "Some Humanistic Aspects of Natural Science"; other lectures dealt with the epoch of Charlemagne, late Roman culture, and classical anticipations of English Romanticism. Cassirer's lecture came after his two-year stay in England and in the spring of his first year of teaching in Göteborg, Sweden (1935–36). The program indicates the chairman of the session was Dr. F. Saxl (1890– 1948), the director of the institute. For Cassirer's relationship to Saxl and the institute see notes 14, 15, 16, and 26 below. This text is taken from a handwritten draft in English (MS #21).–Ed.

> When Bishop Berkeley said "there was no matter,"
>   And proved it—'t was no matter what he said:
> They say his system 't is in vain to batter,
>   Too subtle for the airiest human head;
> And yet who can believe it? I would shatter
>   Gladly all matters down to stone or lead,
> Or adamant, to find the World a spirit,
> And wear my head, denying that I wear it.

In these witty and sarcastic verses of Byron's *Don Juan*[1] there is, I am afraid, expressed a common opinion and a common feeling concerning the problems of philosophical idealism. We do

---

1. Canto 11, stanza 1.—Ed.

not deny that the arguments that may be advanced in favor of a system of philosophical idealism are very strong and very subtle ones, but we are far from really consenting and yielding ourselves to these arguments. Idealism seems to remain a merely speculative view—an airy system that has no power to enforce itself on our true being, to influence our belief and to determine our conduct. Supposing this view to be true, we cannot speak of idealism as a philosophy of culture. For culture is not a merely speculative thing and cannot be based on merely speculative grounds. It does not only consist of a system of theoretical suppositions; it demands a system of actions. Culture means a whole of verbal and moral activities—of such activities as are not only conceived in an abstract way, but have the constant tendency and the energy of realization. It is this realization, this construction and reconstruction of the empirical world, that is involved in the very concept of culture and that makes up one of its essential and most characteristic features.

Before going into the details of our present question we must therefore carefully distinguish between the various meanings that may be given to the term, "idealism." In the whole history of philosophical thought there exists perhaps no other term that has been exposed to the danger of a continual change of meaning to such a high degree. If we compare the first beginnings of idealism with its later developments, if, for instance, we confront the Platonic doctrine of Ideas[2] with the views upheld and maintained by Berkeley, we find that in both systems one and the same term covers two conceptions that are not only divergent from but radically opposed to each other. Kant was the first to denounce this fact and to deplore it.[3] It was one of the principal

2. Cassirer frequently speaks of idealism in the broad sense of the philosophy of the idea and as having its origin in Plato and undergoing a particular line of development in modern thought from Descartes through Kant to Hegel; for example, see *The Philosophy of Symbolic Forms*, trans. Ralph Manheim, 3 vols. (New Haven: Yale University Press, 1953–57), I, 73–85.—Ed.

3. See also Cassirer's comments on Berkeley's thought in relation to Plato and Kant in *Das Erkenntnisproblem in der Philosophie und Wissenschaft der neuern Zeit*, 4 vols. (Darmstadt: Wissenschaftliche Buchgesellschaft, 1971–73), II, 321–27.—Ed.

aims of his *Critique of Pure Reason* to restore, as it were, the Platonic Idea to its original meaning and its original right.

Plato made use of the expression *"idea"* in such a way as quite evidently to have meant by it something which not only can never be borrowed from the senses but far surpasses even the concepts of understanding (with which Aristotle occupied himself), inasmuch as in experience nothing is ever to be met with that is coincident with it. For Plato ideas are archetypes of the things themselves, and not, in the manner of the categories, merely keys to possible experiences. . . .

Plato very well realized that our faculty of knowledge feels a much higher need than merely to spell out appearances according to a synthetic unity, in order to be able to read them as experience. . . .

Plato found the chief instances of his ideas in the field of the practical, that is, in what rests upon freedom, which in its turn rests upon modes of knowledge that are a peculiar product of reason. . . .

If we set aside the exaggerations in Plato's methods of expression, the philosopher's spiritual flight from the ectypal mode of reflecting upon the physical world-order to the architectonic ordering of it according to ends, that is, according to ideas, is an enterprise which calls for respect and imitation. . . .

Yet, before closing these introductory remarks, I beseech those who have the interests of philosophy at heart (which is more than is the case with most people) that, if they find themselves convinced by these and the following considerations, they be careful to preserve the expression 'idea' in its original meaning, that it may not become one of those expressions which are commonly used to indicate any and every species of representation, in a happy-go-lucky confusion, to the consequent detriment of science. There is no lack of terms suitable for each kind of representation, that we should thus needlessly encroach upon the province of any one of them. . . .

Anyone who has familiarized himself with these distinc-

CRITICAL IDEALISM AS A PHILOSOPHY OF CULTURE

tions must find it intolerable to hear the representation of
the colour, red, called an idea. It ought not even to be called
a concept of understanding, a notion.[4]

In order to comply with these critical demands of Kant we
must carefully distinguish between three different kinds of problems which are commonly covered by the class name of idealism
and which, according to this common denomination, are in a
constant danger of being mixed up in philosophical thought.
The first of these problems concerns the nature of truth; the
second concerns the nature of mind and body, of spirit and matter; the third concerns the questions belonging to a philosophy
of culture.

The first and principal aim of the Platonic doctrine of Ideas
was to give an exact definition and a firm and adequate theory of
truth both in its theoretical and in its practical sense, in its logical
and ethical significance. The analysis of the concept of knowledge and the analysis of the Idea of the Good, the definition of
ἐπιστήμη and ἀγαθόν, is at the root of the Platonic system. Outside this field there exists no special problem of reality; for
knowledge and reality not only conform to each other, they coincide with each other. It is the same identity that is affirmed and
maintained by Berkeley but it is no longer grounded upon the
same reasons, on the reasons of abstract and logical thought.
According to Berkeley, abstract thought is not the source of
truth; it is, on the contrary, the source of error. Truth cannot be
based on mere concepts; it must be based on perceptions. For it
is by perception alone that we can come into touch with reality.
Berkeley does not mean to overthrow that concept of reality that
is assumed by common reason. He does not admit that his theory
is a mere offspring of speculative thought; he constantly asserts
that this theory is nothing else than the plain exposition and confirmation of those views which are maintained by "the vulgar."

The vulgar are right in making no distinction between the
world of perceptions and the world of truth; and philosophy has
to accept this view. "We must with the mob place certainty in the

4. *Critique of Pure Reason,* trans. Norman Kemp Smith (London: Macmillan, 1933), A
313–20; B 370–77.—Ed.

senses," says Berkeley in a characteristic and striking passage of
his *Commonplace Book*.[5] It is true that in the later development of
his system Berkeley could not maintain this line of thought. His
empiricism and his sensationalism cannot hold the field. It has to
give way to his metaphysical spiritualism, to his doctrine of God
and the human soul which, especially in the later period of Berkeley's philosophy, gained a complete victory over his original
theory concerning the principles of human knowledge.

But it is from this very side that the idealism of Berkeley is
attacked by Kant. Kant, with the utmost vehemence and with a
personal acerbity that is very rare with him, always protested
against every comparison made between his own system and that
of Berkeley. But it seems, however, that Kant, in spite of all his
efforts to prove this point, did not succeed in convincing his critics and his commentators. Most of them continued in the same
way of interpretation that he himself had denounced over and
over again. Not only the adversaries of Kantian philosophy, but
even its adherents, did not cease to pursue this course. Schopenhauer, for instance, goes so far as to pretend that Kant, in the
refutation of Berkeley's idealism inserted into his second edition
of the *Critique of Pure Reason*,[6] has concealed and obscured his
own thought and that he was induced to such a disfiguration by
merely personal motives. But even rejecting such an imputation,
we may find it sometimes very difficult to draw a sharp line of
demarcation between the thought of Berkeley and that of Kant.
If we consider certain special doctrines as, for instance, the doctrine of the ideality of space and time, the doctrine of matter as a
mere phenomenon, we cannot conceal from ourselves that there
seems to be a close relationship between the critical idealism of
Kant and the psychological and metaphysical idealism of
Berkeley.

As a matter of fact, it is not the content of these doctrines, it is
their form and their foundation that makes the real and essential
difference. The answer may sometimes seem to be the same, but

5. See *The Works of George Berkeley Bishop of Cloyne*, ed. A. A. Luce and T. E. Jessop
(London: Thomas Nelson, 1948), I, 90.—Ed.
6. See B274–79.—Ed.

the fundamental question is always put in a different way. In order to furnish us with this difference, Kant introduces a new term; he adds a special and characteristic attribute to the general conception of idealism. To distinguish his own theory from what he calls the dogmatic idealism of Berkeley and the sceptical idealism of Descartes, he calls it a theory of transcendental idealism. "I entitle *transcendental* all knowledge," says Kant in the introduction to *The Critique of Pure Reason*, "which is occupied not so much with objects as with the mode of our knowledge of objects in so far as this mode of knowledge is to be possible *a priori*."[7] Therefore, transcendental idealism does not begin with any assertion about the nature and essence of the objects themselves; it begins with a critical investigation of the various modes of cognition by which the different classes of objects—the objects of experience, the objects of science, the objects of religious or metaphysical thought—are made accessible to us.

It is this problem of accessibility that has to precede the problem of objectivity. Therefore, Kant does not start from an inquiry into the nature of matter; he proceeds from an inquiry into the presuppositions and principles of science, by which the concept of matter is explained in a clear and exact way. He does not ask what matter is in itself and by what properties it may be distinguished from that other kind of being that we are used to calling spirit. All these contradistinctions of things are declared by Kant to be vain and futile so long as we have not examined and analyzed the special conditions of knowledge under which the different classes of objects are presented to us. Instead of comparing matter and spirit or opposing them to each other we have to compare and to oppose the modes of physical and metaphysical thought.

We cannot speak of the essence of matter before having answered the general question: How is physics, how is a pure science of nature, possible? We cannot treat the problems of the essence of God or of the essence of the human soul before having asked if or in what way metaphysics is possible. By this we are led to quite a different concept and quite a different defini-

7. A 11–12; B 25.—Ed.

tion of objectivity from that contained in former systems of idealism. The true objectivity we are in search of is no longer an objectivity of physical or hyperphysical substances, of empirical or transcendent things. It is not the things themselves, but the possible determinations of things, their determination by the different modes of cognition, that proves to be the true problem of a new idealism. The ontological view of former metaphysics, the view of Descartes or Berkeley, is to be superseded; it is to be replaced by a purely analytical view. Since the principles of the understanding are principles for the exhibition of phenomena only, as Kant declares in the *Critique of Pure Reason:* "the proud name of an Ontology that presumptuously claims to supply, in systematic doctrinal form, synthetic *a priori* knowledge of things in general . . . must, therefore, give place to the modest title of a mere Analytic of pure understanding."[8]

But I do not intend in this lecture to go into the details of the problems of Kantian philosophy. I only wish to ask and to answer the question, How far was a new way prepared for a philosophy of culture by the new element of thought contained in Kant's critical or transcendental idealism? The name of such a philosophy is not mentioned in the work of Kant, and its special theme, its subject matter, does not seem to be alluded to in any part of his system. Kant accepts the classical division of philosophy introduced in Greek thought: the classification of philosophy into physics, ethics, and logic. In a later period of his system he was compelled to enlarge this division; he had to add aesthetics as a special branch of critical philosophy. But if we regard the idealism of Kant not from the point of view of its special historical conditions, but from the point of view of its general systematic tasks, we are led on to an even greater enlargement.

The problem of Kant is not bound to an inquiry into the special forms of logical, scientific, ethical, or aesthetical thought. Without varying its nature we may apply it to all the other forms of thinking, judging, knowing, understanding, and even of feeling by which the human mind attempts to conceive the universe

---

8. A 247; B 303. Cf. "Zur Logik des Symbolbegriffs," in *Wesen und Wirkung des Symbolbegriffs* (Darmstadt: Wissenschaftliche Buchgesellschaft, 1956), pp. 228–30.—Ed.

as a whole. Such a synopsis of the universe, such a synthetic view, is aimed at in myth, in religion, in language, in art, and in science. None of them can be described as a mere copy of what is given in the data of the senses. All these forms not only shine with reflected light; they have a light of their own. They are original sources of light. If we understand the problem in this sense it becomes obvious that all the various and complex systems of symbols that are contained in language, art, science, and mythical and religious thought are not only accessible to a philosophical analysis, but that they call for such an analysis. They must be understood and explained not only as single utterances of the human mind that tend in manifold and diverging directions and that are, so to speak, dispersed over the field of our mental life. They possess, in spite of their differences, an intrinsic unity. It is true that this unity cannot be conceived, in the manner of systematic metaphysics, as a simple and indivisible entity. It cannot be described in terms of mere substantiality. It must be understood and defined in functional terms—that means in terms of relations, of operations and action. That unity which I am in the habit of calling the unity of symbolic thought and symbolic representations cannot be abstracted from its various manifestations. It cannot be conceived as a single, self-existent, isolated being. It is a condition of all the constructive processes of the mind, a force that pervades all our mental operations and energies; but we must not hypostatize this force, we must not conceive it in the way of a separate physical or metaphysical existence.

I cannot think of giving here a full description of this function of symbolic thought in general and of its special applications, for this would require entering into all the various and very complex questions of the philosophy of language, of the philosophy of art, of religion, and of science. All I can attempt here is to give a general delineation of the fundamental problem, a brief and rough draft of a region of thought that is abundant in details, and the main significance and interest of which may, perhaps, be said to consist in these details. To remain within the strict and narrow limits of this lecture, I must restrict myself to a few methodological questions that are involved in the general attempt of a philosophy of culture.

First of all, it is evident that in this sphere the fundamental
concepts and the fundamental problems of philosophical idealism assume a new and different shape. The concept of objectivity and the concept of truth cannot be defined in the same
sense when we are dealing with the problems of language, art, or
religion as when we are concerned with the mere metaphysical
problem of reality. Here at least we are safe against the attacks of
psychological idealism and of scepticism. We need not fear all
the arguments that Berkeley or Hume have advanced against the
assumption of an independent existence of matter. Kant declares
this problem to be the very stumbling-block of philosophy: "It
. . . remains a scandal to philosophy and to human reason in
general that the existence of things outside us . . . must be
accepted merely on *faith,* and if anyone thinks good to doubt
their existence, we are unable to counter his doubts by any satisfactory proof."[9]

This scandal does not return if, instead of dealing with the
problem of a material universe, we are concerned with the universe of culture; for it would be absurd to claim for the latter an
absolute existence and substantiality. But instead of this question
we have to face, in this sphere, another no less important and no
less difficult problem: the problem of objective value and objective significance. Such a significance is presupposed in all the
forms of culture, in language as well as in scientific thought, in
art as well as in religion. But how can we explain and how can we
secure and guarantee this pretended objectivity? There is a fragment of Heraclitus in which he says that men being awake have a
common world τοῖς ἐγρηγορόισιν ἕνα καὶ κοινὸν κόσμον εἶναι,
whereas, while asleep, the individual averts his thoughts from
this common world in order to live in a world of his own.[10] We
may use this saying of Heraclitus as a general expression of our
problem.

The principal aim of all the forms of culture consists instead in
the task of building up a common world of thought and feeling,
a world of humanity which pretends to be a κοινὸν κόσμον

9. *Critique of Pure Reason,* Preface to the Second Edition, B xl, note.—Ed.
10. Fragment 89. See Diels, *Die Fragmente der Vorsokratiker,* 3 vols., 5th ed. (Berlin, 1934–
35), I, 171.—Ed.

instead of being an individual dream or an individual freak and fancy. In the construction of this universe of culture the single forms do not follow a preconceived and predetermined scheme, a scheme that may be once and for all described in an *a priori* way of thought. All we can do is to follow up the slow development that manifests itself in the history of the various forms and to mark, as it were, the milestones of this way.

Language seems to be the first to take and to guide humanity on this way. It cannot be conceived in the way of a *Lingua universalis*. It has no universality which may be compared with the universality of logical thought. It is bound to national, even to individual conditions, but nevertheless it is the first and decisive step to that common world toward which the process of culture strives. Wilhelm von Humboldt was the first to emphasize this point and through this he was led to the basic principle of a new philosophy of language that is developed in his essay on the variety of human speech and its influence on the mental development of mankind. The study of language, he points out, must begin with a quite arid, even mechanical analysis of its material side, with an analysis of sounds and articulate speech, but it cannot confine itself to this problem. Speech means more than a mere mechanism; it means the entrance into the world of spirit, for it is by language alone that man soars above the field of mere particularity.

> Like a true, inexplicable wonder, it bursts forth from the mouth of a nation, and no less amazingly, though this is repeated every day and indifferently overlooked, it springs from the babble of every child; it is the most radiant sign and certain proof that man does not possess an intrinsically separate individuality, that I and Thou are not merely complementary concepts, but that if we could go back to the point of separation, they would prove to be truly identical, that in this sense there are spheres of individuality, from the weak, helpless, perishable individual down to the primeval clan of mankind, because otherwise all understanding would be externally impossible.[11]

11. In the manuscript Cassirer begins this quote in English and moves to the German

But if we think language to be such a miracle, we must acknowledge that the same miracle recurs in all the other forms of mental activity. For there is not only a language composed of sounds, words, phrases, or sentences; there is a much more comprehensive language that is built up by the symbols of art, religion, and science. Each of these languages has its proper use and its proper rules; each of them has a grammar of its own. Karl Pearson wrote a very interesting book to which he gave the title *The Grammar of Science*. In this book he is dealing with the problems of cause and effect, space and time, and matter and motion. But as he points out, all these concepts may be regarded as mere terms belonging to a special vocabulary, to the vocabulary of science. Matter and motion are not things in themselves, the essence of which must remain unknown forever to the human mind. They are concepts and symbols by which we express the order and regularity we meet with in the phenomena of nature. "The whole object of physical science," says Pearson, "is the discovery of ideal elementary motions which will enable us to describe in the simplest language the widest ranges of phenomena; it lies in the symbolization of the physical universe by aid of the geometrical motions of a group of geometrical forms. To do this is to construct the world mechanically; but this mechanism, be it noted, is a product of conception, and does not lie in our perceptions themselves."[12]

text. The manuscript reads as follows: " 'As a true inexplicable miracle it bursts forth out of the mouth of a nation and as the same amazing miracle we meet with it in the first babbling of a child. Speech is the surest proof that man has not a separate individuality of his own, but that he is connected with the primeval stock of humanity' or, to put it in Humboldt's own words, for I feel unable to translate these words into adequate English terms, 'Die Sprache ist die leuchtendste Spur und der sicherste Beweis, dass der Mensch nicht eine an sich abgesonderte Individualität besitzt, dass Ich und Du nicht bloss sich wechselseitig fordernde, sondern, wenn man bis zu dem Punkte der Trennung zurückgehen könnte, wahrhaft identische Begriffe sind, und dass es in diesem Sinne Kreise der Individualität gibt, von dem schwachen hilfsbedürftigen und hinfälligen Einzelnen hin bis zum uralten Stamme der Menschheit, weil sonst alles Verstehen bis in alle Ewigkeit hin unmöglich sein würde.' " The English translation used in the text is from *The Philosophy of Symbolic Forms*, I, 156–57. In Humboldt, see his introduction for his study of the Kavi language, "Über die Verschiedenheit des menschlichen Sprachbaues," *Gesammelte Schriften* (Berlin Academy Edition, 1907), VII, 125.—Ed.

12. *The Grammar of Science*, 3d rev. ed. (London: Adam and Charles Black, 1911), p. 267; orig. pub. 1892.—Ed.

These words were written about forty years ago, without any knowledge of that new development of scientific thought that from the beginning of the twentieth century has reversed all our notions of space and time and matter and motion. But it is just this very reversal that puts the problem of the symbolic character of our fundamental scientific concepts in a new and unexpected light. If we follow up the course of natural philosophy we find that the concept of matter has undergone a perpetual change of meaning. If we continue to use the same word we must remember that it is by no means the same thing that is spoken of in the metaphysical systems of Aristotle or Descartes, in the system of classical physics, and in the modern theories of quantum mechanics. With Aristotle matter is defined in terms of logic and metaphysics, in terms of δύναμις and ἐνέργεια, of potentiality and actuality. With Descartes it is defined in terms of geometry; it becomes equivalent to extension. In the time of Newton it could be defined in terms of those concepts and principles of the type that are laid down and explained in the beginning of Newton's *Philosophiae Naturalis Principia Mathematica*.

But the development of the general principle of relativity and of the theory of quanta seems to lead to an even more surprising and more radical change of meaning. We have to learn from this development that in order to determine the scientific sense of matter we can no longer content ourselves with the use of a single, definite system of physical concepts. We can describe matter, and indeed we must describe it, by completely different schemes of thought. We may think of it in the sense of a particle, but at the same time we are asked to regard it in the manner of a wave. The two conceptions seem completely irreconcilable if we continue in our substantial way of thinking, if we regard matter as a self-existent, independent, absolute being. But the dualism that seems unavoidable in the language of modern physics ceases to be a contradiction if we turn to the proper significance and the proper use of our physical concepts. If instead of conceiving them as immediate pictures, as counterparts of outward things, we conceive them as symbols which, to use Kant's words, are destined for the sole purpose "of spelling out appearances in order to be able to read them as experiences," we understand that it is not only possible, but that it may be necessary to employ in the spelling out of phenomena different symbols and, so to speak, different alphabets of thought that do not contradict each other but complete one another.

It is one of the merits of the theory of Niels Bohr, a merit which, in my opinion, is not only a scientific one, but really a philosophical one, to have made this point clear. In order to account for the fact that in the new theory of quanta we have constantly to combine two different languages—that we cannot desist from using the classical concepts, but that at the same time we are forced to admit concepts and laws, which cannot be explained in terms of classical physics—Bohr has laid down his so-called principle of correspondence. This principle attempts to show how the two different sets of concepts may be reconciled and may be brought into harmony with each other. I cannot discuss here the scientific and epistemological consequences that are involved in the principle of correspondence.[13] But what interests us with regard to our present problem is the fact that Bohr, in order to explain and justify his principle, had to go back to the very nature of the symbols employed in the field of theoretical physics and to reflect on these symbols in an *explicit* way. In constructing his new model of the atom, he had to deviate from the laws of radiation that were maintained in the electromagnetic theory of light, but on the other hand this theory could not be completely abandoned. Speaking of this fact, Bohr adds that it seems to be in flagrant contradiction with all the postulates of classical physics, but that this seeming contradiction is nothing but a very clear and striking proof of the symbolic character of our fundamental physical concepts.

To proceed in a systematic order, it would be my next task to show that there exists not only a grammar of science, but in the same sense a grammar of art, and a grammar of mythical and religious thought. I hope you will not be shocked by this expression, which, of course, must be understood in a very wide and

13. See Cassirer's discussion of causality in *Determinism and Indeterminism in Modern Physics*, trans. O. Theodor Benfey (New Haven: Yale University Press, 1956), pts. 4–5. In relation to Bohr's "principle of correspondence" see esp. pp. 111ff., 165, and 176.—Ed.

free sense. To grasp this sense, we must cease to regard grammar as the arid thing we were taught in our school days. We must not consider it as a dry and abstract study of arbitrary and conventional rules, but as a study of living forms of thought and expression. But for the present moment I cannot and I need not go into the details of these problems. I can give no better proof for the reality and significance of what I have called the grammar of art, and the grammar of religion, than to ask you to have a glance at the library of this institute. By such a glance you will be convinced in a much shorter time and in a much more convincing way of the thesis I wish to maintain here, of the thesis that art and religion have their special language, their special forms of symbolic thought and symbolic representation, but that, in spite of this difference, there exists a profound and intimate connection between both of them. The problems involved in this correlation and cooperation of art and religion may be, as it were, read off the shelves of this library.[14]

14. The classification of books in the Warburg Institute Library was conceived by Aby Warburg (1866–1929) to embody his conception of culture. Fritz Saxl describes the order of the library as it existed in Hamburg (Cassirer's lecture was given in the library after it had been moved to London; see note 16 below): "The books were housed on four floors. The first began with books on the general problems of expression and on the nature of symbols. From here one was led to anthropology and religion and from religion to philosophy and the history of science. The second floor contained books on expression in art, its theory and history. The third was devoted to language and literature, and the fourth to the social forms of human life—history, law, folklore, and so forth." "The History of Warburg's Library (1886–1944)" in E. H. Gombrich, *Aby Warburg: An Intellectual Biography* (London: The Warburg Institute, University of London, 1970, p. 334). Warburg's conception is stated in one of the institute's descriptive booklets as "The Library was to lead from the visual image (*Bild*) as the first stage in man's awareness, to language (*Wort*) and thence to religion, science and philosophy, all of them products of man's search for orientation (*Orientierung*) which influence his patterns of behaviour and his actions, the subject matter of history. Action, the performance of rites (*drōmena*), in its turn is superseded by reflection which leads back to linguistic formulation and the crystallization of image symbols that complete the cycle" (*The Warburg Institute,* University of London: Woburn Square, 1966, pp. 14–15). Cassirer's distinctions between expression (*Ausdruck*), representation (*Darstellung*), and conceptual meaning (*Bedeutung*), which compose the basis for his three functions of consciousness in his "phenomenology of knowledge" in *The Philosophy of Symbolic Forms,* vol. III, resemble in many respects Warburg's threefold division of *Bild, Wort,* and *Orientierung,* as does also Cassirer's threefold distinction which he employs in describing the stages of development within particular symbolic forms—the mimetic, analogical, and symbolic (see *Philosophy of Symbolic Forms,* I, 190).—Ed.

If you look at the work of the founder of this library, if you study the essays of Aby Warburg that a few years ago were collected and republished by Dr. Gertrude Bing,[15] you will immediately become aware of the fact that this work is not exclusively the work of an historian of art or of an historian of human civilization. It is based on an amazing and tremendous knowledge of empirical facts, but at the same time it is directed toward a general philosophical aim and it is inspired by a rare energy of philosophical thought. It is true that even as a philosopher Warburg did not deviate from his own way which, in the main, always remained the way of an historian and of an anthropologist. He was perfectly aware of the strict delimitation which separates the problems of philosophy from the problems of history. When Warburg ten years ago built his new house that was destined to receive his library, he wrote on the door of his new house a single word: the word MNEMOSYNE.[16] By this he has expressed his thought in a suggestive and lapidary way. Mnemosyne— "reminiscence"—is the motto of his work and the maxim adopted by him in the whole of his historical research. He did not only mean to create a collection of books, he aspired to create a recollection of living forms, especially of those forms that have been created by Greek culture, in Greek art, in Greek religion and mythology.

These forms were considered by him to be a living force, a

15. Published in Germany in 1932 under the title of *Gesammelte Schriften*. See Gombrich, *Aby Warburg*, p. 1 and *passim*, for remarks on Gertrude Bing's work as Warburg's assistant and her relationship to the institute.—Ed.

16. This new building for the Warburg Institute in Hamburg was opened on May 1, 1926. With the rise of the Nazi regime the Warburg Institute and library was moved in 1933 to London. Cassirer also left Hamburg for Oxford in that same year. The institute subsequently became a part of the University of London. At the time of Cassirer's lecture the institute was at Thames House. Cassirer had finished his first year of teaching (1935–36) at Göteborg, Sweden. Regarding the Warburg Institute and the time of 1933 see Peter Gay, *Weimar Culture: The Outsider as Insider* (New York: Harper & Row, 1968), pp. 30–34. For a narrative account of the Warburg family see David Farrer, *The Warburgs* (New York: Stein and Day, 1975). For Cassirer's relationship to and feelings concerning the institute and Warburg see his letter of dedication to Warburg of June 13, 1926, in *The Individual and the Cosmos in Renaissance Philosophy*, trans. Mario Domandi (New York: Harper & Row, 1964, p. xiii; orig. pub. as vol. 10 of the *Studien der Bibliothek Warburg*, 1927). See also Cassirer's "Nachruf auf Aby Warburg" in *Hamburger Universitäts-Reden gehalten beim Rektoratswechsel 1929* (Hamburg, 1931), pp. 48–56.—Ed.

perpetual stream of energy that pervades the whole world of our modern civilization. The full comprehension and appreciation of this world means, in the mind of Warburg, the recollection and reconstruction of its origin. I do not know if Warburg, when choosing the device of his new house, was conscious of the fact that this device bears a close relationship with a fundamental conception of the modern philosophy of history. "Mnemosyne"—*Erinnerung*—is the same term that was used by Hegel when at the end of his *Phenomenology of Mind* he was looking back to the way through which he had passed.

> That process of the mind's self-realization exhibits a lingering movement and succession of minds, a gallery of images. . . . The Self has to penetrate and to digest this wealth of its substance. As its perfection consists in coming completely to *know* what it *is* . . . this knowledge is its self-involution in which it discards its external existence and surrenders its shape to recollection. . . . Yet this recollection is a preservation of experience; it is the quintessence and in fact a higher form of the substance. . . . The way to that goal is the internalizing of the minds, as they severally are in themselves, and as they accomplish the organization of their realm. Their conservation, regarded on the side of its free and apparently contingent succession of fact, is history; on the side of their comprehended organization, again, it is the science of mental phenomenology. The two together, or comprehended history, form at the same time the recollection and the graveyard of the absolute Mind, the actuality, truth, and certitude of its throne, without which it were lifeless and alone [*die begriffne Geschichte, bilden die Erinnerung und die Schädelstätte des absoluten Geistes, die Wirklichkeit, Wahrheit und Gewissheit seines Throns, ohne den er das leblose Einsame wäre*].[17]

I had to quote this passage of Hegel's at some length for it indicates in a very characteristic manner the difference between

17. See *Phänomenologie des Geistes*, ed. J. Hoffmeister (Hamburg: Felix Meiner Verlag, 1952), pp. 563–64. The text retains Cassirer's translation. Cf. *The Phenomenology of Mind*, trans. J. B. Baillie, rev. 2d ed. (London: Allen and Unwin, 1949), pp. 807–08.—Ed.

that sort of recollection that is arrived at through empirical knowledge in the history of art, mythology, and religion and that arrived at in speculative metaphysical knowledge. The essential distinction between the two methods is to be found in their relation to the concept and intuition of time. For the historian, time is the true and in a certain sense the only dimension of his thought; it is the element in which history lives and moves and has its being. History must, therefore, always regard truth as an offspring of time: *Veritas filia Temporis*. But speculative philosophy cannot accept this view. Even when concerned with the phenomena of time, with the flux and reflux of history, it is not satisfied within this sphere. It tends to rise above itself, to consider the realm of reality *sub quadam aeternitatis specio*.

The speculative idealism of Hegel claims to be the process by which this transformation, this spiritual metamorphosis of time, is performed. Time and history are nothing but *aufgehobene Momente* or the self-actualization of the absolute idea. The idea itself is exempt from all conditions and all determinations of time. It has no past and no future; it is absolute and omnipresent. .It is *"wesentlich jetzt,"* as Hegel says. From this we may infer in what way our own problem and our own method—the problem and the method of critical idealism—differs both from the empirical view of history and from the speculative view of Hegel's philosophy.

Critical idealism does not confine itself within the sphere of mere facts; it attempts to understand these facts, and that means to order them according to general rules. But that does not mean that these rules can be deduced in a mere *a priori* manner of thought. We have no other way to find them than to ask the special sciences, and we have to accept the data with which we are provided by them, the data of the history of language, the history of art, and the history of religion. But what we are searching for are not the historical phenomena themselves. We try to analyze and to understand the fundamental modes of thinking, of conceiving, representing, imagining, and picturing that are contained in language, myth, art, religion, and even in science.

Instead of following up the phenomena singly and stringing them together on the thread of history, instead of considering them in their succession or in their connection of cause and effect, we inquire into the nature of the different functions on which the phenomena, taken as a whole, depend. We are no longer studying the works of art, the products of mythical or religious thought, but the working powers, the mental activities that are required in order to produce these works. If we succeed in gaining an insight into the character of these powers, if we understand them, not in their historical origin, but in their structure, if we conceive in what way they are different from each other and nevertheless cooperating with each other, we have reached a new knowledge about the character of human culture. We can understand the work of human civilization not only in its historical but also in its systematic conditions; we have entered, so to speak, into a new dimension of thought.

But following all these reflections concerned with the single energies of mind out of which the various forms of culture arise, there remains a different and perhaps the most important problem. We cannot build up a philosophy of culture by mere formal and logical means. We have to face the fundamental ethical question that is contained in the very concept of culture. The philosophy of culture may be called a study of forms; but all these forms cannot be understood without relating them to a common goal. What does, in the end, this evolution of forms mean; what does, so to speak, this gallery of pictures mean as they are displayed in myth, in language, in art, in science? Does it mean nothing but a pastime which the human mind plays, as it were, with itself? Or has this play a general theme and a universal task? This question cannot be answered if we approach the problems of culture from the side of psychology alone, or if we regard them from the point of view of that philosophical anthropology that recently has been developed in modern German philosophy. This anthropology aims at being an *Existenzialphilosophie;* it pretends to be the true interpretation of what may be called the existence of man.[18]

But the term "existence" is in itself an ambiguous one. In the

18. See Martin Heidegger, *Being and Time*, trans. John Macquarrie and Edward Robinson (Oxford: Basil Blackwell, 1962). Cf. *The Myth of the State* (New Haven: Yale University Press, 1946), pp. 292–93, and "Philosophy and Politics" herein. See the remarks on Cassirer and Heidegger in the fourth section of the introduction.—Ed.

sphere of humanity, existence or actuality is to be defined in a
different way from what it is in the sphere of natural things. It
cannot be defined and it cannot be exhausted by pointing at
some special objective properties or qualities. The problem of
the existence of man is not only a problem of objective Being,
but of objective value. If we try to put the philosophical question
of culture in its most pregnant, its most intense and concentrated
form, we are always led back to this decisive problem. The
answers that have been given to this problem are widely different from each other; but in general they may be reduced to
two main principles which mark the essential line of demarcation. The ethical problem of culture leads to the problem of
freedom and necessity. In order to characterize a special philosophy of culture we must inquire after its solution to the latter
problem.

In recent times there has been developed a philosophy of history that boasts of having at last revealed the mystery of culture,
of having found out the way of describing its various forms not
only in an empirical but in a really speculative way.[19] It is true
that these forms of culture can never be described by following
the usual methods of logical thought. They must [according to
this philosophy of history] be intuited; they must be detected not
in an analytical but in a physiognomical way. But such a physiognomical view destroys the belief in a real unity of culture. It
shows that culture is only possible in various shapes that are not
connected with each other by any relationship of thought, or
feeling, or will. Philosophy [in this view] must not seek for such a
unity, it has to give up the belief in this unity. There is no common subject of culture. If we speak of humanity as a common
subject of culture we are deceived by a mere illusion. There is no
common form and no common end of humanity. What we call
by the name of culture must be divided into different souls of
culture. None of these souls of the *Kulturseelen* can be compared

19. See Oswald Spengler, *The Decline of the West*, trans. C. F. Atkinson, 2 vols. (New York:
Knopf, 1926 and 1928). Cf. *The Myth of the State*, pp. 289–92, and "Philosophy and Politics" and "The Technique of Our Modern Political Myths" herein.—Ed.

with the others. Each of these souls has its own mystical being, its mystical origin and its mystical end; its birth, its decay and fall.

But in spite of this radical irrationality we can not only follow the growth and decay of the different souls of culture, we can predict it. For it is [in this view] an infallible and inevitable fate that pervades and governs the universe of culture. Man is not able to resist this fate by any effort of thought and will. He can discover the nature of the process of culture, but he cannot [in this view] control this process or cause it to deviate from its predetermined end. By this we are led to the curious and surprising fact that we are expected to adopt in the region of history a theory of a universal metaphysical determinism—when at the same time natural philosophy and scientific thought are about to give up this narrow and rigid form of necessity and to replace it by a different and more critical conception of causality. But without, for the present moment, entering into the general problem of causality, we may say that it is impossible to introduce the concept of predetermination and predestination into the sphere of culture without sacrificing one of its most distinguished and characteristic features.[20]

Culture cannot be defined and explained in terms of necessity, it must be defined in terms of freedom—a freedom, it is true, that is to be understood in an ethical sense instead of in a metaphysical sense. The relation of this ethical concept to the world of culture is, however, a very complicated one. The problems of a philosophy of culture do not belong, so to speak, to the same dimension as the problems of ethical life, and cannot be immediately reduced to its standards and categories. Both fields are, to be sure, intimately connected with each other, but they are not coextensive with each other. To determine the relative limits between the two spheres, to define their relationship and their peculiarity, therefore, has proved to be one of the most difficult

20. The original manuscript contains two drafts of this discussion of Spengler's view of history which are nearly the same. The text here follows the first version in the manuscript, merging in it several wordings from the second draft. The words in brackets are my insertions from the second version.—Ed.

problems in the evolution of philosophical thought. Without following this evolution, let me illustrate this point by a single characteristic example. With regard to Kant we may say that in spite of his constant effort to distinguish the different regions and the different faculties of the human mind in the most careful way, he does not allow any real and radical distinction between the problems of a philosophy of history and the general problem of morality.

The Kantian philosophy of history is contained in a short but very momentous treatise of Kant's—in his *Ideen zu einer allgemeinen Geschichte weltbürgerlicher Absicht* [*Idea for a Universal History from a Cosmopolitan Point of View*]. In order to understand history in its true philosophical sense, that means not only in its political but in its supra-political, in its cosmopolitan sense, we need not follow the course of its single events. We need not give a detailed account of all the various forms and of all the contingent steps of human civilization. What really matters is nothing but a single and decisive question, the question of the ultimate aim for which all his work is destined. And we cannot hope to find a definitive and satisfactory answer to this question before having laid down the general principles of morality. After having recognized and proved these principles, we find the same fundamental idea at the root of both ethics and history. Both of them are centered in the same point; they are, so to speak, various manifestations and interpretations of the same universal theme, that of freedom. It is freedom, or, which means the same for Kant, it is the autonomy of reason that is the true and ultimate aim of human history.[21]

All these various problems of a philosophy of culture may, therefore, be summed up and concentrated in the question, In which way and by what means this autonomy is to be reached? According to the general presuppositions of the Kantian system the problem can be simplified and concentrated. We need not follow the course of human history nor need we give a detailed

21. From this point to the end of the manuscript Cassirer's handwritten pages do not exist in a smooth order, but the proper order is readily understandable from its content. Several pages have been reordered and several minor repetitions of content have been resolved to produce a continuous text.—Ed.

account of all the various forms of human civilization in order to be able to answer the question which, in the mind of Kant, is the really important and decisive one: the question of the principal aim for which mankind is destined. This aim is a moral one; and it is, therefore, in morality, it is in the system of ethics that we have to seek the true principles of a philosophy of history and a philosophy of civilization.

In Kant's view the idea of freedom is at the root of all the problems of a philosophy of history and of a philosophy of culture. Freedom means the autonomy of reason; and the universal aim of a philosophy of culture is, therefore, contained in the question in which way and by what means this autonomy may be reached in the evolution of human thought and human will. Freedom is for Kant the beginning and the ending of human civilization; in its realization, in the progressive actualization of the demand of the autonomy of reason, there is contained the whole theme of human history. "Nature has willed that man should, by himself, produce everything that goes beyond the mechanical ordering of his animal existence, and that he should partake of no other happiness or perfection than that which he himself, independently of instinct, has created by his own reason."[22]

We may understand this view of Kant and we may explain it by both systematic and historical reasons. But we cannot confine the problem of culture within the limits prescribed by Kant. Kant himself had in a certain sense to pass beyond these limits, in the definitive construction of his critical system. In his first steps he was concerned only with the problem of nature and with the problem of morality. He tried to solve the first problem by going back to the spontaneity of the human understanding, by pointing out that nature in its formal sense, as the complex of

22. "Idea for a Universal History from a Cosmopolitan Point of View," trans. Lewis White Beck in *On History*, ed. Lewis White Beck (Indianapolis and New York: Bobbs-Merrill, 1963), p. 13. In the manuscript Cassirer presents this quotation in German followed by English translation. The German is: "Die Natur hat gewollt: daß der Mensch alles, was über die mechanische Anordnung seines tierischen Daseins geht, gänzlich aus sich selbst herausbringe, und keiner anderen Glückseligkeit, oder Vollkommenheit, teilhaftig werde, als die er sich selbst, frei von Instinkt, durch eigene Vernunft, verschafft hat" (*Idee zu einer allgemeinen Geschichte in weltbürgerlicher Absicht,* "Dritter Satz").—Ed.

rules under which all phenomena must come, in order to be thought as connected in experience, is only possible by means of the constitution of our understanding and its original forms and principles. He tried to found morality on the sole idea of freedom, or what means the same for him, on the pure autonomy of reason. But after having given in his *Critique of Pure Reason* and his *Critique of Practical Reason* his analysis of experience and his analysis of moral consciousness, he is led to a new problem, to the problem of art. He has to recognize the fact that the sphere of art cannot be reduced to the same principles which were sufficient in the field of theoretical and moral investigation. Art has a meaning of its own, an independent significance and an independent value, that is not to be measured according to the standards of theoretical or moral truth. In order to find out and to justify these standards, Kant had to go back to a new faculty that he distinguishes both from the pure understanding and from practical reason, to the faculty of judgment.

With regard to the problem of religion Kant takes a different route. He does not admit any religion that in the last analysis of its content and of its fundamental creeds cannot be reduced to and resolved into the principles of morality. He postulates a *Religion innerhalb der Grenzen der blossen Vernunft*, a *Religion within the Boundaries of Pure Reason;* he acknowledges no other theology than what he calls an ethico-theology. But by this ethical definition and by this restriction of the meaning of religion, Kant deprived himself of the possibility of giving a full analysis and a philosophical appreciation of the concrete phenomena of religious life and religious history. Religion cannot be explained by its ethical contents and its ethical motives alone; it contains a different, nay an opposite moment. It is the world of mythical thought with which religion, in its first beginning and in its historical evolution, is connected. We cannot dissolve this bond that ties together mythical and religious thought if we wish to understand the latter in its concrete meaning and in its concrete historical activity.[23]

23. Cf. Cassirer's treatment of the connection of myth and religion in *The Philosophy of Symbolic Forms,* I, pt. 4, and *An Essay on Man* (New Haven: Yale University Press, 1944), ch. 7.—Ed.

And the same relation holds good for nearly all the other activities of the human mind. Language, art, even science are, in their origin and in their evolution, intimately connected with the elements of mythical thought. They cannot free themselves from these elements, they cannot appear in their proper shape before having traveled a long way in their own history. Even experimental science had to go this way before coming to a true concept of its scope and of its characteristic methods.

There exists a book by Lynn Thorndike, *A History of Magic and Experimental Science,* in which the author has attempted to pursue this slow development of experimental science out of the elements of mythical and magical thought.[24] Myth is, therefore, to be regarded as a common background and a common basis for all the various energies that participate and cooperate in the construction of our human world. By this consideration we are led to a much more complex form of our present problem than could be envisaged in the critical idealism of Kant.

Kant accepts no other theory of God, no other theology than what he calls an ethico-theology. And even in Kantian aesthetics we can find the same characteristic tendency of thought. It is here that Kant always emphasizes the essential difference between the two faculties, on which art and morality are based, the difference between the faculty of pure will and the faculty of aesthetic judgment. Art has, as he attempts to demonstrate, a sphere of its own; it has an independent meaning and an independent value that cannot be measured according to the sole standards of theoretical or moral truth. But without being reducible to morality, art is nevertheless in a close relation to morality, a relation which, according to Kant, must be conceived not as a real and, so to speak, physical one, but rather as a symbolic one.

Beauty by no means coincides with morality nor does it depend on it; but it may be called a symbol of morality. For it is by beauty that a new faculty of the human mind is revealed by which it passes beyond the sphere of empirical individuality, by which it strives after a universal ideal of humanity. As Kant

24. 8 vols. (New York: Macmillan and Columbia University Press, 1923–58).—Ed.

expresses his thought, art and morality, without being the same, are nevertheless connected and coherent with each other by their relation to a common basis—to that basis which in the *Critique of Judgment* is called "das übersinnliche Substrat der Menschheit," the "intelligible substratum of humanity." According to Kant, this intelligible substratum is no datum of our empirical world, but it may be and must be conceived as an ideal of reason, an ideal to which all the different energies of the human mind may be referred and in which they find their unity and harmony.

It is a different conception of freedom and necessity that governs the system of Hegel. Hegel does not accept the moralism of Kant, and from the very beginning of his philosophy he attacked this moralism very vehemently. But there is at least one point on which Hegel perfectly agrees with the main principle of Kantian idealism. Like Kant he is convinced that the problem of freedom is the beginning and the end of idealistic philosophy. This problem pervades the whole work of Hegel. It is the common theme that is developed in manifold variations in Hegel's *Logic,* in his *Phenomenology of Mind,* and his *Philosophy of History.* But in order to come to a full development of this theme we cannot include ourselves in that sphere in the region of subjective mind, which, in the opinion of Hegel, was the sphere of Kantian philosophy.

The analysis of the phenomena of subjective mind, of the phenomena of consciousness, must be supplemented by a more profound and more comprehensive analysis, by a philosophy of objective and absolute mind. It is by such a philosophy alone that the true concept of freedom can be defined and demonstrated. We cannot restrict freedom to morality; for in doing so we should include it within the limits of mere subjectivity, of subjective reflection. But freedom means much more; it means the ultimate end of the absolute mind and at the same time the path it had to traverse in order to come to this end. Freedom is no mere fact of consciousness that must be believed on the testimony of this consciousness, it is to be made and acquired and it cannot be acquired but by the work of the mind's self-realization. And this explains the relation of freedom to the different forms of culture, to art, religion, and philosophy.

Art, religion, and philosophy are nothing but the different and necessary stages of the self-development of the absolute mind. And philosophy, as comprised of all these stages, keeps not only art and religion together, but even unifies them into a simple spiritual vision and thus raises them to self-conscious thought. "Such consciousness" says Hegel, in his *Encyclopaedia*, "is thus the intelligible unity (cognized by thought) of art and religion, in which the diverse elements in the content are cognized as necessary, and this necessity as free."[25] By this Hegel believes he has given the true reconciliation between freedom and necessity. The way of the absolute mind, by which it comes to itself, is a necessary one; but the end of this way is the absolute self-cognition and that means the absolute freedom of mind. Idealism in all its various forms rejects the conception that mind submits to an outward fate. Mind must realize and actualize its own freedom in order to possess it, and the whole work of culture is this very process of self-realization.

Critical idealism puts itself a different and more modest task than the absolute idealism of Hegel. It does not pretend to be able to understand the contents and the scope of culture so as to give a logical deduction of all its single steps and a metaphysical description of the universal plan according to which they evolve from the absolute nature and substance of mind. But in spite of

25. *Encyclopaedia of the Philosophical Sciences* (1830), pt. 3, *Philosophy of Mind*, trans. William Wallace (Oxford: Clarendon Press, 1971), section 572. Cassirer's manuscript contains a loose page which expands this point: "Hegel's philosophy claims to be the systematic description of the path that the absolute mind had to traverse in order to come to itself. All the various forms of culture, art, religion, philosophy are nothing else than the different stages of this self-development of the absolute mind. 'The absolute Mind,' says Hegel, 'while it is self-centered *identity*, is always also identity returning and ever returned into itself: if it is the one and universal substance it is so as a spirit, discerning itself into a self and a consciousness, for which it is a substance' (ibid., sec. 554). Philosophy is therefore the science that does not merely keep together art and religion to make a total, 'but even unifies them into the simple spiritual vision, and then in that raises them to self-conscious thought' (ibid., sec. 572). 'This cognition is thus the *recognition* of this content and its form; it is the liberation from the one-sidedness of the forms, elevation of them into the absolute form.... This movement, which philosophy is, finds itself already accomplished, when at the close it seizes its own notion ...' " (ibid., sec. 573).—Ed.

this critical reserve, it does not think that the single stages and processes by which the universe of culture is built up lack true and real unity, that they are nothing but *disjecta membra*—scattered fragments.

We cannot define and we cannot explain this unity—neither in terms of metaphysics nor in the way of a naturalistic and fatalistic system of history. For it is not a given thing; it is an idea and an ideal. It must be understood in a dynamic sense, instead of conceiving it in a static sense. It must be produced, and in this production consists the essential meaning of culture and its ethical value.

In this way we may consent to the conception of Kant and Hegel that the process of culture is the progress of the consciousness of freedom; for this freedom of consciousness is intended and actualized in every process of thought, will, or feeling that leads us from a mere passive state to a definite form of activity. Critical idealism begins by describing the different forms of this activity, the forms of language, art, religion, and science in a purely analytic way. But we believe that by this it does not exclude, but is preparing for, a synthetic view. It does not aim at a universal formula expressing the absolute nature of mind and the necessary sequence of its single phenomena, nor does it claim to predict and prescribe the future course of the history of culture. Its promise and its hope is a much more unassuming one. It hopes to come to a sort of grammar and syntax of the human mind, to a survey of its various forms and functions, and to an insight into those general rules by which they are governed. By this we may be able to understand in a better way the κοινὸν κόσμον of humanity, that common world in which each individual consciousness participates and which it has to reconstruct in its own way and by its own efforts.

I feel that in the course of this lecture I could give nothing but a rough sketch of the problems to which I wished to direct your attention. But instead of protracting the discussion of the subject, let me conclude with a personal remark and a personal reminiscence. I remember very well the day on which, years ago, I made, under the guidance of my friend Dr. Saxl, the first walk through the library of this Institute. I was strongly impressed by this first inspection; and it was by this impression that I was encouraged to pursue a study that I had been planning for many years—to give a systematic analysis of the problem I have attempted to treat in this lecture.[26] Even now, after having occupied myself with this problem for a long time, I am perfectly conscious of the fact that it is still *in statu nascendi,* in the act of being born. But I hope that the Warburg Institute, in this case like in many others, will prove its special aptitude and talent, that it will pursue its μαιευτικὴ τέχνη, as it is called by Plato—its art of midwifery. I wish to conclude these remarks by the expression of my gratitude toward this Institute and by the wish that, with its help, the problem will grow and come to maturity.

26. Cassirer first visited the library of the Warburg Institute in 1920 shortly after beginning his professorship at the University of Hamburg. Although Cassirer had arrived at his conception of symbolic forms independently of Warburg (as Cassirer makes clear in the preface to *The Philosophy of Symbolic Forms,* vol. II, *Mythical Thought,* the first drafts for this volume were already advanced at the time of his visit), it fit quite closely with the structure of the library.

Fritz Saxl, who joined the institute in 1913 and succeeded Warburg as its director after his death in 1929, recalls this visit: "The study of philosophy was for Warburg inseparable from that of the so-called primitive mind: neither could be isolated from the study of imagery in religion, literature, and art. These ideas had found expression in the unorthodox arrangement of the books on the shelves. Cassirer understood at once. Yet, when he was ready to leave, he said, in the kind and clear manner so typical of him: 'This library is dangerous. I shall either have to avoid it altogether or imprison myself here for years. The philosophical problems involved are close to my own, but the concrete historical material which Warburg has collected is overwhelming.' Thus he left me bewildered. In one hour this man had understood more of the essential ideas embodied in that library than anybody I had met before" ("Ernst Cassirer," in *The Philosophy of Ernst Cassirer,* ed. P. A. Schilpp, Evanston, Ill.: The Library of Living Philosophers, 1949, pp. 47–48).

Cassirer became closely involved with the institute's activities, publishing between 1921–22 and 1932 four of his works as volumes of the institute's series of *Studien der Bibliothek Warburg* and contributing to the *Vorträge* of the institute: "Der Begriff der symbolischen Form im Aufbau der Geisteswissenschaften," *Vorträge der Bibliothek Warburg* (1921–22); *Begriffsform im mythischen Denken* (1922); "Edios und Eidolon. Das Problem des Schönen und der Kunst in Platons Dialogen," *Vorträge der Bibliothek Warburg* (1922–23); *Sprach und Mythos. Ein Beitrag zum Problem der Götternamen* (1925); *Individuum und Kosmos in der Philosophie der Renaissance* (1927); "Shaftesbury und die Renaissance des Platonismus in England," *Vorträge der Bibliothek Warburg* (1930–31); and *Die Platonische Renaissance in England und die Schule von Cambridge* (1932). These were published by B. G. Teubner, Leipzig. Several have appeared in English translation: *Language and Myth,* trans. Susanne K. Langer (New York: Harper and Brothers, 1946); *The Individual and the Cosmos in Renaissance Philosophy,* trans. Mario Domandi (New York: Harper & Row, 1963); and *The Platonic Renaissance in England,* trans. James P. Pettegrove (Austin: University of Texas Press; Edinburgh: Thomas Nelson and Sons, 1953).—Ed.

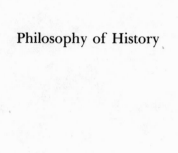

Philosophy of History

Descartes, Leibniz, and Vico

(1941–42)

This lecture is part of a set of lectures labeled "aus Arbeit Seminar 'Phi-losophy of History' Yale 1941–42." It appears to constitute Cassirer's contribution to the graduate course Philosophy 121, The Philosophy of History, which is listed for 1941–42 in the Yale Catalogue as being taught by Cassirer with Charles Hendel and Hajo Holborn of the history department. The course is described as "The philosophy of history and the significance of history for philosophy." The lectures in this manuscript (MS #11) contain discussions of Kant's view of history, philosophy of history in the Renaissance, views of Herder, Hegel's theory of the state, and a general discussion of the nature of the philosophy of history, in addition to this piece. Regarding Hegel's theory of the state and the nature of the philosophy of history, see the two following lectures. Since the lecture on Herder is dated December 17, 1941, and refers to a pre-vious discussion of Leibniz, it is likely that this piece dates from a session in the fall or early winter of 1941.

This manuscript has a connection with an earlier manuscript (MS #161) which is designated as a lecture on Descartes, Leibniz, and Vico for the Warburg Institute, London, a seminar in January and February 1935. (For Cassirer's relationship to the Warburg Institute, see the pre-ceding "Critical Idealism as a Philosophy of Culture.")

Cassirer's discussion of Descartes, Leibniz, and Vico here (MS #161) follows quite closely that of MS #11, indicating that he likely used the former in preparing the latter. Both these pieces were intended for the opening of seminar discussion. Cassirer says at the beginning of MS #161 that he does not intend to take more than half an hour so that "we shall have the full opportunity of discussing the subject thoroughly." Both pieces and all the lectures in MS #11 are in English longhand drafts.—Ed.

In these introductory remarks I do not intend to give you a systematic description of the philosophy of Descartes, Leibniz, and Vico. I must restrict myself to a single problem: to the concept of history and historical truth. A comparison made between the three systems of thought represented by Descartes, Leibniz, and Vico proves to be very instructive for understanding the general development of ideas in the seventeenth century. Here we can pursue, step by step, the rise of a new ideal of science.

In the philosophy of Descartes history has no place. Historical thought is opposed to philosophical thought by its very essence, by its object, and its aim. Philosophical thought means systematic thought. Only those propositions can be said to have a philosophical value and a philosophical relevance which can be brought into a systematic order. Order is the very condition of truth and knowledge; where there is no order there is no science. To understand a proposition means to analyze it into other simpler propositions and ultimately to reduce it to fundamental axioms that are known by themselves, by their coherent clearness and evidence. But it would be perfectly hopeless to seek after a logical order and coherence in history. Here we find nothing else than an aggregate of disconnected facts. The mind of Descartes is a mathematical mind. Mathematical intuition and mathematical deduction are the only sources of knowledge. The highest aim of Descartes is to transmute all science whatever, both physics and metaphysics, into mathematics. But history does not admit of such a transmutation; it is resistant to mathematics.

Personally Descartes may be interested in special historical questions and from time to time he may indulge in the reading of an historical author. But he does not think that such an interest has anything to do with science or philosophy. It is an entertainment of our imagination, not an exercise of our reason. This view is expressed in a very characteristic passage of the *Discours de la méthode:*

> I was quite aware that the memorable deeds related in history elevate the mind and, if read with discretion, aid in forming the judgment. . . . But I believed that I had already given sufficient time to languages and likewise to the read-

ing of the ancients, to their histories and fables. For to hold converse with those of other ages and to travel are almost the same thing. It is useful to know something of the manners of different nations that we may be enabled to form a more correct judgment regarding our own. . . . On the other hand when too much time is occupied in travelling we become strangers to our native country, and the overcurious in the customs of the past are generally ignorant of those of the present. . . . Hence it happens that such as regulate their conduct by examples drawn from this source are apt to fall into the extravagances of the knight-errants of romance.[1]

Who seeks to live in history becomes a stranger to his own native country—that means to the country of reason. Another very characteristic example of the Cartesian antihistoricism is in the *Recherche de la vérité par la lumière naturelle* [*The Search after Truth by the Light of Nature*].[2] This treatise, which has remained a fragment, develops the pedagogic ideals of Descartes; it is in a sense an essay on education. In my opinion it is highly probable that this essay was written during the sojourn of Descartes in Stockholm and that it contains a sort of program for the instruction of Queen Christina of Sweden, who had invited Descartes as her philosophical teacher.[3]

---

1. Part 1.—Ed.

2. The manuscript contains a remark here indicating that the *Recherche de la vérité* was one of the works read in the seminar.—Ed.

3. See Cassirer's study of Descartes and Queen Christina, *Descartes. Lehre-Persönlichkeit-Wirkung* (Stockholm: Bermann-Fischer Verlag, 1939). Cassirer's particular interest in Descartes's *Recherche de la vérité* is shown by the fact that he published two special essays on it: "Über Bedeutung und Abfassungszeit von Descartes' 'Recherche de la Vérité par la Lumière Naturelle,' " *Theoria* 4 (1938), 193–234; and "Descartes' Dialog 'Recherche de la Vérité par le Lumière Naturelle' und seine Stellung im Ganzen der Cartesischen Philosophie. Ein Interpretations versuch," *Lärdomshistoriska Samfundets Arsbok, Lychnos* (Uppsala, 1938), pp. 139–79. This work, along with two other essays on Descartes's thought done the year before, in 1937, form part of Cassirer's *Descartes*. The later writings on Descartes are quite different in their concrete historical approach and tone from Cassirer's earlier studies of Descartes in his inaugural dissertation, "Descartes' Kritik der mathematischen und naturwissenschaftlichen Erkenntnis" (1899), which forms the first part of *Leibniz' System in seinen wissenschaftlichen Grundlagen* (Darmstadt: Wissenschaftliche Buchgesellschaft, 1961; orig. pub. 1902), and his treatment of Descartes's system in *Das Erkenntnisproblem in der Philosophie und Wissenschaft der neuern Zeit*, vol. 1 (Darmstadt: Wissenschaftliche Buchgesellschaft, 1971; orig. pub. 1906), bk. 3.—Ed.

Descartes begins with the question, what an *honnête homme,* what a true gentleman, has to learn, and what is superfluous or even undesirable for his education. Since education has no other and no higher scope than strengthening and cultivating human reason, he says, we can admit no other objects than those which are apt to support the activity of reason and to strengthen its energy. But neither the study of history nor the study of language can perform this task. Historical knowledge depends on memory, not on reason. History is at bottom an idle curiosity that satisfies itself with the accumulation of haphazard facts concerning past ages and the remotest countries. It is clear that the whole life of a man would not suffice for collecting all these facts. But we cannot regret that this wish cannot be fulfilled; we must, on the contrary, convince ourselves that it is an unreasonable wish. He who has no other aim than to cultivate his mind will learn very soon that for this purpose he is not in need of amassing all sorts of historical or linguistic knowledge. He is not obliged to know Greek or Latin—just as little as he is expected to know all the other languages, the idioms and the dialects of the world, for instance, the dialect of the bas-Breton.[4] And he is no more in need of studying the history of the Holy Roman Empire than he has to know all the details concerning the history of the smallest and most insignificant country. The mind of those who are constantly hunting after the discovery of new historical facts is, as Descartes says, in no better condition of health than the body of a man suffering from dropsy; in both cases we are tortured with an insatiable hunger and an unquenchable thirst.

The same conception of history and the same judgment about its educational value is upheld in nearly all the other Cartesian schools. Malebranche is one of the most profound and one of the most original pupils of Descartes. But in this point he does not only agree with his master; he even exaggerates this antihistorical attitude. In his principal work, the *Recherche de la vérité,* Malebranche carries on a true campaign against history and philology. Here we find the most violent invectives against our false ideal of learning and against our false reverence for antiquity.

4. See *Discours de la méthode,* pt. 1.—Ed.

As regards Spinoza it would not be correct to say that his doctrine was without any influence on the development of historical thought.[5] But this influence was only indirect and it was restricted to a special field.

History could find no justification and no new impulse and inspiration in the *Ethics* of Spinoza. But Spinoza's *Tractatus theologico-politicus* opened a new way to the historical study of the Bible and especially to a critical study of the Old Testament. Spinoza was bold enough to give up, and to attack, the principle of verbal inspiration. He did not read the Bible as a sacred book dictated by the Holy Ghost, he read it as a human book and he found in it all sorts of human inconsistencies, errors and incongruities. Through this he prepared a new historical conception of the Old and New Testaments, he paved the way to that criticism of the Bible that later in the eighteenth and nineteenth centuries came into great importance in the history of religion.[6]

But in Spinoza's own philosophical thought and in his system we find no traces of an historical interest. If we follow the principles of his system the mere concept of a philosophy of history becomes a contradiction in terms. History means to look at the world from the point of view of time and temporal evolution; philosophy means to consider the universe from the point of view of eternity—*sub quadam aeternitatis specie*. In Spinoza's theory of knowledge we find the distinction between three modes and forms of cognition that are described by the terms *imaginatio, ratio, intuitio*—imagination, reason, intuition. Imagination is concerned with empirical things and with the order of empirical events. Reason is directed to the mathematical world, especially to the world of geometry; intuition is the very source of metaphysics. All the objects of history belong to the lowest degree of knowledge—to imagination; for, according to Spinoza, time itself is nothing else but a mode of imagination; it is opposed both to reason and to intuition.

5. Cf. Cassirer's similar remark about Malebranche and Spinoza in *Leibniz' System*, p. 447.—Ed.
6. See Cassirer, *The Philosophy of the Enlightenment*, trans. F. C. A. Koelln and J. P. Pettegrove (Princeton, N.J.: Princeton University Press, 1951; orig. German ed. 1932), pp. 184–86.—Ed.

Leibniz was the first to break through this scheme of thought which we find in the systems of classical rationalism. He is by no means opposed to this scheme. At no point does he appear as an adversary of rationalism; on the contrary he is perhaps the greatest representative of rationalism who has appeared in the history of philosophy. In his philosophy rationalism reaches its culminating point and proves its strongest power. Leibniz not only accepts the new ideal of truth introduced by Descartes, he strives to corroborate this ideal and to give it a wider application. He extends the principles of rationalism even to those fields from which they were precluded in the philosophy of Descartes.

Descartes makes a sharp distinction between philosophical and mathematical truth on the one hand and theological truth on the other hand. The latter is not based on rational principles; it depends on revelation. Such a difference between demonstrable logical truth and revealed theological truth no longer exists in the system of Leibniz. According to Leibniz, logic comprises all truth whatever and it is equal to all tasks. No subject matter is resistant to logic, to the forms of reasoning and demonstration. We have a very curious political pamphlet of Leibniz in which he strives to prove by logical arguments, according to the principles of the syllogism, that among all the candidates for the Polish throne Stanislaus Letizinsky is to be regarded as most entitled. We should scarcely expect that such a "logicism" and "mathematicism" could open a new way to understand history.

But in the work of Leibniz we find that historical problems occupy a very large space. In the plan of a complete edition of Leibniz's works that was made by the three academies of Berlin, London, and Paris, the political and historical writings were calculated to fill no less than about fifteen quarto volumes. How can we account for this seeming incongruity? Was the encyclopedic mind of Leibniz of such a sort as to be able to adapt itself to the most divergent subjects and to treat them in one and the same way? Or can we find more profound systematic reasons for the fact that the philosophy of Leibniz gave a new and powerful impulse not only to logical, mathematical, and physical thought but even to historical thought?

In order to find a satisfactory answer to this question I think we have to go back to the first principles of the metaphysics of Leibniz.[7] It is here that its differences with all the former systems of rationalism become evident. In the philosophy of Leibniz the concept of time gains a new meaning and a new importance. To Spinoza, time was a mode of imagination to which we cannot ascribe any philosophical value. The essence of things, the essence of God and nature, cannot be described in terms of time and temporal relations. There is only one substance—and this substance is above time and it is not subject to its conditions. But Leibniz understands and defines the category of substance in a different sense. For him a substance is not only a persistent enduring thing. It is a thing evolving in time; and evolution is one of the principal and indispensable predicates of a true substance. Leibniz is a pluralist, not a monist. For him the universe consists of a plurality, nay of an infinity of individual substances, of monads. And such a monad cannot be understood in a static way, as a being at rest; it must be understood and explained in a dynamic way. The monads are not substances in the traditional sense, as things beyond change and time; they are forces; they are centers of action. Each of these forces has a special indestructible character of its own. "I take it for granted," says Leibniz in the *Monadology*, "that every created thing and consequently the created monad also is subject to change and that change is continual in each one. . . . But besides the principle of change there must be differentiation within that which changes, to constitute as it were the specification and variety of simple substances."[8]

By this conception the two seemingly opposed moments of individuality and universality, of time and eternity, of duration and change are defined in a new sense. They are no longer opposed to each other; they are interlinked and correlated with

7. Leibniz is a central figure throughout Cassirer's thought. Not only is his first published work on Leibniz, *Leibniz' System* (1902), but a good portion of Cassirer's early work involves Leibniz as well as Kant. Cassirer edited a collection of Leibniz's philosophical writings, *G. W. Leibniz. Philosophische Werke*, 3 vols. (Leipzig: F. Meiner, 1924 and 1926; orig. pub. 1904, 1906, and 1915). Cassirer's interest in Leibniz runs throughout his works, including possibly a relationship between the conception of the monad and Cassirer's conception of the symbol.—Ed.

8. See secs. 10 and 12.—Ed.

each other. It was this new metaphysical concept of time and this metaphysical valuation of individuality that proved to be decisive for the evaluation of historical thought. Not the historical works of Leibniz, however rich and interesting in themselves, but his general metaphysics has opened a new way to history.

It is in the works of Herder and Hegel that the fundamental concepts of Leibniz come to their full maturity.[9] Herder was not only influenced by Leibniz, Kant, and Hamann. He had read and studied a work whose importançe was scarcely understood and appreciated in his own time. Vico's *Principi di scienza nuova d'intorno alla comune natura delle nazioni* [*Principles of New Science concerning the Common Nature of the Nations,* (i.e., Vico's *New Science*)] had appeared in the year 1730.[10] What is most impor-

---

9. Cassirer develops this point as follows at the end of his chapter on Herder in the fourth volume of his study the *Erkenntnisproblem,* written about one year before these remarks, in 1940: "There is no break in continuity, therefore, between the eighteenth and the nineteenth centuries, that is, between the Enlightenment and romanticism, but only a progressive advance leading from Leibniz and Shaftesbury to Herder, and then from Herder to Ranke. 'One would not detract too much from Ranke's achievement [said Friedrich Meinecke, in his memorial address on Ranke], if one were to say that the very principles that made his historical writing so vital and so fruitful—feeling for the individual, for the inner forces that shape things, for their peculiar individual development, and for the common basis of life which brings all these together—were won through all the efforts of the German mind during the eighteenth century. All Europe helped . . . Shaftesbury gave valuable intellectual aid to the German movement with his theory of inner form, while at the same time Leibniz in Germany with his theory of the monad and his phrase "universal sympathy" σύμπνοια πάντα kindled the fire which, long smoldering in the young Herder, finally broke out when he adopted that expression from Leibniz and discovered the individuality of nations, rooted in a common and divinely related ground of all life' "; *The Problem of Knowledge: Philosophy, Science, and History since Hegel,* trans. William H. Woglom and Charles W. Hendel (New Haven: Yale University Press, 1950), pp. 224–25.—Ed.

10. See *The New Science of Giambattista Vico,* trans. Thomas Goddard Bergin and Max Harold Fisch (Ithaca, N.Y.: Cornell University Press, 1968). Cassirer discusses Vico in relation to Leibniz's conception of history and the *Geisteswissenschaften* in *Leibniz' System* (1902). In this early work Cassirer presents Vico as the first thinker to raise the question of the foundation of the *Geisteswissenschaften* in the proper form. In his essay for the first *Studien* for the Warburg Institute in 1922 Cassirer states: "Der Plan eines konstruktiven Aufbaus der 'Geisteswissenschaften' wird in der neueren Philosophie zuerst durch Giambattista Vico scharf und bestimmt erfaßt" ("Die Begriffsform im mythischen Denken," in *Wesen und Wirkung des Symbolbegriffs,* Darmstadt: Wissenschaftliche Buchgesellschaft, 1956, p. 5). Cf. Cassirer's endorsement of Vico in *The Logic of the Humanities* [Five Studies], trans. Clarence Smith Howe (New Haven: Yale University Press, 1961; orig. pub. 1942), pp. 52–54.—Ed.

tant in this work from the point of view of our own problem is not its material content. Vico's construction of the history of civilization seems in many points to be very arbitrary and fantastic. The significance and the value of his work does not depend on this construction. But what was much more original and what was momentous for the further development of historical thought was the new methodological ideal introduced and defended by Vico. In a certain sense we may regard the introduction to Vico's works as a new *Discours de la méthode*—applied to history, instead of mathematics or physics.

Vico is perhaps the first thinker who conceived a system of historicism and who dared to oppose this system to Descartes's logicism and mathematicism.[11] According to him it is history in which we have to seek the real truth. For it is by history alone that we can hope to find an approach to reality. Descartes praises and extols mathematics because it is the field of clear and distinct ideas. Vico does not contest this clarity and distinctness. He does not fail to recognize the logical value of mathematics. But according to him this seeming advantage has to be purchased at a very high price. Mathematics has to renounce reality in order to maintain its logical rank. If human knowledge wishes to get into touch with reality, if it does not include itself in its own field, the field of abstract concepts, it has to pass beyond the limit of mathematics. Mathematical concepts owe their clarity and distinctness to the fact that they are conventional and arbitrary concepts. The truth that we may ascribe to them is a hypothetical truth.

If we lay down some fundamental postulates or axioms we may infer from them in a perfectly clear and logically irreproachable way, by mere deduction and reasoning, the truth of subordinate propositions. But what we reach here is not reality. In mathematics we are only conversant with our own concepts and ideas; and we are, so to speak, caught in the snares of these concepts. Modern rationalism has often maintained the principle that the human mind can have no adequate conceptions except of those things that are produced by the mind itself and that

11. See *Logic of the Humanities*, pp. 49–54; and *Problem of Knowledge*, p. 217.—Ed.

originate in its own innate powers. Vico adopts this principle, but he gives it a completely new turn and he draws from it the opposite inference. There is no other field, he declares, in which the human mind is nearer to itself than history. Not the physical world but the historical world is created by man and depends on his own powers. In vain we hope to penetrate into the secrets of nature, to reach an exhaustive knowledge of the physical world. It is true that when passing from mathematics to physics we are approaching reality, we are grasping concrete empirical facts. But our knowledge of these facts remains inadequate; it has verisimilitude, but no real truth. For the physical, the material world is not our own work but the work of God—and God alone, the "maker of the world," can understand his work in a perfect and an adequate way. Nature remains, therefore, in a sense always external to man and beyond the powers of human knowledge. But when dealing with history we are exempt from this restriction and we no longer feel this barrier. Man understands history because he is the maker of history.[12] Neither the mathematical nor the physical but the historical world, the civil society is,

12. In these remarks Cassirer seems to have in mind principally the following passage from the *New Science*, a passage to which he refers in other published works: "For . . . this world of nations has certainly been made by men, and its guise must therefore be found within the modifications of our own human mind. And history cannot be more certain than when he who creates the things also narrates them. Now, as geometry, when it constructs the world of quantity out of its elements, or contemplates that world, is creating it for itself, just so does our Science [create for itself the world of nations], but with a reality greater by just so much as the institutions having to do with human affairs are more real than points, lines, surfaces, and figures are. And this very fact is an argument, O reader, that these proofs are of a kind divine and should give thee a divine pleasure, since in God knowledge and creation are one and the same thing" (par. 349). Presupposed in Cassirer's discussion and in this passage of Vico is Vico's principle of *verum ipsum factum* advanced in his early work, *De antiquissima Italorum sapientia* (1710)—that the truth can only be had of those objects which the knower has himself made. Thus a science, a *scienza*, can only be had of those objects of which the knower is also the creator. Knowledge of other objects not created by the knower can only result in a *coscienza*. Thus, as Cassirer's comments point out, the geometer can have a science of points, lines, surfaces, and figures because he creates them, and man can have a science of the historical world of culture because he is the agent who creates this world. But only God can have a true knowledge of nature because he creates it. He is the "maker of the world." Man can only know the physical objects of nature incompletely as something not of his own making. See Vico, *Opere*, vol. I, ed. Giovanni Gentile and Fausto Nicolini (Bari: Laterza, 1914), pp. 131–32.—Ed.

therefore, the proper study of mankind. What Vico demands is a philosophy of civilization—a philosophy that detects and explains the fundamental laws which govern the general course of history and the development of human culture.

It is the performance of this general task which gives to the work of Vico its philosophical importance. With regard to the special content of the work we must make allowance for the fact that Vico's knowledge of historical fact, when compared with later periods, was only a very insufficient one. Nevertheless he has anticipated many views that later were renewed and corroborated by more detailed historical and philological investigations. Vico's philosophy of civilization has often been regarded as the first step not only to a new philosophy of history but also to our modern science of sociology. As a matter of fact, Vico is perfectly aware of the fact that human culture has to be studied and explained according to sociological principles and methods. He does not strive after a sociological explanation in the modern sense. He regards civilization as an organic whole, as a teleological order. In order to understand the course of civilization we must therefore investigate not only in the *causa efficiens* but much more in the *causa finalis*—in the formal and final causes. In all the variety of human customs, in all the differences depending on external conditions, on physical or geographical circumstances, we can always observe a definite rule of progress. All nations, however separate and divergent from each other, partake in a universal form of humanity.

In particular Vico distinguishes three different stages which in his opinion are to be passed through in the evolution of mankind. There are three ages—called by Vico the age of gods, the age of heroes, and the age of men. These names do not necessarily include a judgment of value. Vico does not maintain a pessimistic theory of the continual degradation of mankind; he is not an admirer or panegyrist of the golden age, of the divine or heroic age. He only wishes to distinguish the early and primitive forms of civilizations from the later stages.[13] To this sequence of the different ages there corresponds in the work of Vico an anal-

13. Cassirer appears here to be interpreting Vico's conception of *storia ideale eterna,* the principle of an "ideal eternal history traversed in time by every nation in its rise, develop-

ogous tripartition of all the fundamental phenomena of human culture and human history. Every age has its own customs, its own laws, its forms of society and civil government, its language, its religion, and its characteristic mode of thought. The two former stages, the divine and the heroic age, are characterized by the preponderance of the faculty of imagination; they are mythical or poetical ages. The last stage is characterized by the preponderance of science and philosophy.

The form of government corresponding to the early stages was a kind of theocracy and military aristocracy. The form appropriate to the present development of mankind is a democracy or a monarchy in which legal rights are conceded to every individual because each individual is regarded as a representative of common humanity. Here we can trace the influence of the general political ideas and ideals of the eighteenth century, of the epoch of Enlightenment, in spite of Vico's opposition to the rationalism of the Enlightenment. As to the problem of language, the language of the first ages is described by Vico as a hieroglyphic one; the language of the second age was a symbolic and poetical one; the language of our own age is an abstract or rational one. For the primeval thought of mankind was a mythical or poetic thought; and the first and original language was poetry.

---

ment, maturity, decline, and fall" (New Science, pars. 245ff.; see also par. 349). Cassirer appears to be suggesting that this be understood as a principle of general cultural development which grounds cultural process in an original state of mythic consciousness, rather than as a principle of historical decline similar to that of Spengler (cf. Cassirer's view of Spengler in other lectures in this volume). The emphasis on the need for a mythical stage of culture in Vico is similar to Cassirer's own conception. In The Philosophy of Symbolic Forms, vol. II, Mythical Thought (New Haven: Yale University Press, 1955; orig. German ed., 1925) Cassirer names Vico and Schelling as the forerunners for his theory of mythical consciousness (p. 3). In An Essay on Man (New Haven: Yale University Press, 1944), Cassirer states: "When Vico made his first systematic attempt to create a 'logic of the imagination' he turned back to the world of myth. He speaks of three different ages: the age of gods, the age of heroes, and the age of man. It is in the two former ages, he declared, that we have to look for the true origin of poetry. Mankind could not begin with abstract thought or with a rational language. It had to pass through the era of the symbolic language of myth and poetry" (p. 153). Cassirer's point in this lecture was intended to focus on the "logic of the imagination" side of Vico's conception of the ideal eternal history, not on its corsi e ricorsi side, its side of historical cycles of rise and decline.—Ed.

The view that later on was expressed by Hamann and Herder in the words "Poesie ist die Muttersprache des Menschengeschlechts" (Poetry is the native tongue of humanity),[14] has been anticipated by Vico. The first nations did not think by concepts; they thought in poetic images, they spoke in fables and wrote in hieroglyphics. In accordance with these forms of thought and language they did not possess a scientific but a poetic geography, a poetic cosmography and astronomy—and even a poetic morality, a morality based upon mythical conceptions. In this conception of history we feel the beginning of a new epoch; we feel the first dawnings of the spirit of Romanticism.

---

14. Cf. *Logic of the Humanities*, p. 55. In *The Problem of Knowledge* Cassirer states: "Giambattista Vico may be called the real discover of the myth. He immersed himself in its motley [*bunt*, "variegated"—ed.] world of forms and learned by his study that this world has its own peculiar structure and time order and language. He made the first attempts to decipher this language, gaining a method by which to interpret the 'sacred pictures,' the hieroglyphics, of myth. Herder followed Vico" (p. 296).—Ed.

Hegel's Theory of the State

(1942)

This lecture is titled "Some Remarks on Hegel's Theory of the State" and forms part of the course on Philosophy of History which Cassirer taught at Yale in 1941–42. (See the manuscript identification note for "Descartes, Leibniz, and Vico" for details.) Two copies of this lecture exist: one in longhand, which is included with the other handwritten lectures of the 1941–42 course that constitute MS #11, and one in typescript, which appears in the material of MS #46. MS #46 is labeled "Hegel Vorles. and Seminar Oxford 1934, Yale 1941/42" and includes, in addition to the typescript of "Some Remarks on Hegel's Theory of the State," some notes and a very long handwritten text of a course on Hegel originally given at Oxford in 1934. This lecture reflects many of the ideas in the text of this Oxford course. The typescript of "Some Remarks on Hegel's Theory of the State" of MS #46 follows word for word the hand draft of MS #11, and must have been made from it. The typescript of MS #46 bears minor corrections, apparently made by Cassirer, and is labeled at the top of the first page: "Cassirer, Meeting 4. February 42."—Ed.

In order to understand the aim of Hegel's philosophy of history we must, first and foremost, have a clear insight into the general character of the Hegelian idealism.[1] Hegel's system

1. Cassirer treats Hegel's system of absolute idealism in an essay of approximately 100 pages in *Das Erkenntnisproblem in der Philosophie und Wissenschaft der neuern Zeit*, 3 vols. (Darmstadt: Wissenschaftliche Buchgesellschaft, 1971; orig. pub. 1920), III, ch. 4. He treats Hegel's political theory, including a summary of its metaphysical background, in *The Myth of the State* (New Haven: Yale University Press, 1946), ch. 17. In his work of thirty years earlier, *Freiheit und Form* (1916), he treats Hegel's doctrine of the state in a brief section showing its relation to the tradition of aesthetic Humanism. See *Freiheit und Form: Studien zur deutschen Geistesgeschichte* (Darmstadt: Wissenschaftliche Buchgesellschaft, 1961; orig. pub. 1916), pp. 357–68.—Ed.

claims to be a system of "absolute idealism." Hegel appears as the heir of the great idealistic tradition. He is believed to complete that great process of thought that begins with Plato and that in modern philosophy reaches its culminating point in Kant's critical philosophy. It is a widely spread opinion that Hegel's philosophy is a direct descendant of the thought of Kant. Its greatest achievement, we are told, depends on the fact that here the fundamental presuppositions and principles which were already involved in the Kantian system are brought to an explicit statement, to a full consciousness of all their systematic complications. In his work, *Von Kant bis Hegel*, Richard Kroner has maintained this view.[2] According to Kroner the system of Hegel is the consummation and fulfillment of all those promises which were contained in Kant's original conception but which Kant himself was unable to carry out.

I cannot accept this view. I do not think that we can construct a continuous process of thought by which we are led from the premises of Kant's Critique to the principles and results of the metaphysics of Hegel.[3] Instead, on the harmony between Hegel and Kant we must, to my mind, lay stress upon the fundamental, the intrinsic and ineradicable opposition between the two systems. We may say that in a sense the essential content of Kant's *Critique of Pure Reason* is contained in that chapter in which he deals with the ground of distinction of all subjects into phenomena and noumena. Kant declares this distinction to be a classical one. He fully accepts the Platonic division between the phenomenal and the noumenal world. But it is just this separation between "phenomena" and "noumena," between a *mundus sensibilis* and a *mundus intelligibilis*,[4] that from the first beginnings of his philosophy is rejected and attacked by Hegel.

Hegel thinks that if we adopt this division of objects into phe-

2. 2 vols., Tübingen, 1921–24.—Ed.

3. See Cassirer, *Kants Leben und Lehre* (Darmstadt: Wissenschaftliche Buchgesellschaft, 1974; orig. pub. 1918), esp. ch. 2, secs. 4–5. This work originally appeared as an eleventh volume of the ten-volume edition of Kant's works [edited by] Cassirer: *Immanuel Kants Werke: Gesamtausgabe in 10 Bänden und einem Ergänzungsband* (Berlin: Bruno Cassirer, 1912).—Ed.

4. Cf. *Kants Leben und Lehre*, p. 148.—Ed.

nomena and noumena and consequently of the world into a sensible and intelligible world, we never can come to a real philosophical truth. Philosophical truth is the dissolution of all oppositions into a perfect unity. Such a unity becomes impossible as long as we maintain any substantial difference between the real and the ideal world, between reason and experience. It is the first task of philosophy to convince us that the real world, the world of nature and history, not only conforms to reason—for such an agreement or adaptation would always presuppose an essential difference between both of them—but that nature and history coincide with each other. There is not only a harmony but an identity between the ideal and the real world, between reason and experience.

As Hegel says in his introduction to the *Lectures on the Philosophy of History,* reason is substance as well as infinite power; its own infinite material underlies all the natural and spiritual life as well as the infinite form. We find a very striking and characteristic expression of this conception in the words that Hegel spoke when, after a long interruption of his academic work, he resumed his philosophical lectures in Heidelberg. "The courage of truth," he says here, "the belief in the power of spirit, is the first condition of philosophy. Man being spirit must esteem himself and ought to esteem himself worthy of the highest rank. He cannot esteem too highly the greatness and power of his spirit. And with this belief nothing will be so hard and unyielding as not to be open to him. The essence of the universe at first hidden and closed has no power by which it can withstand the courage of knowledge: it must become manifest; it must show its wealth and its depth and surrender them to the enjoyment of knowledge. . . ."[5]

These were very proud and magnificent words, and even today we can feel their full vigor and we can understand the inspiring power that they have exerted over the whole younger generation. But from the point of view of the general subject of

5. Cassirer's reference is to Hegel's "Inaugural Address" delivered at Heidelberg on October 28, 1816, as the opening of his "Lectures on the History of Philosophy." See *Vorlesungen über die Geschichte der Philosophie,* vol. 17 of *Sämtliche Werke,* Jubiläumsausgabe, ed. Hermann Glockner (Stuttgart: Fr. Frommanns Verlag, 1959), p. 22.—Ed.

this seminar we have to raise here another question. In which way does this fundamental thesis of the Hegelian system differ from all the other philosophical and political systems of the eighteenth century? Is not the belief in the rationality of the historical world a common conviction that is to be found in all the thinkers of the Enlightenment? Do we not find the same courage of knowledge and the same courage of truth, of which Hegel speaks here, in Montesquieu, in Turgot, in Condorcet? What then is the distinctive trait in Hegel's thought—what makes the specific difference between the type of historical and political thought introduced by him and the systems of the eighteenth century?

We find the answer to this question if we study an early treatise of Hegel: "Über die wissenschaftlichen Behandlungsarten des Naturrechts" ["The Scientific Ways of Treating Natural Law"] published in the year 1802 (contained in the first volume of the great edition of Hegel's works).[6] All the former theories of the state, of the political and historical world, have been theories of "natural law." They are arguing on the presupposition that there is a certain sphere of natural rights that belongs to the individual will as opposed to the will and to the power of the state.[7] The state cannot abrogate these natural and individual rights. They precede all the written laws and statutes; and they maintain, with regard to them, their priority, their superiority, their independence. The freedom of conscience, the religious freedom, the right of personal security, and even the right of property are described in the literature of the seventeenth and eighteenth centuries as such original and inalienable rights.

But Hegel attacks this view. The ideal of freedom proclaimed by the systems of natural right is according to him a mere abstraction. It has no place in our real and concrete world. If the rational *is* the real, if both terms do not mean opposite extremes, but if they pervade and penetrate each other, then we cannot speak of an ideal that is conceived as a pure wish or as an

6. This essay has recently appeared in an English edition: G. W. F. Hegel, *Natural Law*, trans. T. M. Knox (Philadelphia: University of Pennsylvania Press, 1975).—Ed.

7. See "Vom Wesen und Werden des Naturrechts," *Zeitschrift für Rechtsphilosophie* 6 (1932), 1–27, and also *Myth of the State*, ch. 13.—Ed.

abstract demand. All this is a mere formalism that seems to elevate philosophy over the empirical world, the world of facts—but that by this deprives philosophy of its fundamental force—of its force to organize the real world. If we draw such a line of demarcation our so-called ideas and ideals are nothing but chimerical entities. They are regarded, on the one hand, as something far too excellent to have reality, on the other hand as something too impotent to procure reality for themselves.[8]

But it is this dualism between *Sein* and *Sollen*—a dualism that in the system of Kant is declared to be unavoidable and ineradicable—that is denied and rejected by Hegel. He finds the same dualism not only in Kant but also in all the following systems. The idealism of Fichte, for instance, is nothing but a mere subjectivism. In Fichte's philosophy the self, the ego, is declared to be the fundamental principle, both with regard to theoretical and practical philosophy. In one of his earliest writings Fichte declares that the only fundamental right of man, from which all the others may be derived and deduced, is the right of egoity *(Recht zur Ichheit).*

"By the moral law in myself," he says, "I ought to be an Ego, an independent being, a person—I have therefore a right to be a person and to will my duty." It is this ethical subjectivism against which Hegel vehemently protests. "Right and duty," says Hegel in his *Philosophy of Right*, "as the absolute rationality of the categories of the will are essentially not the private property of an individual . . . but have the form of universal characteristics of thought. Conscience, thus, must submit to a criticism of its truth. . . . The State cannot acknowledge conscience in its proper form, *videlicet* as subjective knowledge, just as little as in science the subjective opinion and the appeal to a subjective opinion has any validity."[9] Every attempt to construct a so-called ideal state according to our own subjective moral standards remains, therefore, vain and futile.

Philosophy can plunge into reality and know its principle; but it cannot create reality out of nothing, and it cannot change its

8. *Encyclopaedia, Sämtliche Werke,* VI, 10f.—Cassirer.
9. Sec. 137.—Cassirer.

substance. This thought is expressed in a very striking way in the famous words of Hegel at the end of the preface to his *Philosophy of Right*. "One word more," says Hegel here, "concerning the information of what the world ought to be. For that end philosophy always comes too late. As the thought of the world philosophy first appears when reality has concluded its constructive process and brought itself to completion. What is thus taught by the notion, history also shows to be necessary: only in the ripeness of reality does the ideal appear over against the actual and build up for itself that same world, apprehended in its substance, into an intellectual kingdom. When philosophy paints its grey in grey, some shape of life has become old, and by grey in grey it cannot be made young again, but only known. The owl of Minerva spreads its wings only at the approach of twilight."[10]

If we speak of Hegel as an "idealistic" philosopher we must, therefore, never forget that his philosophical idealism does by no means exclude, that it on the contrary implies and demands, the strictest and most uncompromising political realism. Such a unity of opposite extremes is perfectly in the spirit of the Hegelian system and of the dialectic method. With regard to the political consequences it is difficult to draw a sharp line of demarcation between Hegel and Machiavelli.[11] In his first political writing, in the treatise on the constitution of Germany, Hegel sides without any hesitation with Machiavelli's concept of the *Ragione di stato*, of that reason of the state which must prevail over all other considerations. He defends the *Principe* of Machiavelli in a most energetic way. "In a period of misfortune," Hegel says, "when Italy was hastening towards her ruin and was the battlefield of wars carried on by foreign princes . . . in the deep feeling of this general misery, of hatred, of disorder and blindness an Italian politician conceived with cold circumspection the necessary conception of the deliverance of Italy by the union in one state. . . .

10. *Grundlinien der Philosophie des Rechts*, ed. Johannes Hoffmeister, 4th ed. (Hamburg: Felix Meiner Verlag, 1955), p. 17.—Ed.

11. The text says "as Mr. Hendel has pointed out." This course was jointly taught at Yale by Cassirer and two of his colleagues, Charles Hendel of the philosophy department and Hajo Holborn of the history department. See the manuscript identification note for "Descartes, Leibniz, and Vico."—Ed.

One has to read the *Prince,* taking into consideration the history
of the centuries preceding Machiavelli and the contemporary
history of Italy, and then this book is not only justified, but it will
appear as a highly magnificent and true conception of a genuine
political genius of the greatest and noblest mind."[12]

But in a certain sense Hegel seems to go even farther than
Machiavelli. Machiavelli contents himself with a perfect seculari-
zation of the state—he frees the state from all moral and religious obligations. But in Hegel we find not only a glorification of
the state but a sort of canonization, a religious worship of the
state. "The State," he says, "is the divine Idea as it exists on
earth. It is the ethical substance itself and as such it has its being,
that is its right immediately not in abstract, but in concrete existence. . . . It is the course of God through the world that constitutes the State. Its ground is the power of reason actualizing
itself as will. When conceiving the State, one must not think of
particular States, not of particular institutions, but one must
much rather contemplate the Idea, this real God."[13]

This apotheosis of the state is perhaps the most difficult problem in the Hegelian system. Over and over again Hegel declares
that man holds all his worth and his spiritual reality in fee of the
state, that the state is the object in which freedom finds its reality
and in which it lives enjoying this reality. But is not "freedom"
an empty and meaningless word, if the rights of the individual,
those "inalienable" rights that have been established and
defended in the systems of the philosophy of the Enlightenment,
are declared to be null and void in the face of the omnipotent
state? This fundamental question never could be silenced by the
commentators and adherents of the Hegelian system. Hegel's
preface to the *Philosophy of Right,* first published in the year 1820,
seems to admit but one interpretation. It seemed to involve that
in the political debates of this time, Hegel declared himself the
professed enemy of all the liberal ideas, as an adherent and

12. Cf. "The German Constitution" in *Hegel's Political Writings,* T. M. Knox and Z. A.
Pelczynski (Oxford: Clarendon Press, 1964), pp. 219–21.—Ed.

13. *Rechtsphilosophie,* sec. 258; English trans., Sterrett.—Cassirer. See *The Ethics of Hegel:
Translated Selections from his "Rechtsphilosophie,"* J. Macbride Sterrett (Boston: Ginn and
Co., 1893), p. 191.—Ed.

champion of the darkest political reaction. In his book, *Hegel und seine Zeit,* Rudolph Haym has emphasized this point. "So far as I can see," says Haym, "all that Hobbes or Filmer, Haller or Stahl have taught is relatively open-minded in comparison with the famous phrase regarding the rationality of the real in the sense of Hegel's Preface. The theory of divine free grace and the theory of absolute obedience are blameless and innocuous in comparison with the frightful doctrine which canonizes the subsisting as such."[14]

We meet with similar judgments in recent political and philosophical literature. A German scholar of political law, Hermann Heller, has published a book entitled *Hegel und der nationale Machtstaatsgedanke in Deutschland,* in which he tries to prove that all the later theories of the *Machtstaat,* of power as the unique and essential aim of the state, are based on the principles of the Hegelian system and have their deepest intellectual roots in this system. I do not deny this connection; I think, on the contrary, that Hegel's philosophy is to a very large degree responsible for our modern theories of the omnipotent state. But on the other hand we cannot overlook the opposite moment. When in our next meeting we study the development of the theory of Marx we shall see that it is impossible to interpret this theory without constantly going back to Hegel's system and to his dialectic method.

This opposition has always proved to be the stumbling-block in the interpretation of Hegel's thought. How was it possible and how is it to be understood that immediately after Hegel's death his disciples were divided into entirely different camps, that the Hegelian "Right" and the Hegelian "Left" combatted each other in the most passionate way? In the course of these continual combats Hegel's system seemed to lose its definite shape. Even in our own day it is very difficult to speak of the political system of Hegel without party hate and party favor. But if we wish to elucidate the systematical question, we must first of all take into consideration the historical background of Hegel's philosophy. We must regard the political doctrine of Hegel from a double point

14. Berlin: R. Gaertner, 1857, p. 367.—Cassirer.

of view. Hegel has severely criticized the ideals of the French revolution. But he is by no means an adversary of these ideals as such, and he has never combatted them by those arguments that we find in the systems of political Romanticism. His critical attitude did not prevent him from understanding and appreciating the most profound tendencies of the French revolution and of the political ideals of the Enlightenment. Hegel was in his youth an enthusiastic admirer of the French Revolution.[15] But even later, when his own political ideas had found their definite form, he did not withdraw his judgment. "The thought, the idea of right," he says in the *Phenomenology of Spirit,* "became effective at once, and to this the old edifice of wrong could not resist. In this thought of right there has been erected a constitution and on this foundation everything ought to be based. Hence this was a glorious sunrise; all thinking beings shared in the celebrating of this epoch."

We have a poem of Hegel, written in his youth, in the year 1796, that is one of the most important and most interesting documents in the biography of Hegel. In this poem, entitled *Eleusis,* he reminds his friend Hölderlin, to whom the poem is dedicated, of the alliance into which he entered with him in the seminary of Tübingen. The friends gave each other the promise "to live only for the sake of free truth—and never, never make peace with any convention that regulates opinion and sentiment." Has Hegel in his later life and in his later philosophy kept his promise? Did he remain true to the ideals of his youth or did he deny them? Did he resolve to make his peace with the subsisting political powers and to become the "philosopher of the Prussian state"? I think we must acquit Hegel of this charge that has often been made against him. To be sure, Hegel never was a "radical" in the political sense of this term. But he was a very radical thinker and with regard to his fundamental philosophical and political principles he was not apt to make any compromise.

Hegel's doctrine of the state may in many respects appear paradoxical or even contradictory. But it does not lack a real unity and an inner consistency. If we wish to find this unity we

15. The text here has "as Mr. Holborn has pointed out." See note 11.—Ed.

must not allow ourselves to be led astray by later theories which appealed to the authority of Hegel and tried to interpret the Hegelian system in their own sense. Even in the century after Hegel's death his philosophy of the state never has ceased to exert a decisive influence on the development of our political ideas. But the new generation that came after Hegel no longer understood his metaphysical language. All his fundamental concepts had, as it were, to be translated into a different idiom: into the language of a philosophical naturalism. But by this the notions and the terms of Hegel underwent a complete change of meaning. In the sense of Hegel a naturalistic theory of the state is completely unintelligible; it is a contradiction in terms. The state does not belong to the order of natural things. It belongs to that order which in the language of Hegel is called the realm of objective spirit.

Hegel's doctrine of the *Machtstaat* must be understood and interpreted in this sense. The term "power" itself never means a mere physical but a spiritual force. Hegel declares that the "commonweal" must be the supreme, even the only law which the state has to obey in all its actions. But what does this "commonweal" mean? In an important passage of his greater *Logic* Hegel points out that a mere increase of physical power is by no means the criterion and the true standard of the welfare of a state. The welfare of a state does depend on the maintenance and promotion of its inner form, not upon the growth of its physical force. An enlargement of the territory of a state may enfeeble and dissolve its form and may by this become the beginning of its ruin. But on which conditions does the "inner form" of a state depend? Here we have to distinguish two different moments, an internal and external moment, by which the state is constituted. First of all the state is the representation, the embodiment of a national principle, of the spirit of the nation. "The guarantee of a constitution (i.e., the necessity that the laws be reasonable, and their actualization secured)," says Hegel in the *Encyclopaedia*, "lies in the collective spirit of the whole nation—especially in the specific way in which it is itself conscious of its reason. . . . But the guarantee lies also at the same time in the actual organization or development of that principle in suitable institutions. . . . It is the indwelling spirit and the history of the nation . . . by which constitutions have been and are made."[16]

But what we call the soul, the mind of a people never can be found in external things. It manifests itself in the totality of its spiritual activities, in religion, science, art. In order to embody the true national spirit the state has not only to protect these activities but it has to express them, to make them manifest. "The highest aim that the state can attain," says Hegel is his *Lectures on the Philosophy of History,* "is that art and science are cultivated in it and come to a height corresponding to the spirit of the people. That is the principal end of the state—but an end that it must not bring about as an external work but that must arise from itself."[17] The true power of the state is, therefore, always its spiritual power. In the system of Hegel there can be no separation between the concepts of *Machtstaat* and *Kulturstaat;* the concepts are correlative to each other and coincide with each other.

From this point of view we must also understand the relation between *Staat* and *Sittlichkeit,* between the state and the ethical life. Hegel always insists on the fact that we cannot summon the state before a law court, not even before the court of our moral consciousness. There is no abstract morality, there are no duties or obligations which can be asserted in the face of the state and against its authority. For the state is, as Hegel says, the ethical substance itself and as such it has its being, that is, its right immediately not in abstract but in concrete existence. That is a very dangerous principle that, once and for all, seems to free the state from all moral obligation and all moral responsibility. But does it mean that the state is not only absolutely self-dependent but that it is infallible? Are there no faults, no errors, no crimes in the actions of the state? That is not the opinion of Hegel. He is by no means blind to the deep defects of the state, to the faults and crimes we meet everywhere in actual political life. These defects are unavoidable; for the state does not belong to the

---

16. Sec. 540.—Cassirer.

17. *Vorlesungen über die Philosophie der Geschichte,* ed. Georg Lasson, *Sämtliche Werke,* VIII–IX (Leipzig: F. Meiner, 1919–20), p. 628.—Ed.

highest realm of spiritual reality. It belongs to the sphere of "objective mind," not to the sphere of "absolute mind." It remains, therefore, as Hegel says in the *Encyclopaedia,* "on the territory of finitude."[18]

"The state," says Hegel, "is no work of art. It lives in the world—that is, in the sphere of arbitrariness, of chance and error. Evil conduct can deform and disfigure the state in many respects."[19] But to the mind of Hegel all these inherent evils cannot be cured by any effort of our individual moral wills or by any philosophical or political system. It is only the dialectic process of the history of the world to which we can appeal. "The history of the world is the judgment of the world." The lots and deeds of the particular states and of the particular national minds are, as Hegel says, "The phenomenal dialectic of the finitude of these minds, out of which arises the universal mind, the unlimited mind of the world. This mind wields its right—and its right is the highest—in them, in universal history, the judgment of the world."[20]

There is no *praetor* who can judge of states. The Kantian idea of an everlasting peace by a league of nations settling every dispute and arranging all discords in virtue of a power acknowledged by every single state would presuppose the unanimity of the states, which always would rest upon particular independent wills and therefore be liable to contingency.[21] But there is nevertheless an immanent justice in the fate of nations and of particular states. There is a tragedy in history which reflects the universal tragedy of the world, of the absolute mind. "It is the destiny of the absolute spirit," says Hegel, "to give incessantly birth to itself into objectivity, to submit to sufferance and death and to rise from its ashes to new glory."[22] Even in the reality of the state life and death are not to be separated. It would be the

18. Sec. 483.—Cassirer.

19. *Rechtsphilosophie,* sec. 258.—Cassirer.

20. Ibid., sec. 340.—Cassirer.

21. Ibid., sec. 333.—Cassirer.

22. *Polit. Schriften* (Lasson), 384ff.—Cassirer. See *Schriften zur Politik und Rechtsphilosophie,* ed. Georg Lasson, 2d ed. (Leipzig, 1923). For an English edition see T. M. Knox and Z. A. Pelczynski, *Hegel's Political Writings* (Oxford: Clarendon Press, 1964).—Ed.

real death, the death of its inner vivifying principle, to restrict
the state to an actual finite form. The state must constantly
regenerate itself, it must by a continual dialectic process proceed
to new shapes and stages, and it is only in the totality of all these
shapes that it can find its true reality.

The Philosophy of History

(1942)

This is the text of two lectures that constitute the final part of MS #11, Cassirer's course in the Philosophy of History at Yale University, 1941– 42. (See the manuscript note for "Descartes, Leibniz, and Vico" for a fuller description.) The first of the two lectures indicates that it was for the meeting of March 11, 1942; the second is undated but refers back in content to the previous lecture. As can be seen from Cassirer's remarks, the sessions of the seminar, which were listed in the Catalogue for Wed. 4–6, were attended not only by enrolled students but also by Cassirer's colleagues. This made for the kind of lively philosophical exchange that Cassirer so highly valued in his American teaching experience (see note 10 within).–Ed.

The classification of the different sciences may be attempted in a double way. Science may be determined ontologically or methodologically. In the first case the nature of a science depends on its object, in the second case it depends on its procedure and its logical means. The first view—the ontological view—has prevailed in ancient philosophy and in medieval philosophy. The second view—the methodological view—is introduced and strongly emphasized in modern philosophy, and it may be said to be the very beginning of modern philosophy. We find it in Descartes's *Regulae ad directionem ingenii* [*Rules for the Direction of the Mind*], the first methodological treatise of Descartes. Descartes maintains a strict monism of science. "The sciences taken all together," he says, "are identical with human wisdom, which always remains one and the same, however applied to different subjects, and suffers no more differentiation

121

proceeding from them than the light of the sun experiences
from the variety of things which it illuminates. . . ."[1]

If we accept his view there can be no doubt that we cannot
speak of an insurmountable gulf between history and science.
For it is not the unity of the subject matter but the logical unity
which matters here. And this logical unity must be denied. It is
the unity of a function, not of a thing or substance.[2] History
makes use of concepts and of logical judgments. By these concepts and judgments it tries to find out the truth of things. In
this general aim there is not the slightest difference between history and other sciences, and by this feature it is clearly distinguished from art, with which, in other respects, it may be
compared.[3] In his speech, "Geschichte und Naturwissenschaft"
["History and Natural Science"], Wilhelm Windelband tries to
convince us that there is a fundamental division between two different forms of knowledge. One form is directed to the universal, the other one to the individual; one form is "nomothetic,"
the other "idiographic." The former seeks after general laws; the
latter describes individual facts.

But I do not think that this distinction can be maintained if we
reflect on the logical side of our problem. Every concept and
judgment contains a moment of universality and a moment of
individuality. It gives us a general statement and a general rule;
but this rule must be applied to a particular or a special case. All
empirical knowledge is based on the logical synthesis—on the

---

1. See Rule 1.—Ed.

2. For the basis of Cassirer's distinction between function and substance see *Substance and
Function,* authorized trans. W. C. Swabey and M. C. Swabey (Chicago: Open Court Publishing Co., 1923; orig. German ed., 1910), ch. 1.—Ed.

3. Cf. *An Essay on Man* (New Haven: Yale University Press, 1944), pp. 204–06. Chapter
10 of *An Essay on Man* contains Cassirer's only systematic discussion of the philosophy of
history among his published works. See also *The Logic of the Humanities,* trans. Clarence
Smith Howe (New Haven: Yale University Press, 1961; orig. German ed., 1942), passim;
and *The Problem of Knowledge,* trans. William H. Woglom and Charles W. Hendel (New
Haven: Yale University Press, 1950), pt. 3.—Ed.

correlation and concatenation of both moments. This correlation may not be the same in the case of historical knowledge as it is in mathematical or physical knowledge. But it cannot be missed. Mere individual facts could not be "known" facts—they are not possible objects of knowledge.

To my mind we have, therefore, no other access to our problem than to study the different types of propositions that we find in science and history. This study must, from the point of view of the logician, be made with a perfectly unbiased mind. It does not necessarily imply a judgment of valuation; it must not start with a single ideal of truth in order to make it the only standard, the paragon of knowledge. But it is just this standardization of truth which is very common in the history of philosophy. We find it, to a certain extent, even in the most profound critic of knowledge, in Kant. "Science in the proper sense," says Kant in his introduction to the *Metaphysical Foundations of Natural Science,* "we can only call a knowledge, the certainty of which is *apodeictic,* a knowledge that contains only empirical certainty, is science only in an indirect and inaccurate sense. . . . And I maintain that in every special branch of natural science there is only as much proper science as we find mathematics in it."[4]

But this judgment of Kant seems rather to beg the question than to solve the question. The problem is whether all knowledge must be related to a unique frame of reference or if it is possible and even necessary to introduce various frames of reference. In the midst of the eighteenth century Diderot wrote a very interesting paper, "Pensées sur l'interprétation de la nature" (Thoughts on the Interpretation of Nature).[5] In this

4. See *Metaphysische Anfangsgründe der Naturwissenschaft* in *Immanuel Kant. Werke in zehn Bänden,* ed. Wilhelm Weischedel (Darmstadt: Wissenschaftliche Buchgesellschaft, 1968), VIII, *Vorrede,* pp. 12 and 14.—Ed.

5. See Cassirer, *The Philosophy of the Enlightenment,* trans. F. C. A. Koelln and J. P. Pettegrove (Princeton, N.J.: Princeton University Press, 1951; orig. German ed., 1932), pp. 73–75, 90–91.—Ed.

treatise Diderot makes, so to speak, a methodological prophecy. He declares that mathematics and mathematical physics have attained their culminating point; but that this culminating point will, at the same time, become their turning point. Till now they have governed the world of science in a nearly unrestricted, in an absolute sense. But that will change very soon. We can feel the approach of a new ideal of knowledge. In a hundred years, predicts Diderot, biology will have won the victory over geometry. A hundred years later appeared the work of Darwin on the origin of species.

Here we meet with a different conception of science than in the works of the eighteenth century—in the works of classical physics. From now on even natural science can no longer be regarded as an absolute and indivisible unity. But there is by no means a sudden break of continuity. We may and we must, indeed, make use of mathematical concepts and mathematical methods even in the field of biology. In modern biology we find perhaps an increasing use of these methods, of quantitative concepts. Statistics plays an important role in the solution of biological problems, for instance in the problems of heredity. And we are seeking for biological laws just as much as for physical laws. In this respect there seems to be a perfect continuity. Nevertheless we find that biology has to introduce new and specific concepts that are not to be found in classical physics. I think that modern vitalism—as it was interpreted by philosophers like Driesch, by biologists like Uexküll and others—was wrong when maintaining the thesis that for the explanation of biological phenomena we must necessarily presuppose a new force, a vital principle distinct from chemical and physical forces.[6]

Every organic phenomenon, every phenomenon of life, may be explained according to the same laws that we find in physics and chemistry. But that does not mean that the logical structure of biology coincides with the structure of the sciences of inorganic matter. Biology introduces a new concept, the concept of organic form. And for discovering causal laws it must always make use of this concept. In biology we find not only physical

6. See Cassirer's discussion of vitalism in *Problem of Knowledge*, ch. 11.—Ed.

and chemical concepts but concepts that we may call *morphological* concepts. And even in the biology of the nineteenth century these concepts have by no means become obsolete; they are in constant use, and in the best modern treatises on the logic of biology they are acknowledged as special and irreducible categories.

Let us consider, for instance, a special field of biological problems: the field of embryology. Here we meet with a law that was called by Haeckel *das biogenetische Grundegesetz* ("the fundamental law of biogenesis"). Haeckel is not the first discoverer of this law; it had been introduced before him by Karl Ernst von Baer. But he gave to it a central place in the system of biology. It asserts that an organism in its embryological development has to pass through all the different stages that the species itself had to pass in its evolution. The "ontogenesis" is an abridged repetition of the "phylogenesis"; the development of the individual being follows the same rule as the development of the general history of the species. Even if we accept the truth of this law we cannot compare it side by side to those exact laws that we find in classical physics. It is not a "law" in a strict logical sense; it admits of many exceptions. But we may regard it as a guiding maxim, as a regulative principle of biological research. And this principle becomes applicable only by the introduction of new "morphological" concepts that are created for this classification and for the comparison of biological "forms." We must determine what a fish, a bird, a mammal "is" in order to determine in what temporal sequence these forms, in the ontogenetic and phylogenetic process, follow each other.

In order to characterize this methodological distinction we may perhaps say that physics and chemistry tend toward an *explanation* of natural phenomena, whereas the aim of biology consists in a *description* of natural phenomena. Of course the mere terms "explanation" and "description" are in themselves not unambiguous. We have to define them carefully before we can use them for our problem. There were many modern physicists who preferred to avoid the term "explanation," which they suspected to have a metaphysical purport. Kirchoff declares that even in mechanics we cannot speak of an "explanation" of the phenomena of motion. According to him, mechanics has no other aim than to describe these phenomena in the shortest manner and in an unequivocal way. I do not wish to contest this view. But what matters here is the means that are applied for such a description.

From a logical point of view, in the perspective of a general theory of knowledge, a description by a system of differential equations means something quite different from those descriptions that we find in biology—from descriptions by classificatory morphological concepts. Generally speaking, explanation in the field of physics always implies a process of logical or mathematical deduction. It means the reduction of various classes of phenomena to universal laws from which they may be derived. If you accept the Newtonian theory of central forces you can deduce that all the bodies moving under the influence of these forces must describe certain orbits—a circle or an ellipse, a parabola or hyperbola. These forms can be deduced from a general principle—and if you assume the validity of this principle, they are declared to be the only possible ones. But in biology we have always to introduce concepts and laws which, without contradicting any known physical or chemical law, are not reducible to the same type of knowledge and need a different epistemological foundation. I think that the same general principle holds good for history.

The phenomena of history belong to a special realm: to the realm of man. Outside the human world we do not speak of history in the specific sense of this term. There exists, of course, a natural history; but the treatment of this history contains no new logical problem; it needs no new method beside the methods of general biology. Even when we approach the human

7. Cf. "If . . . one understands Life and Spirit not as substantial essences set over against one another, but takes both of them in the sense of their pure functional activity, the antithesis between the two immediately acquires a different meaning. No longer need the Spirit be viewed as a principle foreign or hostile to all Life, but may be understood as a turning and about face of Life itself—, a transformation which it experiences within itself, insofar as it passes from the circle of merely *organic* creativity and formation into the circle of 'form,' the circle of *ideal* formative activity" (Cassirer, " 'Spirit' and 'Life' in Contemporary Philosophy," trans. R. W. Bretall, in *The Philosophy of Ernst Cassirer*, ed. P. A. Schilpp (Evanston, Ill.: The Library of Living Philosophers, 1949), p. 875.—Ed.

world we cannot speak of a sudden change.[7] We find a continuity—both in a logical sense and in a physical sense. The theory of Darwin seems to be the confirmation of the saying of Spinoza that the world of man is not to be regarded as "a state in a state." There can be no science of man without the presupposition that human phenomena follow the same general rules which we find in inorganic matter and in the general course of organic life. An analysis of concrete historical knowledge entirely confirms this view. The historian cannot dispense with a careful investigation of the physical conditions of human life. Since Montesquieu's *Esprit des lois* the importance of this side of historical investigation could not be overlooked or denied.

Montesquieu tried to prove how much even the moral conditions of human history depend on physical presuppositions. What we call the "national spirit" rests a great deal on special physical facts—on the climate, the soil, the geographical situation of the country. Not every constitution can thrive in every climate; there are, as Montesquieu attempts to show, very characteristic correlations between both elements that can be reduced to general rules. And beside these physical conditions we find as a fundamental fact the economic conditions that in the theory of Marx are declared to be the ultimate source of historical life. But even apart from this we need not resign the hope of discovering general rules governing the course and the evolution of human civilization. The single forms of civilization—myth, religion, art, science—seem to follow a sort of intellectual rhythm that we may attempt to describe in general terms.

Such a description was, for instance, given by Comte in his *Cours de philosophie positive*. Comte was convinced that he had succeeded in finding a universal formula according to which all the phenomena of human culture could be arranged in a fixed order. "From the study of the development of human intelligence in all directions and through all times," he says, "the discovery of a great fundamental law arises to which it is necessarily subject and which has a solid foundation of proof both in the facts of our organization and in our historical experience. The law is this: that each of our leading conceptions—each branch of our knowledge—passes necessarily through three different theoretical conditions, the theological or fictitious, the metaphysical or abstract, and the scientific or positive."[8]

We need not discuss here the objective side of the problem. We need not examine in detail the evidence that may be given for the theory of Marx and Comte or other similar theories. We are only concerned with the formal, the logical and methodological question. From this point of view we may say that the desire "to know the causes of things"—*rerum cognoscere causas,* as Lucretius says—is a common trait in all human knowledge, a feature which, therefore, cannot be used for a logical discrimination and differentiation of the various branches of science. And in order to know "the causes of things" we must always strive to find out some general laws to which these causes ultimately may be reduced. All sciences whatever have, therefore, a "nomothetic" character; we cannot, with Windelband or Rickert, restrict this character to natural science; we cannot restrict history within the limits of a mere "idiographic" knowledge. But we have to ask ourselves whether the search for historical truth coincides with or is equivalent to the search for general causal laws. And this question, I think, we have to answer in the negative. In history there always appears a new factor which is not analyzable into simpler elements. It is that factor which, in a rather vague sense, we express by the term of a historical "character."

In every historical causation there is something more than what we find in physical or biological causation. There is not only causation in general but there is what we call "motivation." Of course "motivation" is by no means opposed to causality; it is a special form of causality. The metaphysical question of the "freedom of will" is not relevant to an investigation of the logical character and the epistemological categories of history. To use the terms of Kant, history is concerned with the empirical character, not with the intelligible character of men. But it always finds this "empirical character" to be one of the ultimate and irreducible sources of human actions.

We may investigate into the causes of a special historical event—let us say, the causes of Caesar crossing the Rubicon. We

8. See *Problem of Knowledge,* pp. 8–10.—Ed.

may allege various reasons which led to the decision of Caesar, the news he had received from Rome about the preparations and the intrigues of his adversaries, and so on. But once all these circumstances are ascertained we have, after all, to go back to what we call the "personality" of Caesar which we think to be the ultimate and decisive motive for this special action. With a different "Caesar" the action would have been different. This seems to be a mere tautology; but this tautology involves a serious methodological problem. For here we meet with the category of "individual causality" that is not used and not admitted in natural science. Of course we may attempt to reduce this individual causality to more general causes.

The individual character of Caesar, it may be said, is a very complex fact that must be analyzable into its simple constituents. If we knew all the causal factors that concur in this fact, if we knew all the conditions that have contributed in bringing about this special being, then we could "understand" Caesar just in the same sense as a scientist understands a natural phenomenon. Even Kant, the most resolute champion of human freedom, admits this view. In the *Critique of Practical Reason* he says that if we had the perfect knowledge of the empirical character of a man, we could predict his actions in the same sense as an astronomer predicts the eclipse of the sun or the moon. In order to gain this knowledge we would have to go back to general psychological and biological causes. We would have to collect all the available evidence concerning the ancestors of Caesar, the biological inheritance he received from these ancestors, and so on.

But the historian, as an historian, does not proceed in this way. He need by no means deny all these facts, but they are not the facts that are important and relevant to him. If he tries to "understand" Caesar, he uses quite a different method; a method that we may describe by the term "interpretation" (*historisches Verstehen*). It is not easy to describe this method in a brief manner and to clear up its special conditions. For the time being I do not wish to elaborate upon this subject but, as I hope, we shall discuss it in a more explicit way in one of our next meetings. My intention was only to suggest a general scheme for this discussion. I propose to use the terms *explanation, description, interpretation* as a general frame of reference that we may employ for a clearer insight into the nature of physical science, of biological and historical knowledge.[9]

In the following remarks I wish to resume the hostilities which in our last meeting were broken off rather abruptly. But before doing so I wish to circumscribe and, if possible, to limit our battlefield.[10] When looking back at the result of our previous discussions I have the impression that all of us agree on some fundamental points. All of us assume that history is a form of human knowledge, that it consists of concepts, of propositions, of judgments; that these judgments claim to be true assertions about the empirical world.

The historian is not like the artist who lives in a world of imagination; he lives in the empirical reality of things and events. He has to describe this reality and he has to investigate the causal relations between particular phenomena. In all this we cannot find any specific difference between historical knowledge and other forms of knowledge. In this respect it seems perfectly arbitrary to draw a sharp line of demarcation between the logic of

9. In relation to the threefold distinction given here compare Cassirer's discussion of the distinction between the natural sciences and the *Kulturwissenschaften* in terms of the process of concept formation in *Logic of the Humanities*, ch. 4.—Ed.

10. That Cassirer saw this "battlefield" as a creative and valuable one for his philosophy is brought out in his remarks to the Yale Philosophical Club in the spring of 1944, which Charles Hendel quotes in his remarks at the memorial service for Cassirer held at Columbia on June 1, 1945: "During my first year I had the pleasure and the great privilege to be invited to a seminar on the philosophy of history . . . ; in my second year I could participate in a seminar on the philosophy of science . . . ; in my third year we had a conjoint seminar on the theory of knowledge. . . . That was, indeed, a new experience to me—and a very suggestive and stimulating one. I look back on these conjoint seminars with real pleasure and gratitude. I am sure I have learned very much from them. . . . Of course, it was in a sense a rather bold enterprise, the bringing together of so many philosophers. . . . And the task that had to be solved here was so much the more doubtful and risky since three different generations were expected to have a share in a common work. To the struggle between philosophers there was added the struggle between the generations. . . . Of course the younger people criticized me sometimes rather severely. They could not always agree with me; they thought perhaps they had outgrown, a long time ago, some of the philosophic ideas and ideals that were still very dear to me. But after all, they listened to me and they tolerated my very old-fashioned philosophy. They could see my point—as well as I could see theirs" (*Philosophy of Ernst Cassirer*, pp. 56–57).—Ed.

history and the logic of natural science. There is only one truth—and there is only one general logic. The forms of thought that we study in logic are the same to whatever object our thought may apply.[11] The formation of concepts and judgments, the forms of reasoning and arguing, the method of hypotheses and verification—all this is to be used in history in the same sense as in any other science. If we look at the problem from this formal point of view, we cannot find any specific difference.

Another fundamental problem is the problem of the so-called historical causality. We had a very lively discussion about this point in our last meeting and we seemed to be divided into different camps. But here too I think there is at least one point in which we can easily come to terms. We no longer discuss the problem of causality in terms of metaphysics but in terms of logic and epistemology. Since the time of Hume and Kant we do not regard causality as a sort of moving force in the things themselves.[12] It is a category, a condition and a prerequisite of our empirical knowledge. And we cannot deny that this category extends over the whole field of our empirical knowledge. There is no domain that is exempt from the rules of causality. Even the principle of the "freedom of the will"—whatever this principle may mean—cannot mean that man stands above nature and that he is not subject to the laws of nature. In a former meeting I quoted the words of Kant, that if we had the perfect knowledge of the empirical character of a man we could predict his actions in the same sense as an astronomer predicts an eclipse of the sun or the moon. And here too we find a fundamental unity in the use of the category of causality.

There are no different and divergent kinds of causality—one for matter and one for life, one for nature and one for history.[13] We can accept neither the thesis of vitalism nor the thesis of an

11. Here Cassirer says: "In this point I do by no means deny or doubt the conclusions that were drawn by Mr. Fitch and Mr. Beardsley."—Ed.

12. Cassirer, *Determinism and Indeterminism in Modern Physics: Historical and Systematic Studies of the Problem of Causality,* trans. O. Theodor Benfey (New Haven: Yale University Press, 1956; orig. German ed., 1936), ch. 2.—Ed.

13. Cf. Cassirer's discussion of form and cause in *Logic of the Humanities,* ch. 4.—Ed.

abstract spiritualistic historicism: we need not introduce new "forces" when passing from the inorganic world to the organic world, from physics and chemistry to biology, as when passing from nature to history. The historian has to accept all the fundamental causal relations that are studied and proved in other sciences. Our human, our historical, our cultural life is not a state in the state. It depends on a very complex system of conditions; on physical conditions, like the soil and the climate, on anthropological conditions, like the race, on economic, social, psychological conditions. Without the careful study of all these conditions history cannot become a science. The question is not whether the knowledge of all these causal relations—detected by physics, biology, anthropology, psychology, economics, sociology—are indispensable for the historian but whether they are sufficient for him, whether they constitute the only and the whole task of history.

The answer to this question cannot be given in a dogmatic way; it must be given in an empirical way. We cannot, by any general speculative theory, prescribe to the historian what he ought to do; we must in a perfectly unbiased mind study what the historian, the great historian, really does. Then I think we shall always find that most of the speculative theories that in the last hundred years were proposed about the task and the method of history are liable to one and the same objection. They construct a logical ideal of history and they try to stretch the real work of the historian into the Procrustean bed of their own theories. Let me quote only a few examples. We have already studied the system of Marx, according to which the whole historical life of man depends on certain general economic conditions. To know and understand these conditions would be the same as to know and understand the whole course of human history.

But side by side to this Marxian doctrine we find other doctrines that, generally speaking, belong to the same type—to the type of a materialistic interpretation of history—but that nevertheless tend in quite a different direction. One of the best known examples is the philosophy of history contained in the work of Taine. Taine sets out from a triad of conditions that are fundamental for all historical life—the triad which he describes by the terms race, milieu, moment—the race, the surroundings, the epoch. These are the three general causes of history which suffice to explain every single event. Once we have ascertained these causes we can understand history, we know its ultimate moving forces, we can deduce the effects from their causes in the same sense as a physicist deduces the orbits of the planets or the movement of a falling body from the general theory of gravitation. That leads to the further result that, in history just as much as in other sciences—in mathematics, in physics, in chemistry or biology—we must resist the temptation to give any judgment of value.

According to Taine, "value" is not a scientific, and, therefore, not a historical category. Scientific thought has to ascertain facts and to inquire into the causes of facts; it has not to ask after the value of facts. "No matter if the facts be physical or moral," says Taine in the introduction to *The History of English Literature*, "they all have their causes; there is a cause for ambition, for courage, for truth, as there is for digestion, for muscular movement, for animal heat. Vice and virtue are products, like vitriol and sugar; and every complex phenomenon has its springs from other more simple phenomena on which it hangs. Let us then seek the simple phenomena for moral qualities, as we seek them for physical qualities. . . . Here lie the grand causes, for they are the universal and permanent causes, present at every moment and in every case, everywhere and always acting indestructible, and in the end infallibly supreme, since the accidents which thwart them, being limited and partial, end by yielding to the dull and incessant repetition of their force; in such a manner that the general structure of things, and the grand features of events, are their work."[14]

Another system of historical causation has been adopted and defended by the German historian Karl Lamprecht. In Germany this theory of Lamprecht's was for a long time the focus of discussions about the logic of history. Lamprecht seeks to reduce all historical life to a few psychological types. In the course of history these types follow each other in a constant and stereotyped

14. Trans. N. Van Laun, 2 vols. (Chicago: M. A. Donohue, n.d.), I, 8–9. See also Cassirer's chapter on Taine in *Problem of Knowledge*, ch. 14.—Ed.

order. In all times, in all countries, in all cultures, this order remains one and the same. A first stage of symbolic thought is followed by another that may be described as the stage of typical thought. Then follows a transition to the era of subjectivism that we find in modern philosophy and modern history and that finally culminates in the romantic movement, which is the reaction of feeling against the cult of reason. Our own time is characterized by Lamprecht as an epoch of *Reizsamkeit,* of sensitiveness and nervous tension. These psychic stages occur in all countries according to the same uniform rhythm, which cannot be altered because it is founded on an invariable psychological law. Lamprecht attempted to prove this thesis by an immense bulk of empirical evidence that he brought together from all sides.[15]

Both Taine and Lamprecht were not only theoreticians of history; they were all their lives absorbed in the solution of concrete historical problems. Taine inserts in his *Philosophy of Art* famous chapters about Greek sculpture, about the great painters of the Renaissance, about the history of art in the Netherlands. And at the end of his life he becomes a great political historian: he writes his work *Les origines de la France contemporaine.* Lamprecht has given us, as a proof and as a specimen of his general theory, his German history, which comprises no less than twelve volumes. But if we analyze these historical works in detail and if we compare them with the general theoretical and philosophical views of their authors, we find that there is very often a striking contradiction between what is *taught* by Taine or Lamprecht as philosophers of history and what is *done* by them as historians. As historians, in the elaboration of their special tasks, they very often tacitly assume some presuppositions and they use some methods that cannot be justified by their general principles but belong to a type of knowledge which is explicitly denied by these principles. But what we wish to understand here are not the different speculative theories *about* history—the anthropological, the economic, or psychological theories—but the work of the historian himself and the logical conditions of this work.

15. See Cassirer's chapter on Lamprecht in *Problem of Knowledge,* ch. 17.—Ed.

In a former meeting I suggested the term "interpretation" as a description of this work. But I entirely admit that without a clearer and more precise definition this term remains dark and ambiguous. Every theory—a physical theory just as much as a historical theory—may be called an interpretation of the facts to which it refers. If, for instance, in optics I adopt the Newtonian theory of light, if I think that light is produced by the emission of imponderable particles from luminous bodies, then I am interpreting light in terms of mechanics; if I adopt the theory of Maxwell I am interpreting the same phenomenon in terms of electrodynamics. We must, therefore, find out the specific difference between these physical modes of interpretation and that sort of interpretation that is characteristic and decisive for the work of the historian. That is, unfortunately, one of the most intricate problems of the theory of knowledge, a problem that needs a very thorough analysis and that we cannot hope to solve by a few remarks. But I may perhaps explain my own view in an indirect way by a sort of mental experiment.

Let me assume that in a shipwreck I am, like Robinson Crusoe, driven to a desert island. I am perfectly abandoned; I can detect no traces of human life or human culture. When walking on the shore I find by chance a stone which by its unusual size or form attracts my attention. I begin to study this stone; I wish to find out its nature. First I may be interested in its physical or chemical qualities; I wish to determine its weight, its chemical composition, and so on. Or I may regard it from the point of view of a mineralogist or geologist.[16] But suddenly my eye is caught by another thing. I remark on the stone some marks that seem to me to recur in a regular order. At a closer examination of these

16. Although Cassirer's example is different and being put to a more specific use, it bears resemblance to the means he employs to explain how the philosophy of symbolic forms is grounded in and can offer an account of the knower's ability to shift perspectives on the object known. Cf. Cassirer's example of the "line-drawing" (*Linienzug*) in "Das Symbolproblem und seine Stellung im System der Philosophie," *Zeitschrift für Aesthetik und allgemeine Kunstwissenschaft* 21 (1927), 295–312. See also Cassirer's use of this perceptual example in *The Philosophy of Symbolic Forms*, trans. Ralph Manheim, 3 vols. (New Haven: Yale University Press, 1953–57; orig. German ed., 1923–29), III, 200–01; and "Zur Logik des Symbolbegriffs" in *Wesen und Wirkung des Symbolbegriffs* (Darmstadt: Wissenschaftliche Buchgesellschaft, 1956; orig. pub. 1938), pp. 211ff.—Ed.

marks I am led to the thought that they are written characters—
and now the interest I took in the stone suddenly changes. Of
course I do not perceive these marks in any other way as all the
other things of my physical surroundings. I have no special
organ for them: I see them by my eyes just as much as I see the
color or the shape of the stone. But now they tell me quite a
different story. I am introduced by them not only into a physical
world, but also into a human world—not into a mere world of
things, but into a world of symbols. I have to interpret these
symbols in order to understand them. I have to decipher the
written characters; I have to combine them into syllables, words,
sentences. And these words and sentences are not single or isolated things; they belong to a system; they are parts of a whole,
of a human language. If this language is unknown to me I am
not able to read it at the beginning. But my interest is now awak-
ened and it tends in a special direction. After some effort I may
succeed, to a certain extent, in finding out the hidden meaning
of the characters. The physical marks have become significant
signs. They begin to "speak" to me. In my perfect seclusion from
all human beings I suddenly hear the message of a human
world.

This example may serve to illuminate the work of the historian. Historical experience has no other objects than physical
experience. All the historian knows he knows by investigating a
special class of physical objects. In his whole work he depends on
those objects; he depends on what we call historical documents
and historical monuments. Without them he could not make a
single step. And all these things, these documents and monuments, are given him as material things. They are written characters, inscriptions on paper or parchment, hieroglyphs,
cuneiform writings, they are colors on a canvas, they are statues
in marble or bronze, they are buildings in stone or any other
material. But in all these material things the historian sees something quite different. This material becomes for him, so to
speak, transparent. He does not study it for its own sake, for the
physical qualities in which natural science, in which the physicist
or chemist is interested. What he finds in it is the testimony and,
as it were, the revelation of past human life. He cannot immedi-

ately understand this life. All he knows about it are only single and scattered fragments. But here his real task begins. He has not only to collect these fragments, he has to complete them and to synthesize them; to bring them into a coherent order, to show us their unity and consistency.

This intellectual and imaginative synthesis is what we call history—just as much as the synthesis of particular material phenomena in space and time according to general laws is called natural science. And it is easy to see why this step is necessary and indispensable for all our understanding of our own human world. Man is not only in all he does but also in all he feels and thinks, a ζῷον πολιτικόν—a social being.[17] He has no separate individual being—he lives in the great forms of social life—in the world of language, of religion, of art, of political institutions. He cannot live his own life without constantly expressing it in these forms. He creates verbal symbols, religious symbols, mythical and artistic images—and it is only by the totality, by the system of these symbols and images, that he can maintain his social life— that he is able to communicate with other human beings and make himself understood by them.

But if we compare this symbolic world with the world of nature we find a great difference between them. Symbolic expressions have a much more unsteady and inconstant character than natural objects. Much more than the material and physical things of our common surroundings, they are liable to change and decay. In the world of meaning, for instance, in the world of language, we always find that characteristic phenomenon which we call "change of meaning." Language, art, religion—all this is in a continual flux. Undoubtedly we can find a definite and constant structure in language, in art, in religion; we can determine their general function in the construction of our common human world. But within the limits of this general structure every single phenomenon may change from one moment to another.

This seems to imply a great uncertainty of all our historical knowledge. When compared with the objects of natural science,

17. Aristotle, *Politics*, I, 2, 1253ª.—Ed.

the objects of historical science seem to be much more fugitive and evanescent. An astronomer who looks at the stars will always find them at the same place and in their due order; a chemist who analyzes a certain stuff will always find the same elements. But in the world of symbols we do not find this same permanence or persistence. After a short time the symbols in which man expresses his ideas and his feelings, his emotions and desires, his thoughts and his creeds, become unintelligible. And here the real task of history begins.

It is for history to revivify these symbols, to restore them to a new life and to render them legible and understandable again. This work is performed in all its great classical works, from the times of Thucydides up to our own time. In this sense Thucydides was right to describe his own work as a κτῆμα ἐς ἀεί, as an everlasting possession of the human mind.[18] In order to possess our human world we have constantly to recover it. Without this recovery brought about by historical thought and historical research all our human works would fade; they would become colorless and meaningless. The historian is, therefore, by no means a mere narrator who tells us the story of past events. He is a discoverer and interpreter of past human life. He who only wishes to relate what has happened during a certain period is an annalist, not an historian. The historian aims at quite a different end. He not only narrates but he reconstructs the past; he inspires in it a new life.

It has often been remarked that the very term "history" is used in a double sense. It means, on the one hand, the *res gestae,* the facts, the events, the deeds of the past. But on the other hand it means something quite different; it means our recollection, our knowledge of these events. From a mere logical point of view that seems to imply a curious and very shocking equivocation that we find in no other branch of knowledge. It is just as much as if a scientist were not able to make a clear distinction between the object and the form of his knowledge—as if he would confuse "physics" and "nature." But we can perhaps account for this incongruity that at first sight seems to be very objectionable. The

18. *History of the Peloponnesian War,* bk. 1, ch. 22.—Ed.

connection between the content and the form of knowledge is much closer in history than it is in any branch of natural science. In our common experience we are all surrounded by physical objects. Science has to describe and to explain these objects, but we would not lose sight of them without the help of science; it seems as if we could perceive, as if we could see and touch them immediately. But we cannot grasp our past life, the life of mankind, in this way. Without the constant and indefatigable labor of history this life would remain a sealed book. What we call our modern historical consciousness had to be built up, step by step, by the work of the great historians.

History reverses, so to speak, the creative process that characterizes our human civilization. Human civilization necessarily creates new forms, new symbols, new material things in which the life of man finds its external expression. The historian traces all these expressions to their very origin; he tries to reconstruct the real life that is at the bottom of all these single forms. In this sense history is a rebirth of life that without its continual effort would vanish and lose its vital force. Without a historical hermeneutic, without the art of interpretation contained in history, human life would be a very poor thing. It would be restricted to a single moment of time, it would have no past and, therefore, no future; for the thought of the future and the thought of the past depend on each other.

Before concluding these remarks I wish to give you once more a quotation from the works of Taine. When referring to Taine I cannot be suspected of citing a witness who is favorable to my own conception of history. Taine belongs to those philosophers who indefatigably and with the strongest emphasis defended the thesis of the unity and homogeneity of science. He admits no difference whatever between scientific knowledge and historical knowledge. His highest ambition and his highest ideal is to reduce history to natural science. But in spite of this general maxim we find in the work of Taine many hints which show us, so to speak, quite a different face and which tend in the opposite direction. "When you consider with your eyes the visible man," he says in his introduction to the *History of English Literature*, "what do you look for?"

The man invisible. The words which enter your ears, the
gestures, the motions of his head, the clothes he wears, visible acts and deeds of every kind, are expressions merely;
somewhat is revealed beneath them, and that is a soul. An
inner man is concealed beneath the outer man; the second
does but reveal the first. You look at his house, furniture,
dress; and that in order to discover in them the marks of his
habits and tastes, the degree of his refinement or rusticity,
his extravagance or his economy, his stupidity or his cunning. You listen to his conversation, and you note the inflec-
tions of his voice, the changes in his attitudes; and that in
order to judge of his intensity, his self-forgetfulness or his
gayety, his energy or his constraint. You consider his writings, his artistic productions, his business transactions or
political ventures; and that in order to measure the scope
and limits of his intelligence, his inventiveness, his coolness,
to find out the order, the description, the general force of
his ideas, the mode in which he thinks and resolves. All
these externals are but avenues converging to a center; you
enter them simply in order to reach that center; and that
center is the genuine man, I mean that mass of faculties and
feelings which are produced by the inner man. We have
reached a new world, which is infinite, because every action
which we see involves an infinite association of reasonings,
emotions, sensations new and old, which have served to
bring it to light, and which, like great rocks deep-seated in
the ground, find in it their end and their level. This under-
world is a new subject-matter, proper to the historian. If his
critical education suffice, he can lay bare, under every detail
of architecture, every stroke in a picture, every phrase in a
writing, the special sensation whence detail, stroke, or
phrase had issue; he is present at the drama which was
enacted in the soul of artist or writer; the choice of a word,
the brevity or length of a sentence, the nature of a metaphor, the accent of a verse, the development of an argument—everything is a symbol to him; while his eyes read the
text, his soul and mind pursue the continuous development

and the ever-changing succession of the emotions and conceptions out of which the text has sprung.[19]

That is precisely the same conception of history that I wished to explain and to defend here—but I think we can scarcely reconcile it with Taine's general principles. So far as I can see the historian in Taine and the philosopher of history are in flagrant contradiction to each other—what the former does, the latter denies.

19. Pp. 5–6.—Ed.

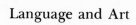

Language and Art

Language and Art I

(1942)

This lecture is the first of two items grouped together in an envelope labeled "Aufsatz: Language and Art/Cornell-U. 23. 4. 42" and "Language, Myth, Art/Sprach-Seminar/11 V. 42" (MS #209). An inside sheet repeats this information. The second of these items constitutes the succeeding essay herein. The first item on "Language and Art" is a typescript with two carbons containing some hand corrections. MS #28 contains the handwritten text for this typescript. The text of "Language and Art I," which is in English, was evidently prepared as an academic, colloquium-style lecture for presentation at Cornell University on April 23, 1942, as the envelope and covering sheet indicate.–Ed.

Language and art may be regarded as two different focal points of all our human activities. There are few things with which we seem to be more familiar. Language surrounds us from the very beginning of our life and from the earliest dawning of our consciousness. It accompanies every step of our intellectual development. Man cannot breathe outside this medium, for it is like a spiritual atmosphere which pervades his thoughts and his feelings, his perceptions and his concepts. Art seems to be confined within narrower limits.[1]

1. Cassirer's principal discussions of art in his published works are *An Essay on Man* (New Haven: Yale University Press, 1944), ch. 9; and "Mythischer, ästhetischer und theoretischer Raum," in *Vierter Kongreß für Ästhetik und allgemeine Kunstwissenschaft*, ed. H. Noack (Stuttgart, 1931), pp. 21–36. For an English translation, see "Mythic, Aesthetic and Theoretical Space," trans. Donald Phillip Verene and Lerke Holzwarth Foster, *Man and World* 2 (1969), 3–17. In this connection Cassirer's earlier study *Freiheit und Form: Studien zur deutschen Geistesgeschichte* (Darmstadt: Wissenschaftliche Buchgesellschaft, 1961; orig. pub. 1916), should be considered as well as his writings on specific literary subjects, esp. on Goethe (see "The Educational Value of Art" herein, note 21). Regarding Cassirer's plan to write a volume on art see the introduction.—Ed.

It appears to be an individual gift, not, like language, a universal gift. Nevertheless we feel that art is not only an addition, a mere supplement to life. We cannot think of it as a mere adornment of human life; we must regard it as one of its constituents, its essential conditions. Those who are sensitive to the great works of art are convinced that without them life would become devoid of significance, that it scarcely would be worth living. But it is a curious and paradoxical fact that this fundamental conviction seems to be obscured, or at least overshadowed, as soon as we transgress the limits of our immediate experience, as soon as we begin to reflect on language and art.

Philosophical reflection never approaches the problems of language and art without being involved in difficult dilemmas and in skeptical doubts. Side by side with an enthusiastic praise of both we find a deep mistrust of both. We can trace this development from early Greek thought down to our day. Plato was the first to feel this discrepancy.[2] Like all the other great Greek thinkers, he was deeply impressed and almost overwhelmed by the power of the Logos. Logos, the "word," meant for him at the same time the faculty of speech and the faculty of reason. But he becomes aware that this gift of the word is a questionable and ambiguous gift. According to the use that man makes of it, it may become a source of truth or a source of illusion. The true, the legitimate use of the word is revealed for Plato in the Socratic dialogue. Here he finds the true method of philosophy, the dia-logical, so to speak, or dialectic method. But side by side with Socrates he sees the Sophists. They are not the philosophers of the word but the artists of the word. They do not employ it for the investigation of truth but for practical purposes, for stirring the emotions of man and for prompting him to certain actions. The art of rhetoric becomes in the hand of the sophist a most dangerous weapon; it becomes the enemy of all true philosophy and of all genuine morality. And according to Plato the fallacies and sophistries of language are increased by the fallacies and

2. Cf. Cassirer, "Eidos und Eidolon. Das Problem des Schönen und der Kunst in Platons Dialogen," in *Vorträge der Bibliothek Warburg* (Leipzig: B. G. Teubner, 1924), II, pt. 1, pp. 1–27.—Ed.

sophistries of art. The sorcery of words that we find in rhetoric is strengthened by the sorcery of poetry and fine arts.

At first sight it may appear as a great historical paradox that Plato became the severe judge and the implacable adversary of art. For is not Plato the greatest artist who ever has appeared in the history of philosophy? But it is precisely this thinker, who was susceptible to all the charms of art, who would be most aware of all its temptations and seductions. In the Platonic dialogue, the *Sophist,* the artist and the sophist are declared to be on the same level. Instead of elevating the human soul to real knowledge, to the intuition of the ideas, as the eternal archetypes of things, they juggle images. By their trickery of our understanding and our fancy they lull us into a world of dreams. The sophist and the artist are not, like the philosopher, the discoverers of the ideas and the teachers of moral and religious ideals; they are on the contrary the εἰδωλοποιοί—the inventors and fabricators of mere idols—they deceive us by the fetishism of words and by the fetishism of images.

These objections seem both unavoidable and unanswerable as long as we argue from the assumption that language and art can have no other and no higher aim than to reproduce and to imitate the empirical reality of things. It is clear that in this case the copy of the world never can reach the perfection and truth of the original. How could we hope to find linguistic or artistic symbols that would express in an adequate way the nature and essence of things? Is not the symbol necessarily a mere symbol, that must be infinitely remote from that which it is designed to delineate and to express? But the problem assumes a new and very different shape as soon as we change our starting point, as soon as we define reality not in terms of a metaphysical system, like the Platonic system of ideas, but in terms of a critical analysis of human knowledge.

It was Kant who by such an analysis paved the way for a new conception of science and scientific truth. But in his last great systematic work, in his *Critique of Judgment,* Kant became at the same time the founder of a new aesthetics. The problem of language, however, is not treated in the work of Kant. He gives us a philosophy of knowledge, a philosophy of morality and art, but he does not give us a philosophy of language. But if we follow the general principles established by his critical philosophy we can fill this gap. According to these principles we must study the world of language, not as if it were a substantial thing which possesses a reality of its own, an original or derivative reality, but as an instrument of human thought by which we are led to the construction of an objective world. If language means such a process of objectification, it is based on spontaneity, not on mere receptivity. According to Kant all the so-called pure concepts of our understanding imply a specific energy, a fundamental spontaneity. They are not intended to depict an absolute reality, a reality of things-in-themselves. They are rules for the connection of phenomena. And, as Kant tries to prove, it is only by this connection, by the synthetic unity of phenomena, that we are able to conceive of an empirical world and to apprehend objects in experience.

If we apply this principle to our present problem, we find that the significance of language and its value must be sought in a different place. Language cannot be regarded as a copy of things but as a condition of our concepts of things. If we can show that it is one of the most valuable aids to, nay a necessary presupposition of, the formation of these concepts, we have done enough. We have proved that language, far from being a substantial thing, a reality of a higher or lower order, is a prerequisite of our representation of empirical objects, of our concept of what we call the "external world." I should like very much to prove this thesis by showing the particular steps by which language gradually fulfills its task. But such a task would be far beyond the compass of this short paper.[3] Here I can only touch on this very complex and intricate problem. I cannot lay before you the

3. In a sentence which Cassirer has crossed out at this point in the manuscript he refers the reader to the French translation of his paper: "Le Langage et la construction du monde des objets," trans. P. Guillaume, *Journal de Psychologie Normale et Pathologique* 30 (1933), 18–44. The original is: "Die Sprache und der Aufbau der Gegenstandswelt" in *Bericht über den XII. Kongreβ der deutschen Gesellschaft für Psychologie. Hamburg* (Jena: G. Fischer, 1932), pp. 134–45. See also Cassirer, "Structuralism in Modern Linguistics," *Word* I (1946), 99–120; and "Reflections on the Concept of Group and the Theory of Perception" herein.—Ed.

empirical evidence on which my contention is based. Apart from general considerations concerning the theory of knowledge my evidence is derived from three different sources: linguistics, discoveries about the psychology of speech, and experiments in the field of psychopathology.[4]

To begin with the third point, psychopathology has taught us that in every study of aphasia, which is the pathological damage or loss of speech, we must distinguish between two different forms of speech. Generally speaking, the patient who suffers from such a disease has not lost the use of words. But he can no longer employ these words in their ordinary meaning; he does not use them for denoting or designating empirical objects. If you ask him for the "names" of things he is as a rule unable to give you the right answer. But he can very well apply his words for a different purpose: for expressing his emotions. If you lead him to a fireplace and if you ask him to tell you the "name" of what he sees there, he will be unable to utter the word "fire"; but he will immediately exclaim "Fire!" in case of danger as an utterance of fright or as a cry of alarm.

The English neurologist, Jackson, who carefully studied such cases of loss or damage of speech, introduced a special terminology in order to point out this difference. He makes a sharp distinction between two forms of speech, that he describes as "inferior" and "superior" speech.[5] In the former our terms are used interjectionally; in the latter they are used "propositionally." Emotional language is not the same as propositional language. In emotional language we have a mere outbreak of feelings; we have, so to speak, a sudden volcanic eruption of subjective states of mind. In propositional language we have an objective concatenation of ideas; we have a subject, a predicate, and a relation between both of them. And it is this type of speech, propositional speech, that for man is the first clue in his discovery of an "objective" world, of a world of empirical things

4. See "Toward a Pathology of the Symbolic Consciousness," ch. 6 of *The Philosophy of Symbolic Forms*, trans. Ralph Manheim, 3 vols. (New Haven: Yale University Press, 1953–57), III, 205–77.—Ed.

5. Cf. ibid., pp. 211—20 and 229.—Ed.

with fixed and constant qualities. Without this guide, access to such a world would seem to be impossible. I do not wish to enter here into the highly debated question of the so-called animal language. The most recent publications in this field show us that this question is still very far from having found a clear and generally accepted solution. What we learn from these discussions is the fact that, in spite of innumerable observations and experiments, we have not the slightest empirical evidence whatever that there is such a thing as a *propositional* language in animals.

Speech remains after all a specifically anthropological concept and a specifically anthropological gift. Even those philosophers and those linguists who are inclined to admit a close relationship between the cries of animals and human speech are finally led to the result that we have to lay stress much more on the negative than on the positive side. "Between the animal utterance and human speech," as, for instance, A. H. Gardiner says in his book, *The Theory of Speech and Language,* "there is a difference so vital as almost to eclipse the essential homogeneity of the two activities."[6] What is always missing in the utterances of animals is the most distinctive feature of human language: its objective "propositional" character. And it is evident that this difference is not simply an accidental feature. It is a symptom of a deeper distinction that governs and determines the totality of our human experience.

A speechless being, an animal, lives in a reality widely divergent from the reality of man. Its modes of apprehending, of knowing or recognizing, cannot be judged according to our human standards. The facts with which we have become acquainted through animal psychology show us that the experience of an animal is, as it were, in a more fluid, fluctuating, indeterminate state than our own experience. For the description of this state modern comparative psychology has coined a special term. The animal, we are told, does not yet live in a sphere of empirical "things"; it lives in a sphere of complex, of diffused qualities. It does not know of those definite and distinct, stead-

6. Oxford: Clarendon Press, 1932, p. 118.—Ed.

fast and permanent objects which are the characteristic mark of our own human world. To these objects we ascribe a constant "nature." They are identifiable and recognizable under very different conditions.

But it is just this identification that seems to be missing in animal experience. An animal that reacts to a special stimulus in a certain way shows very often quite a different and even opposite reaction if the same stimulus presents itself under unusual circumstances. Let me illustrate this fact by a single characteristic example. A German psychologist has observed the habits of the domestic spider.[7] This spider weaves a web which becomes a craterlike structure narrowing into a funnel. In this tube the spider awaits her prey. Whenever a fly is caught in the outer meshes of the web, the spider rushes forth immediately, inserts her fangs in the victim, and paralyzes him. But if the smallest fly comes into the tube or if it is encountered anywhere except in the entanglement of the net the spider will not touch it and may even flee from it. We see by this example that any alteration of the particular conditions under which a stimulus presents itself to an animal may suffice to render the process of "recognition" impossible.

It is in man, and in man alone, that we find this solidification, this coalescence of various sense-data into one and the same conceptual unity, which is the very condition of the thought of a constant and permanent reality, a reality consisting of objective things and objective qualities. In this process of solidification language plays a decisive role. It is obvious that even the representation of a simple object of our common experience, let us say, the representation of a house, does not consist in a single image or in a mere aggregate of images, in a sum of sense-data. A simple phenomenological analysis shows us clearly that our apprehension of a house contains a great number of various elements. It is not given in a single perception; it contains a whole class of perceptions that are combined with each other and related to each other by a definite rule. According to the greater or smaller

7. Cf. "Language and Art II," herein.—Ed.

distance from the observer, according to his point of view, his special perspective, according to the various conditions of illumination the appearance of a house incessantly changes its shape. But all these widely different appearances are nevertheless thought to be the representation of one and the same "object," of an identical thing. For maintaining and preserving this objective identity, the identity of the name, of the linguistic symbol, is one of the most important aids.

The fixation brought about in language is the support of that intellectual consolidation on which the apprehension and recognition of empirical objects depends. If a child is taught that various and shifting appearances which present themselves under very different conditions are to be designated by one and the same "name," then it learns to look at them as a constant unity, not as a mere multiplicity and diversity. It has won a fixed center to which all the single appearances may be referred. The name creates, so to speak, a new focus of thought, in which all the rays that proceed from different directions meet each other and in which they fuse into that intellectual unity which we have in view when speaking of an identical object. Without this source of illumination our world of perception would remain dim and vague. "Apart from language," says the distinguished French linguist, Ferdinand de Saussure, in his *Cours de linguistique générale,* "our thought is only an amorphous and unorganized mass. . . . Taken in itself, thought is like a misty veil. There are no pre-established ideas and nothing is distinct before the appearance of language."[8]

But can we adopt this view without restriction? We must admit that language is in a sense at the root of all the intellectual activities of man. It is his principal guide; it shows him a new way that gradually leads to a new conception of the objective world. But can we say that this way is the only one; that without language man would be lost in the dark, that his feelings, his thoughts, his intuitions would be wrapped in dimness and mystery? In giving such a judgment we should not forget that besides the world of language there is another human world which has a meaning

8. 2d ed. (Paris, 1922), p. 155.—Cassirer.

and a structure of its own. There is, as it were, another symbolic universe beyond the universe of speech, of verbal symbols. This universe is the world of arts—of music and poetry, of painting, of sculpture and architecture.

Language grants us our first entrance into the objective. It is, as it were, the key word that unlocks the door of understanding to the world of concepts. But concepts are not the only approach to reality. We understand reality, not only by subsuming it under general class-concepts and general rules, but also by intuiting it in its concrete and individual shape. Such a concrete intuition cannot be attained by language alone. It is true that our ordinary speech has not only a conceptual but even an intuitive character and purport. Our common words are not mere semantic signs but they are charged with images and with specific emotions. They speak not only to the understanding but to our feeling and imagination.

In early stages of human culture this poetical and metaphorical character of language seems decisively to prevail over its logical, its "discursive" character. But if from a genetic point of view we must regard this imaginative and intuitive tendency of human speech as one of its most fundamental and most original features, we find on the other side that in the further development of language this tendency is gradually diminished. Language becomes so much the more abstract the more it expands and evolves its inherent faculty. From those forms of speech that are the necessary instruments for our everyday life and our social intercourse language develops into new forms. In order to conceive the world, in order to unify and systematize his experience, man has to proceed from ordinary speech to scientific language—to the language of logic, of mathematics, of natural science.

It is only by this new stage that he can overcome the dangers, the mistakes, and fallacies to which he is subject in the ordinary use of words. Over and over again these dangers have been described and denounced in the history of philosophical thought. Bacon describes language as the perpetual source of illusions and prejudices, as *"idolon fori,"* as the idol of the marketplace. "Although we think we govern our words," he says, "yet certain it is that we are possessed and governed by them. Words strongly influence the understanding of the wisest and they are prone to entangle and pervert his judgments." And, "It must be confessed," adds Bacon, "that it is not possible to divorce ourselves from these fallacies and false appearances, because they are inseparable from our nature and condition of life; nevertheless the caution of them does extremely import to the true conduct of human judgment."[9]

After many and pointless attempts to evade these dangers of common words human science seems at last to have found the true way. Scientific language is not the same as ordinary language. Its symbols are of a different kind and they are formed in a different way. Man develops a series of scientific languages in which every term is defined in a clear and unambiguous way and by which he may describe the objective relations of ideas and the concatenation of things. He proceeds from the verbal symbols used in ordinary speech, to the symbols of arithmetic, geometry, algebra, to those symbols that we find in a chemical formula. That is a decisive step in the process of objectification. But man has to pay for this gain by a severe loss. His immediate, his concrete experience of life fades away in the same degree in which he approaches his higher intellectual aims. What remains is a world of intellectual symbols, not a world of immediate experience.

If this immediate intuitive approach to reality is to be preserved and to be regained, it needs a new activity and a new effort. It is not by language but by art that this task is to be performed. What is common to language and art is the fact that neither of them can be considered as a mere reproduction or imitation of a ready-made, given, outward reality. As long as we look at them in this way all the objections made against them in the course of the history of philosophy remain unanswerable. In this case Plato would be perfectly right in saying that the artist is less than a copyist; that his work has no original purport and value but is a mere copy of a copy. Later philosophers tried to avoid this conclusion by ascribing to art a higher aim. They tell

9. Cf. Francis Bacon, *The Advancement of Learning,* Book II in *The Philosophical Works of Francis Bacon,* ed. J. M. Robertson (London, 1905), p. 119.—Ed.

us that art reproduces, not the phenomenal, the empirical world, but the supra-sensuous world. This view prevails in all the later systems of idealistic aesthetics; in Plotinus, in Schelling, in Hegel. Beauty, it is declared, is not a mere empirical or physical quality of things; it is an intelligible, a supra-sensuous predicate. In English literature we find this conception, for instance, in the works of Coleridge and Carlyle. In every work of art, says Carlyle, we discern eternity looking through time, the godlike rendered visible.

From a speculative point of view that is a very tempting solution to our problem. For it seems that by this we have not only a metaphysical justification of art, but, as it were, a deification of art. Art becomes one of the highest revelations of the Absolute. According to Schelling beauty is "das Unendliche endlich dargestellt"—"the infinite represented in a finite shape."[10] Beauty becomes by this an object of religious worship, but at the same time it is in danger of losing its ground. It is so highly elevated above the world of sense that we forget its earthly, its human roots. Its metaphysical legitimation threatens to become the denial of its specific essence and nature. As a matter of fact in the system of Hegel art could not escape this fate. It appears here as one of the forms of the absolute spirit. But its splendor vanishes before a new light, before the sunrise of philosophy. Art has only a relative and subordinate, not a definitive truth. It is inferior both to religion and to philosophy. "To us," Hegel says, "art is no longer the highest manner in which truth procures existence to itself. Its form has ceased to be the highest need of spirit. We do no longer believe in images."[11] But not to

---

10. Schelling states: "Jede ästhetische Produktion geht aus von einer an sich unendlichen Trennung der beiden Thätigkeiten, welche in jedem freien Produciren getrennt sind. Da nun aber diese beiden Thätigkeiten im Produkt als vereingt dargestellt werden sollen, so wird durch dasselbe ein Unendliches endlich dargestellt. Über das Unendliche endlich dargestellt ist Schönheit." *System des transzendentalen Idealismus* (1800) in *Schellings Werke*, ed. Manfred Schröter, 6 vols. (Munich: E. H. Beck and R. Oldenbourg, 1927), vol. II, p. 620.—Ed.

11. Cf. Hegel's introduction to part I of his "Lectures on Aesthetics": "Uns gilt die Kunst nicht mehr als dei höchste Weise, in welcher die Wahrheit sich Existenz verschafft." *Vorlesungen über die Aesthetik, Erster Band*, vol. 12 of *Sämtliche Werke*, Jubiläumsausgabe (Stuttgart: Fr. Frommanns Verlag, 1953), p. 150.—Ed.

believe in images, in concrete intuition, does not mean the philosophical interpretation or legitimization of art; it means the
death of art.

The modern followers of Hegel were perfectly aware of this
danger and they endeavored to avert it. It is on this point that
Benedetto Croce deviates from his philosophical master. Croce
declares that art rests on an independent and perfectly autonomous activity of man that must be measured by its own standards and that possesses an inherent value incomparable with
religious or philosophical truth. But when we study the work of
Croce we meet, in regard to our own problem, with a great surprise. Croce completely denies the possibility of distinguishing
between language and art. According to him they are not only
closely related to each other, but they coincide with each other.
We find this thesis in the very title of Croce's book on aesthetic,
*Estetica come scienza dell' espressione e linguistica generale (Aesthetic as
Science of Expression and General Linguistic)*.

Philosophically speaking, aesthetic and linguistic are not concerned with different problems; they are not two branches of
philosophy, but only one branch. "Whoever studies general Linguistic, that is to say, philosophical Linguistic, studies aesthetic
problems, and *vice versa*."[12] The only reason that Croce alleges
for this paradoxical statement is the fact that both art and language are "expressions" and that expression is an indivisible
process that admits of no degrees and no possible differentiations. We cannot speak of different kinds of expression. In the
theory of Croce a letter is, therefore, on the same level and it is
just as much a work of art as a painting, or a drama, as far as it is
a mode of expression. But to my mind this theory fails in a double respect.

First of all, the mere fact of expression cannot be regarded as
an artistic fact. If I write a letter in order to give or to get information about empirical facts or in order to serve a practical pur-

12. Trans. Douglas Ainslie, rev. ed. (New York: Macmillan, 1922; orig. pub. 1909), p.
142. Cf. Cassirer's discussion of Croce in *The Logic of the Humanities*, trans. Clarence Smith
Howe (New Haven: Yale University Press, 1961; orig. German ed., 1942), pp.
204–08.—Ed.

pose I am not, by this act of writing, an artist. But a man may even write a most passionate love letter, in which he may succeed in giving a true and sincere expression to his deepest feelings, without by this fact alone becoming an artist. I do not think that R. G. Collingwood, an English adherent and follower of Croce, is right when, in his book, *The Principles of Art,* he defines art as the function of making "a clean breast of one's feelings" and when from this he concludes that every utterance and every gesture that each of us makes is a work of art.[13] The artist is not the man who indulges in the display of his emotions or who has the greatest facility in the expression of these emotions. To be swayed by emotions means sentimentalism, not art. If an artist, instead of being absorbed in his work, is absorbed in his own individuality, if he feels his own pleasure or if he enjoys "the joy of grief," then he becomes a sentimentalist. The artist does not live only in our common reality, in the reality of empirical practical things. But just as little does he live in the sphere of his inner personal life, in his imagination or dreams, in his emotions or passions. Beyond these two realms he creates a new sphere—the sphere of plastic, architectural, musical forms, of shapes and designs, of melodies and rhythms.

To live in this sphere—in colors or sounds, in lines or contours, in tones and meters—that is the beginning and, in a certain sense, the end of a truly artistic life. I do not wish to defend here the device *l'art pour l'art*—art for art's sake. Art is not a display and an enjoyment of *empty* forms. What we intuit in the medium of art and artistic forms is a double reality, the reality of nature and of human life. And every great work of art gives us a new approach to and a new interpretation of nature and life. But this interpretation is possible only in terms of intuition, not of concepts; in terms of sensuous form, not of abstract signs. As soon as I lose these sensuous forms from sight, I lose the ground of my aesthetic experience. We may, therefore, be allowed to subsume art under a more general concept, under the concept of expression. But in this case we must at the same time take into consideration the specific difference of aesthetic phenomena.

13. See *The Principles of Art* (Oxford: Clarendon Press, 1938), pp. 279–85.—Ed.

Expression is not in itself an aesthetic process; it is a general biological process. Darwin wrote a book wholly concerned with this, *The Expression of the Emotions in Man and Animals*.[14] In this book he tries to show that the various modes of expression we find in the animal sphere originally have a biological meaning and purport. They are remnants of, or preparations for, biological action. The uncovering of the teeth of monkeys means, for instance, that the animal wishes to show to its enemy that it is provided with a formidable weapon. We need not enter here into the details of this biological theory. But even if we restrict ourselves to the human sphere, it is easy to show that not all expressions are equivalent and that not all of them have an aesthetic significance. A mere utterance of emotion—of joy or grief, of love or hate, of fear or hope—is by no means an aesthetic phenomenon.

For Croce language and art are identical because he finds in both of them one and the same decisive character, that character which in his terminology is called *liricità* (lyricism). Every man who succeeds in expressing his thoughts or feelings is, according to Croce, a sort of poet; we are all lyricists in our measure. But verbal expression, expression by linguistic symbols, is not the same as lyrical expression. What impresses us in lyric is not only the meaning, the abstract significance of the words; it is the sound, the color, the melody, the harmony, the concord and consonance of the words.

The great lyrical poet, Wordsworth, defines poetry as "the spontaneous overflow of powerful feelings." But it is not the mere power or the mere overflow of feelings that creates poetry. The mere abundance and profusion of his own sentiments is only a single element and moment in poetry; it does not constitute its essence. This abundance must be governed and dominated by a different power, by the power of form. Every act of speech includes this power of form and is an immediate witness of it. But our usual language tends in a different direction than lyrical expression. It is true that even ordinary speech may contain and, indeed, must contain a certain lyrical element.

14. Cf. An *Essay on Man*, pp. 115–18.—Ed.

When speaking to you at this moment I have no other intention than to communicate to you my ideas and thoughts about a general philosophical problem. But on the other hand I can scarcely forbear from conveying to you some other impressions. From my manner of speaking, from the pitch and stress, the modulation and inflection of my voice, you may feel my personal interest in special sides of the problem. You may feel my pleasure in addressing this audience; you may feel, at the same time, my discontent and my embarrassment that I have to speak here in a language that is not my mother tongue, in a foreign language of which I only have a very inadequate command. But neither you nor I are interested in this side of my lecture. What is important and relevant to us is quite a different thing. It is the objective, the logical purport of our problem. We are engaged in a certain theoretical question that we try to solve by a common intellectual effort. The language we have to make use of is, therefore, not emotional, but propositional language; it is logical, not lyrical language.

But as soon as we enter the aesthetic sphere all our words seem to undergo a sudden change. They are not only significant in an abstract way; they are, so to speak, fused and melted with their meanings. If a practical man, say an engineer, who wishes to construct a railway or a canal, gives us a description of a certain area, or if a geographer or geologist describes the same region in scientific terms and for theoretical purposes, they are very far from any aesthetic mode of expression, from a lyrical poem or the painting of a landscape. They are interested in empirical facts, in physical things or qualities. The artist ignores these qualities. He is absorbed in the pure form of things; he intuits their immediate appearance. He does not apprehend nature as an aggregate of physical things or as a chain of causes and effects. But just as little does he regard nature as a subjective phenomenon, as a sum of sense-perceptions.

With regard to ordinary sense-perception we may to a certain degree accept the theories of sensationalism. We may say, with Hume, that every idea is a copy of an impression. But in our experience of art this theory breaks down. The beauty of things is not a predicate that can be perceived and enjoyed in a mere passive way. In order to apprehend beauty we always need a fundamental activity, a specific energy of the human mind. In art we do not simply react to outward stimuli and we do not simply reproduce the statements of our own mind. In order to enjoy the forms of things we have to create these forms. Art is expression, but it is an active, not a passive mode of expression. It is imagination, but it is productive, not merely reproductive, imagination.

Artistic emotion is creative emotion; it is that emotion which we feel when we live the life of form. Every form has not only a static being; it has a dynamic force and a dynamic life of its own. Light, color, mass, weight are not experienced in the same way in a work of art as in our common experience. In the latter case we look at them as given sense-data out of which we build up by processes of logical thought or empirical inferences our concept of a physical universe, of an external world. But in art not only is the horizon of our sense-experience enlarged, but our perspective, our prospect of reality, is changed. We see reality in a new light, in a medium of living forms. Plotinus says in his treatise on beauty that Phidias, in creating his statue of Zeus, gave to the god the same form as Zeus himself would have chosen if he had decided to appear in a human shape. Phidias could inspire into the passive marble the life and the breath of the god because for him, as a great sculptor, the marble itself was not a dead stuff, a mere piece of matter, but was filled up with an inner life, with a vital movement and energy.

From this point of view we must deny another fundamental thesis of Croce's *aesthetic*. Croce denies emphatically that there exist any different or separate kinds of art. Art is intuition, and intuition is unique and individual. A classification of works of art is, therefore, devoid of philosophical value. If we try to classify the works of art, if we speak of lyric, epic, or drama as different kinds of poetry, or if we oppose poetry to painting or music, we are using quite superficial and conventional standards. According to Croce such a classification may have a practical purpose, but it has no theoretical significance whatever. In this case we are acting like a librarian who, without being concerned with the content of his books, might choose to arrange these books according to the alphabetical order of the names of their authors, or according to their size or format. But even this paradox vanishes if we bear in mind that art is not only expression in general, in an unspecified manner, but expression in a specific medium. A great artist does not choose his medium as a mere external and indifferent material. To him the words, the colors, the lines, the spatial forms and designs, the musical sounds are not only technical means of reproduction; they are the very conditions, they are essential moments of the productive artistic process itself.

But this dependence of every art on its specific material leads to an intricate problem in the case of poetry. When compared with other arts poetry has to face a new and serious difficulty. As we pointed out, language always implies an element of lyricism. It has its poetic side; it speaks in images and metaphorical expressions. But the more language develops and the more it performs its characteristic theoretical task the more this lyrical element is suppressed and replaced by other elements. The words and forms of ordinary speech were not designed for artistic purposes. They were made for practical needs; for prompting certain actions or for designating and classifying the objects of our common experience. But poetry does not move in this practical or theoretical sphere; it strives toward a different aim. How is it possible that to reach its end, poetry can use the same means? How can we employ the general terms of language, the class names of things, in such a way that they may become adequate to a perfectly new task, that they may convey to us concrete and individual intuitions?

Every great poet is a great creator, not only in the field of his art but also in the field of language. He has the power not only to use but to recast and regenerate language, to mold it into new shapes. The Italian language, the English language, and the German language were not the same on the day of the death of Dante, of Shakespeare, and Goethe as they were on the day of their birth. They had undergone by the work of Dante, of Shakespeare, and Goethe an essential change; they were enriched not only by new words but also by new forms. Nevertheless the poet cannot coin a perfectly new language. He has to respect the fundamental structural laws of his language; he has to adapt its grammatical, morphological, and syntactical rules. But in obeying these rules he is not simply subject to them; he is able to govern them and to turn them to a new purpose.

The work of every true poet may in a sense be compared with the work of an alchemist who tries to find the philosophers' stone. The poet has, as it were, to transmute the baser metals of ordinary speech into the gold of poetry. We feel this gift of transmutation in every stanza of Dante or Ariosto, in every Shakespearean tragedy, in every lyrical poem of Goethe or Wordsworth. All of them have their peculiar sound, their characteristic rhythm, their inimitable and unforgettable melody. Each of them is, so to speak, wrapped in its special poetical atmosphere. Lessing says in his *Hamburgische Dramaturgie* that it is just as impossible to steal a verse of Shakespeare as to steal the club of Hercules.[15] Every verse of Shakespeare bears the stamp of his mind. It cannot be borrowed from him, it cannot be appropriated by another poet. And what is even more astounding is the fact that Shakespeare never repeats himself. He not only speaks a language that never had been heard before, but every figure of Shakespeare speaks its own unmistakable language. In Lear and Macbeth, in Coriolanus and Othello, in Brutus and Hamlet, in Juliet and Desdemona, in Beatrice and Rosalind we hear this personal language, this individual accent which is the mirror of an individual soul.

This is only possible because a poet has the peculiar gift of throwing the abstract and general names of ordinary speech into the crucible of his poetical imagination and molding them into a new shape. Through this he becomes able to express all those innumerable nuances, those delicate shades of joy and grief, of delight and distress, of despair and ecstasy that are inaccessible to and ineffable in every other mode of expression. The poet does not merely describe in words; he calls forth, he conjures up

15. Lessing states: "Über was man von dem Homer gefragt hat, es lasse sich dem Herkules eher seine Keule, als ihm ein Vers abringen, das läßt sich vollkommen auch vom Shakespeare sagen. Auf die geringste von seinen Schönheiten ist ein Stempel gedruckt, welcher gleich der ganzen Welt zuruft: ich bin Shakespeares!" *Hamburgische Dramaturgie*, vol. V of *Lessings Werke*, ed. Georg Witkowski (Leipzig: Bibliographisches Institut, n.d.), p. 243.—Ed.

our deepest emotions. That is the privilege of poetry, but, at the same time, it is its boundary. For it follows from this that what we call the context of a poem cannot be separated from its form. "Hence," says Shelley in his *Defense of Poetry*, "the vanity of translation: it were as wise to cast a violet into a crucible that you might discover the formal principles of its color and odor, as seek to transfuse from one language into another the creations of a poet. The plant must spring again from its seed, or it will bear no flower—and this is the burthen of the curse of Babel."[16]

In this, I think, we find the true defense of poetry, and of art in general, against the attacks of philosophers like Plato or of moralists like Tolstoi.[17] Tolstoi sees in art a continuous and dangerous source of infection. "Not only is the infectiousness a certain sign of art," he says, "but the degree of the infection is the only standard of the value of art."[18] But it is easy to see where this theory fails. What Tolstoi ignores or minimizes is the most fundamental moment and motive of poetry, the moment of form. He who forms a passion does not infect us with a passion. In listening to a play of Shakespeare we are not infected with the ambition of Macbeth, with the cruelty of Richard III, or the jealousy of Othello. What the poet gives us is the deepest emotion; but it is, as Wordsworth says, "emotion recollected in tranquillity." Even in the most emotional form of poetry, in drama and tragedy, we feel this sudden change; we feel, as Hamlet says, a temperance in the very torrent, tempest, and whirlwind of our passions. It is only in the realm of forms that we can win this temperance. I cannot enter here into the Aristotelian theory of tragedy and I cannot try to interpret the meaning of the term "catharsis," an interpretation that would entangle us in very difficult philological questions.

16. *The Complete Works of Percy Bysshe Shelley*, ed. Roger Ingpen and Walter E. Peck, 10 vols. (London: Ernst Benn Ltd. and New York: Charles Scribner's Sons, 1930), VII, 114.—Ed.

17. Cf. "Language and Art II," herein.—Ed.

18. Cf. Tolstoi, *What is Art?*, trans. Aylmer Maude (Indianapolis and New York: Liberal Arts Press, 1960), ch. 5.—Ed.

But setting aside all philological considerations we may say that, in a systematic sense, the "catharsis" brought about by tragedy or any other work of art cannot be understood in a moral sense, let alone in a physiological sense.[19] It is no purification or purgation of our emotions. It means that our emotions are elevated to a new state. A man who in real life had to live through all the emotions we feel when listening to a tragedy of Sophocles or Shakespeare would not only be oppressed but crushed and annihilated by the power of these emotions. But in art we are not exposed to this danger. What we feel here is the full life of emotions without their material content. The burden of our passions is taken off our shoulders; what remains is the inner motion, the vibration and oscillation of our passions without their gravity, their pressure, and their weight. The very word "passion," when understood in its original etymological sense, seems to indicate a passive state of our mind.

But in art passion seems suddenly to change its nature; it becomes an active state. It is not a mere state of emotion; it implies at the same time an activity of contemplation. Art does not deceive us by a mere phantasmagoria of words or images. It enchants us by introducing us into its own world, the world of pure forms. In this specific medium the artist reconstructs the world. That is the real power that we find in every great genius of art. "The pen of an original writer," said Edward Young in his *Conjectures on Original Composition* (1759), "like Armida's wand, out of a barren waste calls a blooming spring. ... A genius differs from a good understanding as a magician from a good architect; that raises his structure by means invisible; this by the skillful use of common tools."[20]

Within the compass of this short lecture I could only give a very rough sketch of a problem which is very rich in most important systematic consequences. It was impossible to enter here into any detailed discussions of special questions. I have intended to stress only that point which seems to me to be of paramount

19. Cf. "The Educational Value of Art" herein.—Ed.

20. Ed. Edith I. Morley (Manchester, 1918), p. 6, p. 13.—Cassirer.

importance both from the point of view of the philosophy of culture and from the point of view of a general theory of knowledge. We miss the real clue to a deeper understanding of language and art as long as we content ourselves with the traditional view that they imitate a given, a ready-made reality. This view, that is expressed in the well-known slogan, *"Ars simia naturae"*— "Art is the ape of nature"—has for many centuries dominated our aesthetic theories, and even in the development of the philosophy of language it has always played a fundamental role.

But neither art nor language are simply a "second nature." They are much more; they are self-dependent and original human functions and energies. It is by virtue of these energies that we succeed in building up and organizing the world of our perceptions, our concepts, and intuitions. In this sense they possess not only a reproductive, but a really productive and constructive character and value; and it is this character that gives to both of them their true place in the universe of human culture.

Language and Art II

(1942)

This is the second of two items of MS #209 (see remarks on the first in preceding essay). The envelope containing these lectures labels this item "Language, Myth, Art/Sprach-Seminar/11 V 42." Inside on a covering sheet is stated: "Lang Myth Art/Seminar: Sprachphilos./Material zur Umarb. des aufs 'L & A.'" From this and the content of the text it seems clear that this is a presentation prepared by Cassirer for the final sessions of his seminar on the philosophy of language, shown in the Yale Catalogue for 1941–42 as Philosophy 126, Seminar in the Philosophy of Language and the Principles of Symbolism. The material is an "Umarbeit," a reworking and expansion of the ideas of Cassirer's "Language and Art" lecture of late April 1942. The first seminar session appears to be May 11, 1942. The manuscript is in English longhand and at several points indicates the incorporation of pages from "Language and Art I." It also repeats some quotations and examples from it. See my remarks on the overlap of Cassirer's papers on art in the preface to this volume.—Ed.

In our last two meetings I wish to give you a general survey of that problem that I regard as the fundamental question of a philosophical anthropology. I wish to study in its different stages that general process that I call the process of objectification. My thesis is that we cannot regard the world of empirical objects as an immediate datum—as a hard and brute fact. Objectivity is, from the point of view of a philosophical analysis, not the *terminus a quo* but the *terminus ad quem;* it is not the starting point but the terminating point of human knowledge.[1] Of course every philosophy

---

1. See also Cassirer's discussion of the sign and "transcending the copy theory of knowledge" in *The Philosophy of Symbolic Forms,* 3 vols., trans. Ralph Manheim (New Haven: Yale University Press, 1953–57), I, 93–114.—Ed.

contains an ontology—a general theory of being. In this regard we may perfectly agree with Aristotle if he defines metaphysics as the doctrine of the ὄν ἡ ὄν, as the doctrine of being as such—as being qua being. A critical philosophy does by no means deny the necessity or the importance of such an ontology. But it does no longer understand it as a description of an absolute being—of a thing in itself and its qualities. It restricts the task of ontology to that field of phenomena, of objects that are given us by the different modes of empirical knowledge.

In this sense Kant says, in a famous chapter of the *Critique of Pure Reason,* in the chapter on the ground of distinction of all subjects into phenomena and noumena, that all the fundamental concepts of the human understanding are principles for the exhibition of phenomena only: "and the proud name of Ontology, which presumes to supply in a systematic form different kinds of synthetical knowledge a priori of things by themselves— for instance the principle of causality—must be replaced by the more modest name of a mere Analytic of the pure understanding."[2] From this critical and analytical point of view we must say that what we call "objectivity" is not *gegeben,* but *aufgegeben;* it is not an immediate and unquestionable datum; it is to be regarded as a task.

This thesis gains its particular strength if instead of beginning with the physical or metaphysical universe, we choose the human world, the world of civilization, as our starting point. It is obvious that this world does not exist as a ready-made thing. It has to be constructed; it has to be built up by a continual effort of the human mind. Language, myth, religion, art, science are nothing but the single steps made in this direction. They are not imitations or reproductions of a ready-made nature of things. They are, as it were, only different stations or halting-places in our way to objectivity. What we call human culture may be defined as the progressive objectification of our human experience—as the objectification of our feelings, our emotions, our desires, our impressions, our intuitions, our thoughts and ideas.

In order to study this general process that leads to the world of human culture we may choose different methods. The first

2. A247; B303.—Ed.

method that seems to recommend itself is a comparative method. A philosophical anthropology has to conform to the maxim of Spinoza that man is not to be regarded as a "state in the state."[3] He is only a single link in the general chain of evolution. Cultural life is always bound up with the conditions of organic life. We must therefore begin with studying these conditions. For such a comparative study of the different forms of organic life modern biology and modern animal psychology have provided us with a very interesting material. The biologist Johannes von Uexküll has written a book, *Umwelt und Innenwelt der Tiere.* Here he declares that every organism has its special *Umwelt* and its special *Innenwelt*—a specific mode of its outward life and its inward life. We cannot perceive or observe both of them immediately, we have to employ an indirect method. The anatomical structure of an animal gives us the clue to the reconstruction of its inner and outward experience. Animals that widely diverge in this respect do not live in the same reality. An animal that possesses a brain or a complicated nervous system cannot have the same experience as an animal that belongs to a lower type of organization. According to Uexküll there exists, therefore, no common world of objects that is one and the same for men and for all animal species. "In the world of a fly," he says, "we find only fly-things; in the world of a sea-urchin we have only sea-urchin things."[4]

By the observations of Uexküll and other investigators in the field of animal psychology we cannot attain a positive solution of our problem. But we may draw from the facts ascertained by them an important negative conclusion. When compared with our own human experience the experience of an animal seems to be, so to speak, in a much less solidified state. It is, as it were, in a state of liquefaction. In order to describe this state modern comparative psychology has coined a special term. The animal, we are told, does not yet live in a sphere of fixed and determi-

3. Cf. Cassirer, "Spinozas Stellung in der allgemeinen Geistesgeschichte," *Der Morgan,* vol. 3, no. 5 (1932), 325–48.—Ed.

4. *Umwelt und Innenwelt der Tiere* (1909; 2d ed. Berlin, 1921). See *An Essay on Man,* pp. 23–24.—Ed.

nate things, it lives in a sphere of complex or diffused qualities. It does not know of those definite and distinct, steadfast and permanent objects which are the characteristic mark of our own human world. To these objects we ascribe a constant "nature." They are identifiable and recognizable under very different conditions. But it is just this identification that seems to be missing in animal experience. An animal that reacts to a special stimulus in a certain way shows very often quite a different and even opposite reaction if the same stimulus presents itself under unusual circumstances.

Let me illustrate this fact by a single characteristic example. A German psychologist has observed the habits of the domestic spider.[5] This spider weaves a web which becomes a craterlike structure narrowing into a funnel. In this tube the spider awaits her prey. Whenever a fly is caught in the outer meshes of the web, the spider rushes forth immediately, inserts her fangs in the victim, and paralyzes him. But if the smallest fly comes into the nest proper of the labyrinth or if it is encountered anywhere except in the entanglement of the net, the spider will not touch it and may even flee from it. We see by this example that any alteration of the particular conditions under which a stimulus presents itself to an animal may suffice to render the process of "recognition" impossible. It is in man, and in man alone, that we find this solidification, this coalescence of various sense-data into one and the same conceptual unity, which is the very condition of the thought of a constant and permanent reality, a reality consisting of objective things and objective qualities.

It is, indeed, the character and the privilege of our own human experience that we not only reach to a general unspecified biological situation, that our actions are not only brought about and prompted by some vague impressions or emotions, by desires and feelings. Of course we are not exempt from these vague impressions and feelings—and in a certain sense they may even be regarded as the first stimulus of all our human activity. Even Locke, who follows quite a different method of psychological observation and psychological analysis, who argues upon the

5. Cf. "Language and Art I" herein.—Ed.

principle that the first unquestionable data to which all the complex phenomena of the human mind are to be reduced are the simple and fixed elements of sense-perception—even Locke has, in his *Essay on Human Understanding,* a very interesting chapter in which he tries to explain that a certain ill-defined and very vague "uneasiness" is one of the first and one of the most important and indispensable motives of all human life and even of all our intellectual activity.[6]

But man never perseveres in his primitive state. He does not simply submit to the powers of his feelings, his emotions, his dim and vague impressions. Out of this state of primitive dimness and uncertainty he passes to a new state of mind. He does not only live in reality but he becomes conscious of reality. And it is not before he has reached this new intellectual state that he can speak of a world of "objects," of empirical things and of definite and permanent qualities of these things. We may designate this process by very different names, and in the history of philosophy we meet with various terms that attempt to describe it. The variety of these terms does not matter, as long as we bear in mind the general character of the process itself. The most common term, the oldest and in a certain sense the classical term, is of course the term "reason," which is a translation of the Greek *Logos.* It is by the *Logos,* by the power of reason that man is distinguished from animal.

But this term that in Greek philosophy meant something very clear and definite has been obscured in the course of its long history. It has assumed some metaphysical connotation that we wish to avoid when dealing with the problems of a philosophical anthropology. For this purpose we need not presuppose that there is a separate, a substantial thing, called reason, mind, spirit. In his chapter on the "Paralogisms of Pure Reason" Kant warns us against all the fallacies and illusions contained in this metaphysical use of the term "reason." We can no longer define reason or spirit in a substantial, ontological way—we have to define it as a function. It is not a separate substance or power; it is a way, a method of organizing our human experience. Such an

6. See Book II, ch. 21, sec. 29.—Ed.

organization is brought about by language, by myth, by religion, by art, by science. If we seek after a common name that should be apt to cover all these different activities, we may be inclined to use the term "apperception" that in this sense was first introduced by Leibniz.

According to Leibniz we may describe the world of an animal as a world of "perceptions," of *petites perceptions,* whereas we have to describe the world of man as an apperception of reality. This apperception—in the sense of Leibniz—implies a new state of consciousness and a new concept of objectivity. Or we may prefer to use the term "reflection"—a term that likewise has a very long and a very complicated history but that was defined in a special sense by Herder in his classical treatise on the origin of language. According to Herder language does not originate in perception or emotion, but in reflection.

> Man demonstrates reflection when the force of his soul works so freely that in the ocean of sensations that flows into it from all the senses, he can, in a manner of speaking, isolate and stop One wave, and direct his attention toward this wave, conscious that he is so doing. He demonstrates reflection when, emerging from the nebulous dream of images flitting past his senses, he can concentrate upon a point of wakefulness, dwell voluntarily on One image, observe it calmly and lucidly, and distinguish characteristics proving that this and no other is the object. He demonstrates reflection when he not only knows all attributes vividly and clearly, but can *recognize* one or more distinguishing attributes: the first act of this recognition yields a clear concept; it is the soul's first judgment—and what made this recognition possible? A characteristic which he had to isolate and which came to him clearly as a characteristic of reflection. Forward! Let us cry εὕρηκα! The first characteristic of reflection was the word of the soul. With it human speech was invented![7]

7. Herder, "Über den Ursprung der Sprache" (1772), *Werke*, ed. B. Suphan, vol. 5, pp. 34ff. (see *Philosophy of Symbolic Forms,* I, 152–53).—Ed.

I do not wish to dispute here about the use of terms. My contention is that the whole process that we may describe by the words reason, apperception, and reflection implies the constant use of symbols—of mythical or religious, of verbal, of artistic, of scientific symbols. Without symbols man would, like the animal, live in reality. He could preserve his state by giving characteristic responses to different physical stimuli. For this preservation of his mere biological existence he would not need to transgress the limits of animal, of instinctive life. In his *Principles of Psychology* William James says that every animal instinct involves a practical relation to the subject.[8] Great provinces of human life and innumerable human actions are still on the same level: they are practical responses to practical needs. But in the world of his symbols—in language, art, science—man begins to take a new course, the course of his theoretical or reflective life which gradually and continuously leads him to a new conception of the objective world.

It is not easy to follow up and to describe this gradation in the process of objectification. What seems to appear first is by no means that world of physical objects, that world of "nature" that is studied in natural science. Natural science is a very late and a very complicated product of human thought. It is by mythical, not by physical or mathematical thought that man first approaches nature. And mythical thought does not know of any fixed order of objects that are bound up with invariable rules. Myth is by no means devoid of any principle; it is not a mere mass of absurd, incoherent, contradictory statements concerning the reality of things. But in its interpretation of this reality it follows quite a different principle than scientific thought. Scientific thought presupposes that concept of nature that is defined by Kant as the existence of things as far as it is determined by general laws. But myth does not know of any general laws. Its world is not a world of physical things obeying causal laws but a world of persons. Therefore the world of myth is not a world of natural powers that may be reduced to certain causal laws but a dramatic world—a world of actions, of supernatural forces, of

8. 2 vols. (New York: Henry Holt and Co., 1890), II, 442.—Cassirer.

gods or demons. This, too, is without any doubt a sort of objectification; but it is an objectification of a special direction and
tendency.

In myth man objectifies his own deepest emotions; he looks at
them as if they had an outward existence. But this new objectivity is throughout bound up within the limits of personality. In
the organic world, in the life of animals we cannot find anything
that bears an analogy to this process of mythical imagination and
mythical thought. Without any doubt the higher animals possess
not only a very wide scale of emotions but they have also the
faculty of expressing these emotions in many and various ways.
Darwin has made a special study of this problem—and he has
written a very interesting and important book, *The Expression of
The Emotions in Man and Animals.* But here too the animal, however expressing its emotions, remains, so to speak, captured in
the sphere of these emotions. It cannot exteriorize them—it cannot realize them in outward forms.

But it is just this exteriorization and realization that we find in
mythical thought. All sorts of affections—fear, sorrow, anguish,
excitement, joy, orgasm, exultation—have, so to speak, a shape
and a face of their own. In this respect we may define myth not
as a theoretical or causal interpretation of the universe but as a
physiognomical interpretation.[9] Everything in mythical thought
assumes a special physiognomy. Man lives in the multiplicity and
variety of these physiognomic characters and he is constantly
influenced and impressed by them. He looks at the world in the
same sense as, in our own human intercourse, we are used to
look at other persons, at our own fellow creatures. The things
that surround him are not a dead-stuff; they are filled and
impregnated with emotions. They are benignant or malignant,
friendly or dreadful, familiar or uncanny, they inspire confidence or awe or terror. By this we can easily explain what seems
to be one of the fundamental features of mythical thought. If
this thought is bound to any definite rule it is not a rule that may
be compared with the rules of nature and of scientific thought.

9. Cf. Cassirer's discussion of the expressive function *(Ausdrucksfunktion)* in *The Philosophy
of Symbolic Forms,* III, pt. 1.—Ed.

Scientific thought constantly strives to find the permanent qualities and the constant relations of things.

But myth does not acknowledge such permanent characters. It does not interpret nature in terms of our usual empirical thought or in terms of physics; it interprets it rather in terms of our physiognomic experience. And nothing seems to be more unstable and fluctuating than this experience. A human face may very often and very rapidly and unexpectedly pass from one state to the very opposite: from joy to grief, from elation to depression, from mildness and benevolence to anger or fury. Mythical thought expands this experience over the whole universe. Nothing has a definite and permanent shape; everything is liable to sudden transformations and transfigurations. We know all these mythical metamorphoses and we remember their poetical description in the work of Ovid. A human being may at every moment be changed into a new form. Niobe becomes a stone, Daphne becomes a laurel, Arachne becomes a spider, and so on.

Nevertheless it would be wrong to consider the world of myth as a mere dream, as a perfectly unorganized mass of crude superstitions, of illusions or hallucinations. Even myth obeys a rule of its own. It does not only invent at random but it has a tendency to organize its feelings and imaginations. In an early stage of mythical thought we find those mythical figures that in the work of a German scholar, in the work of Hermann Usener, have been described as *Augenblicksgötter*, as momentary gods. They seem to be unconscious and involuntary creations made on the spur of the moment. They have not yet won a fixed and determinate shape; they are fugitive and fluctuating; demonic powers the presence of which man feels without being able to describe them, to give them a definite form and a definite name. But according to the theory of Usener this primitive state of mythical thought undergoes a change in its further evolution. The momentary gods are replaced by other gods that in the work of Usener are called *Tätigkeitsgötter* and *persönliche Götter*.[10]

10. See Hermann Usener, *Götternamen. Versuch einer Lehre von der religiösen Begriffsbildung* (Bonn: F. Cohen, 1896), secs. 16 and 17.—Ed.

I cannot debate here upon this theory, the importance of which for the history of religion and for the philosophy of civilization I have emphasized in a special treatise: *Sprache und Mythos,* published in the Studies of the Warburg Institute in the year 1925.[11] But if we follow up this development we may say that even in this field we find a continual development that leads us from singularity to particularity, from particularity to universality. In polytheistic thought the world is no longer an amorphous mass that is at the mercy of incalculable demonic powers. It is divided into definite provinces, into certain spheres of actions, each of which is under the guidance and control of a special god. And among these gods themselves we find a hierarchical order. We find a supreme god, we find Zeus in his double function, in his cosmological and ethical function, as the god of the heavens and as the father of the gods and man, as the protector and guardian of justice. All this shows us very clearly that even mythical thought is not devoid of a very clear and a very keen sense for organization and objectification, although its objectification is not a work of the intellect, but a work of the imagination.

And the same progress we find not only in the field of mythical images and mythical representations but also in those fundamental emotions that seem to be the motive of all mythical and religious thought. It has often been said that all religion originates in fear—*"Primus in orbe deos fecit timor."*[12] But fear alone is a more passive state of the human mind, that can scarcely account for that free activity, that creativeness and productivity, that we always find in mythical and religious thought. Fear may create demons; but it does not create the higher gods; nor can we derive from it the doctrine of monotheism, the doctrine of a unique god. It is true that even very profound religious thinkers seem to be inclined to reduce religion more to a sense of passivity than to an original, autonomous, active function. In his *Reden über die Religion,* Schleiermacher defines religion as "the

11. *Language and Myth,* trans. Susanne K. Langer (New York: Harper & Brothers, 1946), esp. chs. 1–3.—Ed.

12. The manuscript here reads "says Lucretius," with "Lucretius" crossed out. The quotation is, in fact, from Petronius, Fr. 27.—Ed.

feeling of absolute dependence on the Divine."[13] Kierkegaard thinks that all religious thought, especially all Christian thought, has one of its deepest roots in our feeling of anxiety. Anxiety is a central problem in Kierkegaard's philosophy of religion. He has written a special treatise about the concept of anxiety in which he declares that the more original a human being is, the deeper his anxiety is.[14]

But I do not think that we can accept this doctrine. I do not deny that in a genetic sense fear and anxiety may be regarded as one of the first and the most important phenomena of our religious consciousness. But in the evolution and in the progress of religion they give room to other and very different feelings and emotions. In a book of the English anthropologist Marett, the way of religion is described as the way "From Spell to Prayer."[15] Magical thought and magical rites may be interpreted as products of fear or as attempts to get rid of this fear by controlling the powers of demons and gods. But religious thought leads to another conception. It is no longer fear and anxiety, and it is no longer mere submission, mere passive obedience, that is the principle of the higher religions. What we find here are other affections, the affections of confidence and hope, of love and gratitude, and it is on these affections that religious belief depends. In philosophical religion, first of all in the religion of Plato, the idea of God itself becomes equivalent to the idea of the Good; to the summit and zenith of the whole realm of ideas.

But if now from the field of mythical thought we pass to another sphere, to the field of language, we find ourselves transposed into a new world. It is true that myth and language are so strongly connected with each other that at first sight it may appear impossible to separate them. Linguistic thought is, so to

---

13. Cf. Friedrich Schleiermacher, *On Religion: Speeches to Its Cultured Despisers*, trans. John Oman (London: Kegan, Paul, Trench, Trübner and Co., 1893), "Second Speech," esp. p. 45. See "The Dialectic of Mythical Consciousness," pt. 4 of *The Philosophy of Symbolic Forms*, II, esp. 259–60; and "Myth and Religion," ch. 7 of *An Essay on Man.*—Ed.

14. Søren Kierkegaard, *The Concept of Dread*, trans. Walter Lowrie (Princeton, N.J.: Princeton University Press, 1944).—Ed.

15. In *The Threshold of Religion* (London, 1909).—Cassirer. Cf. *Philosophy of Symbolic Forms*, II, 16.—Ed.

speak, impregnated and permeated with mythical thought. This impregnation becomes so much the more obvious the more we go back to more primitive stages of language. But even in our own highly developed languages it has by no means lost its power. In common speech we do not speak conceptually, but metaphorically; we cannot escape the use of metaphors. And this imaginative, this metaphorical speech seems closely related to the fundamental function of mythical thought. At the same time all human language wishes to convey certain feelings, wishes, desires. It is not only a communication of ideas and abstract thought; it is filled with emotions. But if we look at language as a whole and if we follow up its general development it proves to be impossible to reduce it to this emotional background.

In the speculative theories about the origin of language we find two theories that in the history of linguistics and in the history of philosophy were in constant combat against each other. The one is the onomatopoetic theory, the other is the interjectional theory. Jocularly they have been described, by Max Müller and others, as the bow-wow theory and the pooh-pooh theory. The onomatopoetic theory, the theory that all language originates in the imitation of natural sounds, has always played an important role. A delineation of this theory which at the end turns into its travesty was given by Plato in his dialogue *Cratylus*. In modern times this view seems to have lost its credit; we can scarcely find a modern philosopher or a modern linguist who maintains it in its former sense. But the other theory, the theory of interjections, seems still to have many adherents.

That the only possible explanation of human language is to reduce it to a general phenomenon, to the phenomenon of animal cries, is, for instance, the thesis that is upheld in American philosophical literature, in the book of Grace deLaguna: *Speech, Its Function and Development*.[16] And one of the veterans of modern linguistics, Otto Jespersen, maintains the same theory and thinks that all the facts of the history of language tend in this direction. Jespersen has developed his theory both in an earlier book, *Progress in Language*, published in the year 1897, and his

16. New Haven: Yale University Press, 1927.—Ed.

last comprehensive work: *Language, Its Nature, Development and Origin* (1922). He does not wish to appeal to any general speculative reason; he thinks that he can prove his point by a mere empirical analysis. "The method I recommend," he says, "and which I am the first to employ consistently, is to trace our modern twentieth-century languages as far back in time as history and our materials will allow us. . . . If we should succeed in discovering certain qualities to be generally typical of the earlier as opposed to the later stages of languages, we shall be justified in concluding that the same qualities obtained in a still higher degree in the earliest times of all. . . .

"But if the change witnessed in the evolution of modern speech out of older forms of speech is thus on a larger scale projected back into the childhood of mankind, and if by this process we arrive finally at uttered sounds of such a description that they can no longer be called a real language, but something antecedent to language—why, then the problem will have been solved; for transformation is something we can understand, while a creation out of nothing can never be comprehended by human understanding."[17] But it is just on this point that the real methodological difficulty begins. We may by a series of intermediate links contrive to connect our own language with a primitive state of mere emotional cries. But even in this case the "transformation" that we have to admit does not cease being a sort of logical creation. What in the primitive state was supposed to be a mere instinctive utterance, an emotional cry, must on a higher stage be declared as something quite different. What was the expression of a feeling, an exclamation of joy or fear, becomes an objective statement, a proposition and a judgment about things and the concatenation of things.

This new use of language is a prerequisite of Jespersen's own theory. It is not only admitted by him but it is testified by the very examples he chooses for explaining his conception. "We get the first approach to language proper," he says, "when communicativeness takes precedence of exclamativeness, when sounds are uttered in order to 'tell' fellow creatures something. . . . How

17. New York: Henry Holt, 1922, p. 418.—Cassirer.

did what originally was a jingle of meaningless sounds come to be an instrument of thought? ... Suppose some dreaded enemy has been defeated and slain: the troop will dance round the dead body and strike up a chant of triumph. ... This combination of sounds, sung to a certain melody, will now easily become what might be called a proper name for that peculiar event. ... Under slightly altered circumstances it may become the proper name of the man who slew the enemy. The development can now proceed further by a metaphorical transference to similar situations."[18]

But this explanation does not solve our question, it begs the question. It is a vicious circle to reduce language to emotional cries and at the same time to assume that these cries have in a certain stage changed their meaning—that they were used as "names." The very concept of a "name" contains our whole problem in a nutshell; it presupposes the transition to a new function, to the "symbolic" function in its strict and proper sense. It is by this function that—to use the words of Jespersen—communicativeness takes precedence over exclamativeness.

All the theories belonging to this type indeed focus on one and the same point and are liable to the same objection. By considering language in its simplest form they hope to decrease or to minimize its distance from other elementary processes. But after a few steps made in this direction they are inevitably brought to a standstill. They have to admit a specific difference—a difference that is not merely quantitative but a qualitative one. This difference remains the same in the lower and the higher, in the "primitive" and the highly developed stages. In *The Theory of Speech and Language,* Gardiner is inclined to admit an "essential homogeneity" between human and animal language. But he immediately adds that those "emotional monologues" we find in the animal world are far removed from speech.[19] He declares that no amount of variety either in the stimuli or in the reactions ever could give rise to anything resembling a "real" language. "Between the animal utterance and

18. Ibid., p. 437.—Cassirer.

19. Oxford: Clarendon Press, 1932, pp. 118ff.—Ed.

human speech," he says, "there is a difference so vital as almost to eclipse the essential homogeneity of the two activities." The seeming homogeneity is indeed a mere material homogeneity that does not exclude but, on the contrary, accentuates the formal, the functional heterogeneity. "Between interjection and word," it has been rightly said, "there is a chasm wide enough to allow us to say that the interjection is the negation of language, interjections are employed only when one either cannot or will not speak."[20]

That the function of describing or designating things by giving them a "name" is a new and independent function, that it implies a new step in "objectification" that cannot be reduced to the lower emotional level of speech can be shown also by referring to the facts with which we have become acquainted by the modern psychopathology of speech. For this I only wish to give a special characteristic example. The study of the so-called amnestic aphasia—that means the study of such cases in which the patient by an injury of the brain has lost his use of names—have taught us that we have to distinguish between two different forms of human speech. Generally speaking, the patient who suffers from such a disease has not completely lost the use of words. But he can no longer employ these words in their ordinary meaning, he does not use them for denoting or designating empirical objects. If you ask him for the "names" of things he is as a rule unable to give you the right answer.[21] But he can very well apply his words for a different purpose: for expressing his emotions or for describing the use of things. If you show him a glass of water he will not call it by this name; but he will tell you that what he sees is something to drink; if you show him a knife he will tell you that it is something to cut with. If you lead him to a fireplace he will be unable to utter the word "fire"; but he will immediately exclaim "Fire!" in the case of danger as an utterance of fright or as a cry of alarm.

The English neurologist Jackson, who carefully studied such

20. Benfey, *Geschichte der Sprachwissenschaft* (München, 1869), p. 295. Cf. Jesperson, p. 415.—Cassirer.

21. Cf. "Language and Art I" herein.—Ed.

cases of loss or damage of speech, introduced a special terminology in order to point out this difference. He makes a sharp discrimination between two forms of speech that he describes as "inferior" and "superior" speech. In the former our terms are used interjectionally; in the latter they are used "propositionally." Emotional language is not the same as propositional language. In emotional language we have a mere outbreak of feelings; we have, so to speak, a sudden volcanic eruption of subjective states of mind. In propositional language we have an objective concatenation of ideas; we have a subject, a predicate, and a relation between both of them. And it is this type of speech, it is propositional speech that for man is the first clue in his discovery of an "objective" world, of a world of empirical things with fixed and constant qualities. Without this guide the access to such a world seems to be impossible. It is by language that we first learn to classify our perceptions; to bring them under general names and general concepts. And it is only by this effort of classification and organization that the apprehension and the knowledge of an "objective" world, of a world of empirical things, can be reached.

A simple phenomenological analysis may show us very clearly that even the apprehension of our common empirical objects, let us say, our apprehension of a house, contains a great number of various elements and depends on very complex psychological and logical conditions. Such an object is not given us in a single perception. It is a class of perceptions that are combined with each other and related to each other by a definite rule. According to the greater or smaller distance from the observer, according to his point of view, his special perspective, according to the various conditions of illumination, the appearance of a house incessantly changes its shape. But all these widely divergent appearances are nevertheless thought to be the representation of one and the same subject, of an identical thing. For maintaining and preserving this objective identity, the identity of the name, of the linguistic symbol, is one of the most important helps.

The fixation brought about in language is the support of that intellectual consolidation on which the apprehension and recognition of empirical objects depend. If a child is taught that

various and shifting appearances which present themselves
under very different conditions are to be designated by one and
the same name, then it learns to look at them as a constant unity,
not as a mere multiplicity and diversity. It has now a fixed center
to which all the simple appearances may be referred. The name
creates, so to speak, a new focus of thought, in which all the rays
that proceed from different directions meet each other and in
which they fuse into that intellectual unity which we have in view
when speaking of an identical object. Without this source of illumination our world of perception would probably remain dim
and vague. By this we understand that a comparative study of
language has not only a philological or historical but a fundamental philosophical interest and a philosophical value.

For it is by this comparison that we can understand and appre-
ciate much better the real function of language. Only by the dis-
cernment of its individual features we can gain a true insight
into the general nature and function of language. "Wer fremde
Sprachen nicht kennt, weiss nichts von seiner eigenen," says
Goethe, "he who does not know foreign languages does not
know anything about his own language." We have to penetrate
into foreign languages in order to convince ourselves that the
true difference does not consist in the learning of a new vocabulary, that it does not consist in a formation of words, but in a
formation of concepts. To learn a new language is, therefore,
always a sort of spiritual adventure; it is like a journey of discovery in which we find a new world. Even when studying closely
related languages—let me say German and Swedish—we seldom
find real synonyms, words that are entirely coextensive in meaning and usage. The different words always convey a slightly different sense. They combine and correlate the data of our
experience in a different way and lead, therefore, to different
modes of apprehension. The terms of two languages show no
real congruence with each other; they cover, so to speak, various
areas of thought.

When comparing different languages we always find that their
manner of classifying and organizing the world of sense-experience does not follow one and the same rigid, unique, predetermined logical scheme. There exists no fixed pattern of thought

or intuition according to which our linguistic concepts have to be molded. Everywhere we find the greatest elasticity and the greatest mobility. It is by this mobility that language becomes able to reflect the whole life of a nation or a speaking community. The richness or poverty, the deficiency or abundance of names is always very characteristic for the particular direction of feeling and life. But the general aim remains always the same, the organization and classification of our perceptual world. "Apart from language," says a distinguished modern linguist, Ferdinand de Saussure, in his *Cours de linguistique générale*, "our thought is only an amorphous mass. . . . Taken in itself, thought is like a misty veil. There are no pre-established ideas and nothing is distinct before the appearance of language."[22]

I do by no means wish to contradict this statement that is in perfect accordance with my own position. But I do not think that from a comprehensive philosophical point of view we can accept it without any restriction. We must admit that language is in a sense at the root of all the intellectual activities of man. It is his principal guide; it shows him a new way that gradually leads to a new conception of the objective world. But can we say that this way is the only one; that without language man would be lost in the dark, that his feelings, his thoughts, his intuitions would be wrapped in dimness and mystery? When giving such a judgment we should forget that beside the world of language there is another human world which has a meaning and a structure of its own. There is, as it were, another symbolic universe beyond the universe of speech, of verbal symbols. This universe is the world of arts—of music and poetry, of painting, of sculpture or architecture.

Language gives us the first entrance into the world of concepts. But concepts are not the only approach to reality. We have not only to understand reality by subsuming it under general class concepts and general rules, we wish to intuit it in its concrete and individual shape. Such a concrete intuition cannot be reached by language alone. It is true that our ordinary speech

22. 2d ed. (Paris, 1922), p. 155.—Cassirer. See Saussure, *Course in General Linguistics*, trans. Wade Baskin (New York: McGraw-Hill, 1966), pp. 111–12.—Ed.

has not only a conceptual but even an intuitive character and purport. Our common words are not mere semantic signs but they are charged with images and with specific emotions. They speak not only to the understanding but to our feeling and imagination—they are poetical and metaphorical expressions, not merely logical or "discursive" expressions. In early stages of human culture this poetical and metaphorical character of language seems to prevail over its logical, its "discursive" character—poetry is the native tongue of mankind says a German thinker, Georg Hamann, the teacher and the friend of Herder. But if from a genetic point of view we must regard this imaginative and intuitive tendency of human speech as one of its most fundamental and most original features, we find, on the other side, that in the further development of language this tendency is gradually diminished. Language becomes so much the more abstract the more it expands and evolves its inherent faculty. From those forms of speech that are the necessary instruments for our everyday life and our social intercourse, language develops into new forms.

In order to conceive the world, in order to unify and systematize his experience, man has to proceed from ordinary speech to scientific language—to the language of logic, of mathematics, of natural science. It is only by this new stage that he can overcome the dangers, the mistakes and fallacies, to which he is subject in the ordinary use of words. Over and over again these dangers have been described and denounced in the history of philosophical thought. Bacon describes language as the perpetual source of illusions and prejudices, as an *idolon fori*, as the idol of the market place. "Although we think we govern our words," he says, "yet certain it is that we are possessed and governed by them." Words strongly influence the understanding of the wisest and they are prone to entangle and pervert his judgments. "It must be confessed," adds Bacon, "that it is not possible to divorce ourselves from these fallacies and false appearances because they are inseparable from our nature and condition of life; nevertheless the caution of them does extremely import to the true conduct of human judgment."[23]

23. Cf. Bacon, *Novum Organum*, secs. 43 and 59; and "Language and Art I," herein.—Ed.

After many and pointless attempts to evade these dangers of
common words, human science seems at last to have found the
true way. Scientific language is not the same as ordinary language. It cannot dispense with the use of symbols—but its symbols are of a different kind and they are formed in a different
way. Man develops a series of scientific languages in which every
term is defined in a clear and unambiguous way and by which he
may describe the objective relations of ideas and the concatenation of things. He proceeds from the verbal symbols used in
ordinary speech, the symbols of arithmetic, geometry, algebra, to
those symbols that we find in a chemical formula. That is a decisive step in the process of objectification. But man has to pay for
this gain by a severe loss. His immediate, his concrete experience
of life is fading away in the same degree in which he approaches
his higher intellectual aims. What remains is a world of intellectual symbols—not a world of immediate experience.

If this immediate intuitive approach to reality is to be preserved and to be regained, it needs a new activity and a new
effort. It is not by language but by art that this task is to be
performed. What is common to language and art is the fact that
neither of them can be considered as a mere reproduction or
imitation of a ready-made, given, outward reality. As long as we
look at them in this way all the objections made against them in
the course of the history of philosophy become in fact unanswerable. In this case Plato would be perfectly right when saying that
the artist is less than a copyist; that his work has no original purport and value but is a mere copy of a copy.

These arguments can only be refuted if we remember that art
and language, far from being imitations or copies, are autonomous, independent, self-contained activities, and that it is only
by the medium of these activities that man can build up a world
of objective experience. But in this task art and language do not
go the same way; they tend to different directions. Common language develops in the direction of generalization and abstraction; and by this effort it finally leads to a new stage, to the stage
of scientific language. But in art this process of abstraction and
generalization is, so to speak, arrested by a new effort; it is
brought to a standstill. Here we take the opposite route. Art is
not a process of classifying our sense-data. Far from proceeding

to more and more general concepts, it is absorbed in individual intuitions.

In art we do not conceptualize the world, we perceptualize it. But the percepts to which we are led by art are by no means those perceptions which in the traditional language of the systems of sensationalism are described as the copies, the faint images of sense-perception. The imagery of art is of quite a different, nay of the opposite character. Art is not reproduction of impressions; it is creation of forms. These forms are not abstract, but sensuous. They would immediately lose their ground, they would evaporate as soon as we abandon the sphere of our sense-experience. But what is given us in art are not the so-called secondary qualities of things. An artist does not know of these qualities. The concept of secondary qualities is nothing but an epistemological abstraction that may be fruitful and even necessary for building up a coherent theory of knowledge, a philosophy of science.

But art and the artist have to confront and to solve quite a different problem. They do not live in a world of concepts; nor do they live in a world of sense-perceptions. They have a realm of their own. If we wish to describe this world, we must introduce new terms. It is a world not of concepts, but of intuition, not of sense-experience, but of contemplation. In this sense, I think, we have to understand the definition of Kant, that beauty is what pleases in pure contemplation. This aesthetic contemplation is a new and decisive step in the general process of objectification.

The sphere of art is a sphere of pure forms. It is not a world of mere colors, sounds, tactile qualities—but of shapes and designs, of melodies and rhythms. In a certain sense all art may be said to be language, but it is language in a very specific sense. It is not a language of verbal symbols, but of intuitive symbols. He who does not understand these intuitive symbols, who can not feel the life of colors, of shapes, of spatial forms and patterns, harmony and melody, is secluded from the work of art—and by this he is not only deprived of aesthetic pleasure, but he loses the approach to one of the deepest aspects of reality.[24]

24. See "Language and Art I," herein, n. 1, for indication of Cassirer's works on art.—Ed.

Looking back at our general analysis of myth, language, and art, we may perhaps be tempted to condense the results of this analysis in a short formula. We may say that what we find in myth is imaginative objectification, that art is a process of intuitive or contemplative objectification, that language and science are conceptual objectifications. I think that such a formula would not be without value and that it would contain a certain truth. But of course we must be careful in its application. When using it we must not relapse into the errors of the so-called *Vermögens-Psychologie* (faculty-psychology). There are no strictly separate provinces of the human mind. From the point of view of our scientific analysis it may be allowed and it may even appear necessary to bring the various phenomena of the human mind under general titles. But when doing so we must not allow ourselves to be deceived by that fallacy that was described and denounced by William James as the "psychologist's fallacy." We must not think that what we have called by a separate name is a separate entity or a separate function. Man is not a mixture of single and isolated faculties. His activity tends in different directions, but it is not divided into different parts.

In all these activities we find the whole of human nature. There is no branch of human culture in which feeling and emotion, imagination and contemplation, thought and reason have not their definite share. Therefore we cannot reduce myth, art, language to one of these faculties to the exclusion of all the others. Myth is by no means a mere product of the imagination. It is not the work of an unsound or unbalanced mind, an aggregate of dreams or hallucinations, of extravagant and fantastic ideas. In the development of the human mind myth plays quite a different role. It is the first answer given to the riddles of the universe. It attempts, although in an incomplete and inadequate way, to find out the beginning and the cause of things. In this, myth appears not only as a product of fancy but as the work of men's first intellectual curiosity. Myth does not content itself with a description of what things are; it strives back to their origin, it wishes to know why they are. It contains a cosmology and a general anthropology. And many of the great mythological cosmologies—we may for instance think of Egyptian or Jewish cosmology—do not lack a real acuity and profundity of thought.

On the other hand, art seems to be connected with myth in its origin and first beginning, and even in its progress can never completely escape the domain and the power of mythical and religious thought. It is just in the greatest artists—in Dante and Milton, in a Mass of Bach or in the *Sistina* of Michelangelo that we feel this power in its full strength. The greatest modern artists still feel a continual longing for the mythical world; and they mourn for it as a lost paradise. In German literature this longing is expressed in Schiller's poem, "Die Götter Griechenlands," and we feel it, incessantly and in the highest intensity, in the poetry of Hölderlin.[25] The poet—the true poet—does not live and cannot live in a world of dead things—of physical or material objects. He cannot approach nature without by the very manner of this approach constantly vivifying and animating nature. In this respect genuine poetry always preserves the fundamental structure of mythical feeling and mythical imagination. Myth and art are living in a personal world, not in a physical world. In English literature I think that Wordsworth gave one of the strongest and the most striking expressions of this side of the poet's feeling, which he describes in a famous passage of his *Preludes:*

> To every natural form, rocks, fruits, or flower
> Even the loose stones that cover the highway
> I gave a moral life: I saw them feel,
> Or linked them to some feeling: the great mass
> Lay bedded in a quickening soul, and all
> That I beheld respired with inward meaning.

When reading such a passage—or any other great poem—we immediately feel in which respect poetical language is radically distinct from conceptual language. It contains the strongest emotional and intuitive elements. The symbolism of language is not a

25. See Cassirer, "Hölderlin und der deutsche Idealismus," *Logos* 7–8 (1917–18), 262–82, 30–49; reprinted in *Idee und Gestalt. Fünf Aufsätze* (Berlin: Bruno Cassirer, 1921). Also, "Die Methodik des Idealismus in Schillers philosophischen Schriften," in *Idee und Gestalt*, and "Schiller und Shaftesbury," *Publications of the English Goethe Society* (New Series), 11 (1935), 37–59.—Ed.

mere semantic, but it is at the same time an aesthetic symbolism. Not only in the language of poetry but also in ordinary language this aesthetic element cannot be excluded. Without it our language would become colorless and lifeless.[26]

In our last meeting I tried to give you a general survey of that slow and continuous process that to my mind we have to regard as one of the essential and most characteristic features of human culture. I attempted to describe this process as a process of objectification. What man seems to strive at and what he really attains in the different forms of human activity—in myth and religion, in art, in language, in science—is to objectify his feelings and emotions, his desires, his perceptions, his thoughts and ideas.

At the end of our last meeting I quoted a passage from the work of Ferdinand de Saussure, *Cours de linguistique générale,* in which he expresses this view with regard to language. "Apart from language," says Ferdinand de Saussure, "our thought is only an amorphous mass. . . . Taken in itself thought is like a misty veil. There are no preestablished ideas and nothing is distinct before the appearance of language." This is obvious, as soon as we follow the device that in the study of language was first introduced by Wilhelm von Humboldt, the very founder of a critical philosophy of language. Humboldt incessantly admonishes us to look at language not as a work but as an activity—not as an *Ergon* but as an *Energia.*[27] Language can never be defined in a mere static way as a system of fixed grammatical forms or of logical forms. We have to consider it in its actual performance— in the act of speech. And this act is always pervaded with the totality of our subjective, personal life. The rhythm and the measure, the accent, the emphasis, the melody of speech are unavoidable and unmistakable indications of this personal life—

26. The text has a break here with a sentence beginning "This is evident" not completed.—Ed.

27. Cf. "Die Kantischen Elemente in Wilhelm von Humboldts Sprachphilosophie," in *Festschrift für Paul Hensel* (Greiz i.V.: Ohag, 1923), pp. 105–27; and *Philosophy of Symbolic Forms,* I, 155–63. There is a break in Cassirer's text between the beginning of the quotation from Saussure and this sentence.—Ed.

of our emotions, our feelings, and interests. Our analysis remains incomplete if it does not constantly bear in mind this side of the problem. Modern linguistics has often laid special stress upon this fact.[28]

But the conceptual meaning and the conceptual value of language is not diminished by these considerations. Croce is wrong when thinking that lyricism (liricità) is the proper and essential root of language.[29] Lyricism is not missing in language, but it is always counterbalanced by another element, by its inherent logicism. Karl Vossler says—referring to Croce—that stylistics, not grammar, is the real basis of language. But I cannot see how stylistics without grammar could be possible. And it is not only poetry that is bound to the words of our common language, but also all the other arts have a strictly objective side and, so to speak, a logic of their own. In music this logic is perhaps to be felt most distinctly—and without it there would not be such a thing as a "musical theory." We all admit the saying of Plato, that nobody can become an artist without a sort of θεία μανία, without a divine inspiration. But inspiration is not the only source of art. A great intellectual effort, a clarification, intensification, concentration of the original conception, a sound judgment, a severe criticism—all that is necessary to produce a great work of art.

What, therefore, is characteristic for myth, language, or art is not the fact that in one of them we find a marked process or faculty that is completely missing in the other. It is not the presence or absence of one of these faculties but the relation they

28. Here Cassirer cites J. Vendryes, Language, A Linguistic Introduction to History, trans. Paul Radin (New York: Knopf, 1925), and indicates that he intends to quote a passage from this work, but the specific reference is not given. Cassirer perhaps has in mind Vendryes's emphasis on language as based in sound and the speech act and his placement of language within the study of the development of culture and social structures: "Language is thus the social fact par excellence, the result of social contact. . . . Psychologically the original linguistic act consists in giving to a sign a symbolic value. This psychological process distinguishes the language of man from that of animals" (p. 11). Cf. Cassirer's discussion in An Essay on Man of the definition of man as an animal symbolicum and his discussion of the differences between signs and symbols as related to "animal reactions" and "human responses" (see ch. 3).—Ed.

29. Cf. "Language and Art I" herein.—Ed.

bear to each other that makes the real difference. In myth the power of imagination is prevailing; and in its premature stage it seems to be overwhelming. In language the logical moment, the Logos in its proper sense, is gradually increased; and in the passage from common language to scientific language it definitely gains the victory. But in art the combat seems to be reconciled, and this reconciliation is one of its essential privileges and one of its deepest charms. Here we feel no longer the conflict between opposed tendencies. All our different powers and all our different needs seem to be melted into a perfect harmony. In this way we may interpret the Kantian definition of beauty. What we enjoy in beauty, says Kant, is "des freien Spiels der Vorstellungskräfte," "the free play of the powers of representation with reference to knowledge in general."[30]

In a great genius of art this free play reaches its highest development and its full power. What are the faculties of the mind, asks Kant, which constitute genius? And he answers the question by saying that "genius" means *Geist* (spirit) and that *Geist* is that which brings about the perfect harmony and equipoise of all the different faculties of the mind. "Thus, properly speaking, genius consists in a happy disposition which cannot be taught by science or acquired by industry, a disposition which enables us to find Ideas for a given concept and moreover to *express* those Ideas in such a way that the subjective state of mind accompanying the concept can be communicated to others."[31] It was for this reason that Kant refused the name "genius" to the great scientists, yet admired them. For science, when compared with art, is always a one-sided activity, in which the intellect masters and in a certain sense oppresses all the other human powers. We may remember the anecdote of a famous French mathematician who, after having attended a representation of Racine's *Iphigénie*, asked his friends the question, "Qu'est-ce que cela prouve?"—What does that prove?

Such a question is the very opposite to the spirit of art. A work of art is not only composed of different elements; it always con-

30. *Kritik der Urteilskraft,* sec. 9.—Cassirer.

31. Ibid., sec. 49.—Cassirer.

tains opposite poles. To use the words of Heraclitus, we may call it a ἕν διαφερόμενον ἑαυτῷ—a unity divided and distinguished in itself. It is unity and multiplicity, it speaks to the imagination and to the intellect, it is emotion and rest. For it would be erroneous to reduce art to a mere expression of emotions. The facility to express emotions is regarded by Croce and his adherents as the fundamental aesthetic fact. But here, too, we have to make a restriction and a sharp distinction. Of course we cannot deny the fact that the greatest artists are capable of the deepest and richest emotions. They possess a variety and intensity, a scale of feeling that none of us can reach or imitate. But that does not make a qualitative difference but only a difference of degree. The capability of expressing his emotions is not a particular but a general human gift. But a man may write a most passionate love letter in which he may succeed in giving a true and sincere expression to his feelings without by this fact alone becoming an artist. And even if he uses a metrical form he does not necessarily by this become a poet.

Therefore I cannot agree with the statement I find in a recent book of R. G. Collingwood, an English adherent and follower of Croce's, that art may be described as the function of making a clean breast of one's feelings. Everyone can do this—and, as a matter of fact, Collingwood draws from this definition the inference that "every utterance and every gesture that each of us makes is a work of art."[32] But that is a very questionable and paradoxical statement. The artist is not the man who indulges in the display of his emotions or who has the greatest facility in the expression of these emotions. To be swayed by emotion means sentimentalism, not art. If an artist, instead of being absorbed in the intuition of his material, of sounds, of bronze or marble, or in his creation of forms is engrossed in his own individuality, if he feels his own pleasure or enjoys "the joy of grief"—then he becomes a sentimentalist; he ceases being an artist.

Art does not live in our common, average, empirical reality of material things. But it is just as little true that it simply lives in

32. *The Principles of Art* (Oxford: Clarendon Press, 1938), pp. 279–85.—Cassirer. Cf. "Language and Art I" herein.—Ed.

the sphere of the inner personal life, in imaginations or dreams, in emotions or passions. Of course all that the artist creates is based on his subjective and objective experience. An artist like Dante or Goethe, like Mozart or Bach, like Rembrandt or Michelangelo gives us his intuition of nature and his interpretation of human life. But this intuition and interpretation always means a transfiguration and, so to speak, a transubstantiation. Life and nature no longer appear in their empirical or material shape. They are no longer opaque, impermeable facts; they are filled with the life of forms.

It is in these forms, not only in his personal emotions; it is in shapes and designs, in lines and patterns, in rhythms, melodies, harmonies that a true artist lives. And that means a new and an opposite pole of life. Wordsworth defines poetry as the "spontaneous overflow of powerful feelings." But we find in Wordsworth also a second and different definition. Poetry, he tells us, is "emotion recollected in tranquillity." Even in the most emotional form of poetry, in drama and tragedy, we feel this sudden change, we feel—as Hamlet says—a temperance in the very torrent, tempest, and whirlwind of our passions. That is the objectification of human life brought about by art—and it is perhaps its most characteristic achievement, an achievement that we cannot find in any other sphere.

Let me conclude these general considerations by a quotation taken from the work of Goethe. "Das Wahre, mit dem Göttlichen identisch,"—says Goethe, "läßt sich niemals von uns direkt erkennen; wir schauen es nur im Abglanz, im Beispiel, Symbol, in einzelnen ʻund verwandten Erscheinungen; wir werden es gewahr als unbegreifliches Leben und können dem Wunsch nicht entsagen, es dennoch zu begreifen." "Truth or, what means the same, the Divine is never to be grasped directly. We can see it only in a reflected light, in an example, a symbol, in single and related phenomena. We become aware of it as incomprehensible life and yet we cannot renounce the wish to comprehend it."[33] The fundamental reality, the *Urphänomen*, in the

33. "Versuch einer Witterungslehre (1825)," in *Schriften zur Naturwissenschaft, Zweiter Teil,* vol. 40 of *Goethes Sämtliche Werke,* Jubiläumsausgabe (Stuttgart and Berlin: F. G. Cotta'sche Buchhandlung Nachfolger, n. d.), p. 55.—Ed.

sense of Goethe, the ultimate phenomenon may, indeed, be designated by the term "life."[34] This phenomenon is accessible to everyone; but it is "incomprehensible" in the sense that it admits of no definition, no abstract theoretical explanation. We cannot explain it, if explanation means the reduction of an unknown fact to a better-known fact, for there is no better-known fact. We can neither give a logical definition of life—*per genus proximum et differtiam specificam*—nor can we find out the origin, the first cause of life.

Life, reality, being, existence are nothing but different terms referring to one and the same fundamental fact. These terms do not describe a fixed, rigid, substantial thing. They are to be understood as names of a process. Man is the only being that is not only engaged in this process but who becomes conscious of it; myth, religion, art, science are nothing else than the different steps made by man in his consciousness, in his reflective interpretation of life. Each of them is a mirror of our human experience which, as it were, possesses its own angle of refraction. Philosophy, as the highest and most comprehensive mode of reflection, strives to understand them all. It cannot comprise them in an abstract formula; but it strives to penetrate into their concrete meaning. This meaning is based on general principles—and these principles are studied by a philosophy of language, a philosophy of art, of religion, and of science.

In our former discussions I often had the impression that some of you were thinking that what I defend here is a system of subjective idealism in which the ego, the subjective mind, the thinking self is considered as the center and as the creator of the world, as the sole or ultimate reality. I do not wish to argue here about terms. We know that Kant felt very much surprised and very much scandalized when his *Critique of Pure Reason* at its first appearance met the same objection, when it was described by a reviewer as a system of subjective idealism. He wrote a special treatise, his *Prolegomena,* in order to refute this view. In this sem-

34. See Cassirer's discussion of the relation between "life" *(Leben)* and "spirit" *(Geist):* " 'Spirit' and 'Life' in Contemporary Philosophy" in *The Philosophy of Ernst Cassirer,* ed. P. A. Schilpp (Evanston, Ill.: Library of Living Philosophers, 1949), pp. 857–80; orig. German pub. 1930.—Ed.

inar we could only touch on this question. In order to clear this point we had to enter into the general theory of knowledge. For it is only on such a theory that we can hope to find a clear and satisfactory answer to the question what the terms "realism" and "idealism," subject and object, consciousness and being really mean. Without a thorough epistemological analysis all these terms remain vague and obscure. It is, for instance, not easy to understand a philosopher who, like Hegel, has no less than four terms—*Sein, Dasein, Existenz, Wirklichkeit*—that are to be carefully distinguished from each other and that in their meaning widely diverge from each other.

But I think that the problems with which we were concerned here scarcely need these epistemological subtleties. They are to a very large degree independent of any metaphysical theory about the absolute nature of things. The metaphysical realist and the metaphysical idealist may answer them in the same way. For the fact of human culture is, after all, an empirical fact that has to be investigated according to empirical methods and principles. And all of us, I think, are empirical realists, whatever metaphysical or epistemological theory we may assume.

The ego, the individual mind, cannot create reality. Man is surrounded by a reality that he did not make, that he has to accept as an ultimate fact. But it is for him to interpret reality, to make it coherent, understandable, intelligible—and this task is performed in different ways in the various human activities, in religion and art, in science and philosophy. In all of them man proves to be not only the passive recipient of an external world; he is active and creative. But what he creates is not a new substantial thing; it is a representation, an objective description of the empirical world.

The Educational Value of Art

(1943)

This lecture is written in English longhand, marked on its envelope as "Seminar of Education, March 10th 1943" (MS #219). It is possible that it is a lecture for Cassirer's seminar for the spring term of 1942–43, which is listed in the Yale Catalogue as Philosophy 123b, Seminar on Aesthetics: Symbolic Problems, and bears the description: "Good, beauty, and truth; imitation; nature and genius; emotion and expression; aesthetic form; the objectivity of beauty, etc." This constituted the second half of a year-long seminar; the first half was titled Philosophy 123a, Seminar on Aesthetics: Fundamental Types, and treated various types of aesthetic theories, both ancient and modern. It is also possible that this was a guest lecture in a seminar dealing with education, as it is so labeled and its style is quite self-contained. Cassirer makes no references to other meetings of the course, as he frequently does in other seminar lectures. It is, however, concerned with several of the "symbolic problems" listed for Philosophy 123b.–Ed.

Of all the problems that we have to study in a philosophy of education, the problem of the educational value of art is one of the most difficult ones. From its first beginnings philosophy had to face this problem. But it seems as if we are still very far from a generally admitted solution. We are still confronted with the same fundamental dilemma that we find in the great systems of Greek thought; we are struggling with the same systematic difficulties as Plato or Aristotle. Plato was the first great thinker who felt the problem in its full strength.[1] But he could not untie the Gordian knot; he had to cut it.

1. See "Eidos und Eidolon. Das Problem des Schönen und der Kunst in Platons Dialogen," in *Vorträge der Bibliothek*, vol. 2 (Leipzig: B. G. Teubner, 1924), pt. 1, pp. 1–27.—Ed.

There is an old tradition according to which Plato began not as a philosopher but as a poet. But when he made his first acquaintance with Socrates he changed his mind; he became aware of a new mission that he had to fulfill. This mission, this philosophical vocation, required a great sacrifice. He burned all the poems that he had written before. If this story is true—and there seems to be no reason to doubt it—this was a very characteristic and significant symbolic act. It was a symbol not only of a change in Plato's personal life but of a change in Greek culture and in the Greek system of education. Until then the poems of Homer had been the center and the very focus of Greek education. Every Greek boy knew these poems by heart. They were the principal sources of his education; they formed his religious and moral ideals. But all this had to be negated and destroyed by Plato. In order to build up his own theory—the theory of the ideal state— he had to contest and to challenge the deepest and most powerful instincts of Greek cultural life. If we read the famous words contained in the *Republic* of Plato, we still feel all the great personal and systematic difficulties of this new task; we are aware of all the obstacles that Plato had to overcome in order to attain his end. But his intellectual courage did not shrink back from these obstacles. He did not seek for a compromise; he gives us a radical solution.

If education is one of the principal tasks of the state—the task in which all the others are, so to speak, contained and concentrated—poetry and fine art can have no place in the constitution of the state. They are not constructive but dissolving powers— they are destructive and anarchic forces. It is for the philosopher and for the legislator to restrain these anarchic forces. Plato says:

> As in a city when the evil are permitted to have authority and the good are put out of the way, so in the soul of man, as we maintain, the imitative poet implants an evil constitution, for he indulges the irrational nature ... he is a manufacturer of images and is very far removed from the truth. But we have not yet brought forward the heaviest count in our accusation: the power which poetry has of harming even the good. ... The best of us, as I conceive, when we listen to

a passage of Homer, or one of the tragedians, in which he
represents some pitiful hero who is drawling out his sorrows
in a long oration, or weeping, or smiting his breast—the best
of us, you know, delight in giving way to sympathy, and are
in raptures at the excellence of the poet who stirs our feelings most. But when any sorrow of our own happens to us,
then you may observe that we pride ourselves on the opposite quality—we would fain be quiet and patient; this is the
manly part, and the other which delighted us in the recita-
tion is now deemed to be the part of a woman. Now can we
be right in praising and admiring another who is doing that
which anyone of us would abominate and be ashamed of in
his own person? . . . And the same may be said of lust and
anger and all the other affections, of desire and pain and
pleasure, which are held to be inseparable from every
action—in all of them poetry feeds and waters the passions
instead of drying them up; she lets them rule although they
ought to be controlled, if mankind are ever to increase in
happiness and virtue.[2]

Have these blames, cast on the educational value of art, ever
been refuted? In the whole history of aesthetics we find the continuous echo of Plato's accusations. It became one of the most
important tasks of every theory of art to refute or at least to
enfeeble the Platonic arguments. The greatest pupil of Plato was
the first to make an effort to vindicate the rights of poetry. Aristotle's theory of tragedy has its basis in this tendency. I do not
wish to debate here upon the philological interpretation of the
Aristotelian term, *catharsis*. But what seems to be clear and undeniable is that the real purpose of the Aristotelian theory was to
dispel the doubts of Plato. Art, he objects, is not destined to stir
and arouse our emotions. Such art, especially the art of tragedy,
shows us the opposite effect. "We see in the case of the sacred
songs," says Aristotle in his *Politics*, "that while usually their
effect upon the mind is a sort of intoxication, yet when they are

2. *Republic*, X, 605b–606d, Jowett trans.—Ed.

heard by persons in ecstasy, these are calmed, as though they had gone through a medical cure and a catharsis."[3]

By great tragic poetry we are not thrown into a chaos of violent and contradictory emotions; we find, on the contrary, calmness and relief—a discharge of fear and pity. In Greek ethics this state of calmness had been described by the term *euthymia*. In the ethical system of Democritus *euthymia* is regarded as the highest moral end, the *summum bonum*. It does not mean a special positive pleasure; it means the inner harmony of the soul, a peace undistracted by overwhelming and overmastering passions—a composure or equanimity similar to the smooth mirror of the stormless sea. But can art ever have this cathartic effect? Can it lead to such a composure?

If we look at the development of modern aesthetics we find that this difficulty has not been solved. The problem is still as controversial as it ever was before. It may suffice to quote here one special example—the example of a man who was not only a deep thinker, but at the same time one of the great modern poets. In his treatise, *What is Art?*, Leo Tolstoi repeats all the accusations of Plato against the moral and educational value of art. "We are surrounded," he says, "by productions considered artistic. Thousands of verses, thousands of poems, thousands of novels, thousands of dramas, thousands of pictures, thousands of musical pieces follow one after another. . . . But among these productions in the various branches of art there is in each branch one among hundreds of thousands, not only somewhat better than the rest, but differing from them as a diamond differs from paste. The one is priceless; the others not only have no value but are worse than valueless, for they deceive and pervert taste. And yet, externally, they are . . . precisely alike."[4]

Where can we find a criterion to distinguish between all these things that call themselves works of art? For Tolstoi it is clear and undeniable that this criterion can only be a moral and religious one. Whether art has an inner value depends not on the

3. 1342^a—Ed.

4. Trans. Aylmer Maude (Indianapolis and New York: Bobbs-Merrill, 1960), pp. 132–33.—Ed.

mode of expression and on the thing expressed, or on the character of the feeling which it describes. If it describes and expresses simple, unsophisticated, good feelings, it is good; if it arouses wild, violent, disordered emotions, it is bad. Tolstoi compares the impression made on him by the loud singing of a large choir of peasant women who were welcoming his daughter, celebrating her return home after her marriage, to a sonata of Beethoven played in his house that same evening by an admirable musician. He prefers by far the former to the latter. "The song of the peasant women," he says, "was real art, transmitting a definite and strong feeling; while the 101st sonata of Beethoven was only an unsuccessful attempt, containing no definite feeling. . . ."[5]

It is clear that what Tolstoi attacks is by no means only the art of his own time—the so-called decadent art of the nineteenth century. The greatest and most powerful artists of all times—Beethoven and Shakespeare—are included in his judgment. Every sort of aestheticism, every variant of the theme *l'art pour l'art,* is unsound and dangerous. To speak of a purposeless art, or of an art that has its end in itself, is a mere juggling with words. Art has a very definite purpose; the purpose not only to describe or express, but to improve our feelings. If it forgets this purpose it forgets itself; it becomes as futile and meaningless play. "As the evolution of knowledge proceeds by truer and more necessary knowledge, dislodging and replacing what is mistaken and unnecessary, so the evolution of feeling proceeds through art—feelings less kind and less needful for the well-being of mankind are replaced by others kinder and more needful for that end. That is the purpose of art. . . . The more art fulfills that purpose the better the art, and the less it fulfills it, the worse the art."[6]

Wordsworth described poetry as the "spontaneous overflow of powerful feelings." Tolstoi could not accept such a definition. According to him it is not the power, but the quality of the feeling, it is the inherent moral and religious value which is decisive

5. Ibid., p. 135.—Ed.
6. Ibid., p. 143.—Ed.

for the worth of a work of art. "Art is not a pleasure, a solace, or an amusement; art is a great matter. Art is an organ of human life, transmitting man's reasonable perception into feeling. In our age the common religious perception of man is the consciousness of the brotherhood of man—we know that the well-being of man lies in union with his fellow man. True science should indicate the various methods of applying this consciousness to life. Art should transform this perception into feeling."[7]

If we look at the theory of art of Plato and Tolstoi we are confronted with the same great historical paradox. How was it possible—we must ask ourselves—that the most serious attacks against the value of art came from these two thinkers, who obviously did not underrate or despise the power of art but had the richest experience in art and the deepest feeling of its power? Plato is the greatest artist who has appeared in the history of philosophy; Tolstoi is a great and incomparable poet who in his novels gave one of the deepest and richest descriptions of modern life. In the case of Plato and in the case of Tolstoi it was precisely this susceptibility to the most subtle nuances and to all the charms of art which made them, as it were, chastize art for its weakness, for its inherent dangers and temptations. They tried to create a theory of art by which man should be enabled to resist these temptations. Plato spoke as a politician and as an idealistic philosopher; Tolstoi spoke as a moralist and as a religious thinker. But their criticism is directed to one and the same point. What they attack is the hedonistic theory of art—the conception that the highest, nay the only aim, of the work of art is to give us a special and specific kind of pleasure.

If this hedonistic interpretation were true, it would, indeed, be almost impossible to ascribe to art any *educational* value. Education needs stronger powers and a firmer basis than pleasure. The hedonistic interpretation of art has been sharply criticized in our modern aesthetic theories—for instance, in the theory of Croce. Nevertheless it still maintains its place; and it has found many and strong defenders, especially in American philosophi-

7. Ibid., p. 189.—Ed.

cal literature. One of the best-known books in American philosophical literature—Santayana's book, *The Sense of Beauty*, is a
typical example of this aesthetic hedonism. "Science," says Santayana, "is the response to the demand for information, and in it
we ask for the whole truth and nothing but the truth. Art is the
response to the demand for entertainment, and truth enters into
it only as it subserves these ends."[8] If this definition were correct,
art would indeed be liable to all the objections of Plato or Tolstoi. To describe beauty as "a relatively stable or real pleasure," a
description contained in a book of Marshall, is indeed a very
inadequate and misleading description of our aesthetic experience.[9] The demand for entertainment may be satisfied by much
better and cheaper means. To think that the great artists worked
for this purpose—that Michelangelo constructed Saint Peter's
church, that Dante or Milton wrote their poems, that Bach composed his Mass in B-minor for the sake of entertainment—is an
absurdity. All of them would have subscribed to the words of
Aristotle in the *Nicomachean Ethics* that to exert oneself for the
sake of amusement seems silly and utterly childish.[10]

The systems of hedonism have a common flaw that appears
both in the field of ethics and aesthetics. What seems to recommend these systems is their simplicity. From a psychological
point of view it is always very tempting to explain all the phenomena of human life by a uniform principle and to reduce
them to one and the same fundamental instinct. But a closer
systematic analysis shows us that this advantage is a very questionable one. Here we must, first and foremost, account for
those specific differences which in the traditional theories of an
ethical or aesthetical hedonism are completely ignored or obliterated. Pleasure and pain are the most general phenomena, not
only of human life, but, as it seems, of all organic life. They
accompany all our activities—our bodily functions as well as our
mental functions. But it is precisely for this reason that they can-

8. New York: Charles Scribner's Sons, 1896, p. 22.—Cassirer.

9. Henry Rutgers Marshall, *The Beautiful* (London: Macmillan, 1924), p. 78.—Ed.

10. 1776[b] 33.—Cassirer.

not be used as definitions or explanations of any *special* function—its characteristic and its prerogative.

If pleasure is regarded as the common denominator it is only
the degree, not the kind of pleasure which really matters. There
is a very striking remark in Kant's *Critique of Practical Reason*
which lays stress on this point: "If the determination of will,"
says Kant, "rests on the feeling of the agreeableness or disagree-
ableness that we expect from any cause it is all the same to us by
what sort of ideas we will be affected. The only thing that concerns us, in order to decide our choice, is, how great, how long
continued, how easily obtained, and how often repeated this
agreeableness is. And as to the man who wants money to spend,
it is all the same whether the gold was dug out of the mountain
or washed out of the sand, provided it is everywhere accepted at
the same value, so the man who cares only for the enjoyment of
life does not ask whether the ideas are of the understanding or
the senses, but only how much and how great pleasure they will
give for the longest time."[11]

There was always *one* argument that could be propounded for
a theory of aesthetic hedonism. If we accept this theory we can
avoid every severance between "art" and "life." The chasm
between them is filled; art is no longer a separate sphere, a state
in the state, it becomes the fulfillment of our deepest and inevitable natural instincts. The defenders of the principle *l'art pour l'art*
had often put the work of art on such a high pedestal that it
became inaccessible to the *profanum vulgus*–to the mass of the
uninitiated. "A poem," said the poet Stéphane Mallarmé, "must
be an enigma for the vulgar, chamber-music for the initiated."[12]
Such an esoteric view seems to give to art its highest value, but at

11. Trans. T. K. Abbott (London: Longmans, Green and Co., 1873), p. 110.—Cassirer.
Cassirer alters the personal pronoun from third person singular to first person
plural.—Ed.

12. See William A. Nitze and E. Preston Dargan, *A History of French Literature*, 3d ed.
(New York: Holt, Rinehart and Winston, 1950), p. 708. Cf. *Essay on Man*, p. 166, n. 39, in
which Cassirer employs this quotation, with citation to Katherine Gilbert, *Studies in Recent
Aesthetic* (Chapel Hill: University of North Carolina Press, 1927), p. 18 [sic], p. 20. Gilbert's citation is to Nitze and Dargan's *History*, and although the line appears therein it
does not appear as a direct quote from Mallarmé.—Ed.

the same time it deprives it of one of its principal tasks. For an energy that does not prove its power in the organization of our actual and concrete human life would be *sterile*. It seemed better to make art a more "common" thing, an experience of our everyday life. "When we look at a picture, or read a poem, or listen to music," it was objected to such a view, "we are not doing something quite unlike what we were doing on our way to the Gallery or when we dressed in the morning. . . . Our activity is not of a fundamentally different kind."[13] But did any great artist ever feel in this way—did he regard his activity as such a commonplace and trivial thing? And even we, the spectators, rise to have a very keen feeling of the difference between listening to a play of Shakespeare or a concerto of Beethoven and innumerable other things that give us the greatest and indubitable pleasure. That is provided by common experience; but it is one of the first and fundamental tasks of an aesthetic theory to account for this specific difference.

The history of aesthetics seems constantly to oscillate between two opposite poles—between an intellectual and an emotional approach to art. The former prevails in all the classical and neoclassical theories of art; the second seems now accepted by most of our modern theories. Art may be described and interpreted as "imitation of nature" or as "expression of feelings." The term "imitation" always contains a theoretical element. Aristotle describes imitation (μίμησις) as a fundamental instinct and an irreducible fact of human nature. "Imitation," he says, "is natural to man from childhood, one of his advantages over the lower animals being this—that he is the most imitative creature in the world and learns at first by imitation."[14] That explains the pleasure we feel in art. For to be learning something is the greatest of pleasures not only to the philosopher, but also to the rest of mankind, however small their capacity for it. The reason for the delight in seeing the picture is that one is at the same time learn-

---

13. I. A. Richards, *Principles of Literary Criticism* (New York: Harcourt, Brace, 1926), pp. 16–17.—Cassirer.

14. *Poetics*, 1448b 5–10.—Ed.

ing—gathering the meaning of things, e.g., that the man there is so and so. This general theory of imitation (μίμησις) prevailed for many centuries and stamped its mark upon the whole development of aesthetic thought.

But from the beginning of the eighteenth century we feel a new tendency that constantly increases in strength. If we read a work like the work of the French critic Batteux, *Les beaux arts réduits à un même principe,* published in 1747, we find that Batteux strongly upholds the traditional view. Nevertheless, even he cannot refrain from a certain uneasiness about the truth of his theory of imitation when speaking of a special branch of art, of lyrical poetry. "Is not lyrical poetry," he asks himself, "something very different from imitation? Is it not a song inspired by joy, admiration, gratitude? Is it not a cry of the heart, an enthusiasm in which nature does everything and art nothing? I do not see in it any painting or picture—but only fire, feeling, intoxication. So two things are true first: lyrical poetry is true poetry, second it is not an imitator."[15] From the point of view of a resolute champion of the classical and neoclassical theory of beauty, this was a very interesting admission. Batteux himself did not think that the objection was unanswerable. But the arguments by which he tried to prove that lyrical poetry—like all other kinds of art— could be comprehended under the general scheme of imitation were weak and inconclusive. All these arguments were suddenly swept away by the appearance of a new force. Even here the name of Rousseau marks a decisive turning point in the history of ideas, in the theory of art as well as in the theory of education. Rousseau rejects the whole classical and neoclassical tradition. When he wrote his *Nouvelle Héloïse* his work proved to be a new

15. Batteux states: "Quand on n'examine que superficiellement la Poësie lyrique, elle paroît se prêter moins que les autres espéces au principe général qui raméne tout à l'imitation. . . . La Poësie n'est-elle pas un chant, qu'inspire la joie, l'admiration, la reconnoissance? N'est-ce pas un cri du coeur, en élan, où la nature fait tout, l'art rien? Je n'y vois point de tableau, de peinture. Tout y est feu, sentiment, ivresse. Ainsi deux choses sont varies: la première, que les Poësies lyriques sont de vrais poëmes: La seconde, que ces Poësies n'ont point le caractre de l'imitation." *Les beaux arts réduits à un même principe,* vol. I of *Principes de la littérature,* nouvelle édition (Paris, 1764), pt. 3, sec. 1, ch. 12, pp. 299–300.—Ed.

revolutionary power.[16] The mimetic principle had, henceforward, to give way to a new conception and a new ideal of art. Art
is not a reproduction of the empirical world, an imitator of
nature. It is an outbreak of emotions and passions, and it is the
strength and the depth of these passions which gives to a work of
art its real meaning and value.

That lyrical art is the prototype of all art whatever is the
theory that, in contemporary philosophy, has found its best and
most characteristic expression in the work of Benedetto Croce.
According to the classical and neoclassical theories, the highest
task of art was to imitate nature. But there was always a restriction on this view. The artist has not given a simple copy of
nature; he has to perfect, to beautify, to idealize nature. His
object is not nature in a general and indiscriminate sense, but
"beautiful nature," *la belle nature,* as it was called by the French
classicists. But it is this very concept of a so-called beautiful
nature that is emphatically denied by Croce. His philosophy is a
philosophy of spirit, not of nature. From the point of view of this
notion, an ideal or beautiful nature is a contradiction in terms, a
wooden iron. "Beauty," says Croce, "is no quality of things,
whether trees or pigments, but like all other values only comes
into being as a result of a spiritual activity."[17] In Croce's theory,
art is identified with language. *"Estetica come scienza dell'expressione
e linguistica generale"* (*Aesthetic as Science of Expression and General
Linguistic*) is the title of his book. Philosophically speaking, aesthetics and linguistics are not concerned with different prob-

16. See Cassirer, *The Question of Jean-Jacques Rousseau,* trans. Peter Gay (New York:
Columbia University Press, 1954; orig. pub. 1932), pp. 43, 85, 93–99; and *Rousseau, Kant
and Goethe,* trans. James Gutmann, Paul Oskar Kristeller, and John Herman Randall, Jr.
(Princeton, N. J.: Princeton University Press, 1945), p. 14. "The spell that rested on
French language and poetry was broken only by Rousseau. Without creating a single
piece of what might properly be called lyrical poetry, he discovered and resurrected the
world of lyricism. It was the revelation of this almost forgotten world in Rousseau's *Nouvelle Héloïse* that so deeply moved and so strongly shook his contemporaries. They saw in
this novel no mere creation of the imagination. They felt transplanted from the sphere of
literature into the core of a new existence and enriched with a new feeling for life"
(*Jean-Jacques Rousseau,* p. 85).—Ed.

17. Cf. *Aesthetic as Science of Expression and General Linguistic,* trans. Douglas Ainslie, rev.
ed. (New York: Macmillan, 1922), p. 97.—Ed.

lems; they are not two branches of philosophy, but one branch only. "Whoever studies general Linguistic, that is to say, philosophical Linguistic, studies aesthetic problems, and *vice versa*."[18] Art and language are "expressions," and expression is an indivisible process.

Undoubtedly this theory of Croce's contains an element of truth. He has vigorously attacked and he has by very good and plausible reasons refuted the traditional theory of imitation and the hedonistic theories. But at one point his own thesis is open to the same objections. Even he fails to recognize the true specific difference of the aesthetic activity. What he describes is a common genus under which we may subsume this activity; but it is not its specific character, its distinctive mark. Croce does not admit that there is any difference between "expression" in general and "aesthetic expression." By this he is led to very paradoxical conclusions. We cannot speak of different kinds of expression. Expression is a unique act that admits of no degrees and no possible differentiation. A letter, for instance, in which I succeed in expressing my thoughts or my feelings, is, therefore, just as much a work of art as a painting or a drama. Croce's theory is only interested in the *fact* of expression, not in the *mode* of expression. To him all expression is a lyrical act—it contains that characteristic element which he describes by the term "lyricism" *(liricità)*.

But to my mind this theory fails in a double respect. The mere fact of expression cannot be regarded as an artistic fact. If I write a letter destined for a practical purpose, I am, in this act of writing, by no means an artist. But a man may even write a most passionate love letter in which he may succeed in giving a true and sincere expression to his deepest feelings without, by this fact alone, becoming an artist. Without doubt the great artists are capable of the deepest emotions. They possess a rarity and intensity, a scale of feeling that we do not find in the average man.

18. Ibid., p. 142. Cf. Cassirer's remarks on Croce's aesthetics, "Language and Art, I and II," herein. Also, Cassirer, *The Logic of the Humanities*, trans. Clarence Smith Howe (New Haven: Yale University Press, 1961; orig. pub. 1942), pp. 204–08.—Ed.

But this strength and multiformity of feeling is in itself no proof of a great artistic capacity and it is not the decisive feature of the work of art. The artist is not the man who indulges in the display of his emotions and who has the greatest facility in the expression of these emotions. To be swayed by emotions means sentimentalism, not art. If an artist, instead of being absorbed in the creation of his work, in the embodiment of his intuition, is absorbed in his own individuality, if he feels his own pleasure or enjoys the "joy of grief," then he becomes a sentimentalist. The artist, as such, does not live in our common reality, in the reality of empirical things or empirical ends. But it is just as little true he simply lives in the sphere of his inner personal life, in his emotions and passions, in his imaginations and dreams. What characterizes him and what assigns to him his particular place is his power to create a new sphere beyond these two realms—the sphere of pure sensuous forms.

Not expression alone, but creative expression, is the fundamental character of art. Expression, when taken in an unspecific and indiscriminate sense, is a general biological phenomenon. Darwin has written a special book on this, *The Expression of the Emotions in Man and Animals.* In this book he tries to show that the various modes of expression we find in the animal sphere have a biological meaning and purport. They are remnants of past or preparations for future biological actions. The uncovering of the teeth in monkeys means, for instance, that the animal wishes to show its enemy that it is provided with a formidable weapon. I do not wish to enter here into the details of this theory of Darwin. But it shows us very clearly that there is a sharp line of demarcation between the biological and the aesthetic part of expression. Even in the human sphere we find innumerable acts of expression that have a practical or biological relevance without having any aesthetic significance. This fact is overlooked or minimized by Croce and by all the adherents of his theory. In his work *Principles of Art,* R. G. Collingwood declares that the function of lyrical poetry—and the function of art in general—simply consists in the artist's making "a clean breast of his feelings." "What the artist is trying to do," he says, "is to express a given emotion. To express it and to express it well, are the same thing. . . . Every utterance and every gesture that each one of us makes is a work of art."[19]

But in this definition the whole constructive process that is a necessary prerequisite and a decisive feature both of the production and of the contemplation of the work of art is entirely obliterated. Our ordinary gestures are just as little works of art as our interjections are acts of speech. They are involuntary and instinctive reactions; they possess no real spontaneity. The moment of purposiveness is necessary both for linguistic and aesthetic expression. In every act of speech and in every artistic creation we find a definite teleological structure. An actor in a dramatic play really acts his part. All his single utterances are parts of a coherent structural whole—the accent and rhythm of his words, the modulation of his voice, the countenance of his body, the motions of his face. And all are to the same end—to the representation and embodiment of a human character. Even lyrical poetry—the most "subjective" form of art—is by no means devoid of this tendency. It contains the same sort of embodiment and objectification. "Poetry", says the French poet Mallarmé, "is not written with ideas, it is written with words."[20] It is written with images, sounds, and rhythms that, just as much as in the case of dramatic poetry and dramatic representation, must coalesce into each other and form an indivisible whole.

The life and the art of Goethe are perhaps the best and the most typical example of the mutual penetration of all those different elements which in their union constitute the work of the lyrical poet.[21] Goethe himself has described this process in his autobiography. "And thus began," he says, speaking of his early youth, "that bent of mind from which I could not deviate my

19. Oxford: Clarendon Press, 1938, pp. 279, 282, 285. Cf. "Language and Art, I and II," herein.—Ed.

20. Cf. *An Essay on Man*, p. 142.—Ed.

21. For Cassirer's interpretations of Goethe see *Freiheit und Form. Studien zur deutschen Geistesgeschichte* (Berlin: Bruno Cassirer, 1916), ch. 4; *Idee und Gestalt: Fünf Aufsätze* (Berlin: Bruno Cassirer, 1921), chs. 1–2; and *Goethe und die geschichtliche Welt: Drei Aufsätze* (Berlin: Bruno Cassirer, 1932). Also, "Thomas Manns Goethebild. Eine Studie über Lotte in Weimar," *Germanic Review* 20 (1945), 166–94, and "Goethe and the Kantian Philosophy" in *Rousseau, Kant and Goethe*, pp. 61–98.—Ed.

whole life through: namely, that of turning into an image, into a poem, everything that delighted or troubled me, or otherwise occupied my attention, and of coming to some certain understanding with myself thereupon, as well to rectify my conceptions of external things, as to set my mind at rest about them. The faculty of doing this was necessary to no one more than to me, for my natural disposition whirled me constantly from one extreme to the other. All the works therefore that have been published by me are only fragments of one great confession."[22] Croce is right to say that lyricism (liricità) is a necessary and indispensable element in every art. But even lyric is not a mere effusion of feelings. Like all other forms of art it possesses not only a subjective but also an objective pole. It is the tension between these two poles and the evolution of this tension that we feel in every great lyrical poem, in a poem of Goethe or Hölderlin,[23] of Wordsworth or Leopardi.

If we bear in mind this double character of the work of art we can answer the question of its educational value. We need no longer be afraid of its charms; we need not see in it a disturbance of our ethical life. The great moralists and the great religious thinkers, like Plato or Tolstoi, were always afraid of the infectiousness of art. Not only is the infectiousness a certain "sign of art," says Tolstoi, but the degree of infection is the only standard of the value of art. But it is easy to see at which point this theory fails. It forgets and minimizes the most fundamental moment and motive—the moment of form. He who forms a passion, who gives to it an objective shape, does not infect us with a passion. When listening to a play of Shakespeare we are not infected with the ambition of Macbeth, with the jealousy of Othello, or the cruelty of Richard the Third. What we feel here is the highest tension of all our passions, but it is, at the same time, the highest energy of creative form—and it is this active, creative energy which possesses the power to transform the passions

22. *Dichtung und Wahrheit*, VII; *Truth and Poetry*, trans. Parke Godwin, 2 vols. (New York: Geo. P. Putnam, 1850), vol. II, pt. 2, book 7, p. 66.—Cassirer.

23. See "Language and Art II," herein, n. 25.—Ed.

themselves—to give us, as Hamlet says, a temperance in the very torrent, tempest, and whirlwind of our passions.

The tragic catharsis of which Aristotle speaks is not to be understood in a moral sense, let alone in a psychological sense. It is no purification or purgative of our emotions. But it means that our emotions themselves become a part of our active life, not of our passive life. They are elevated to a new state. A man who in real life had to live through all the emotions we feel when listening to a tragedy of Sophocles or Shakespeare would be crushed and annihilated by the power of those emotions. In art we are not exposed to this danger. What we feel here is the full life and the full strength of emotions without their material content. The burden of our emotions is, as it were, taken off our shoulders; what we feel is their inner motion, their vibration and oscillation—without their gravity, their oppressive power, their weight and pressure.

Imitation of nature and expression of feelings are the two basic elements of art. They are, as it were, the stuff of which the garment of art is woven. But they do not express art's fundamental character, they do not exhaust its meaning and value. If art were nothing else than a mere copy of nature or a mere reproduction of human life, its intrinsic worth and its function in human culture would be rather doubtful and questionable. But it is much more. It adds, so to speak, a new dimension to human life; it gives to it a depth that we do not reach in our common apprehension of things. Art is not a mere repetition of nature and life; it is a sort of transformation and transubstantiation. This transubstantiation is brought about by the power of aesthetic form. Aesthetic form is not simply given; it is not a datum of our immediate empirical world. In order to become aware of it, we have to produce it; and this production depends on a specific autonomous act of the human mind. We cannot speak of aesthetic form as a part or element of nature; it is a product of a free activity. It is for this reason that in the realm of art even all our common feelings, our passions and emotions, undergo a fundamental change. Passivity itself is turned into activity; mere receptivity is changed into spontaneity. What we feel here is not a single or simple emotional state. It is rather the whole gamut of human life, the continuous oscillation between all its extremes—between joy and grief, hope and fear, exultation and despair.

It could perhaps be objected that this is only a one-sided description of the aesthetic process. To be sure, it may be said, the *creation* of the work of art implies the greatest activity and energy of the human mind. But does this principle also hold for ourselves—for the spectators and auditors? When listening to a fugue of Bach or a concerto of Mozart, we seem to be in a sort of quietism, in a state that has often been described as a state of "aesthetic repose." We may accept this term if by "aesthetic repose" we understand the absence of the immediate power and pressure of passions and emotions. But that does by no means reduce the aesthetic state to a state of mere passivity. It means just the contrary. Even the spectator of the work of art is not restricted to a mere passive role. In order to contemplate and to enjoy the work of art he has to create it in his measure. We cannot understand or feel a great work of art without, to a certain degree, repeating and reconstructing the creative process by which it has come into being.

Artistic experience is always a dynamic, not a static attitude—both in the artist himself and in the spectator. We cannot live in the realm of artistic forms without participating in the creation of these forms. The artistic eye is not a passive eye that simply receives or registers the impressions of outward things. It is a constructive eye. "Beauty," said Schiller in his *Letters on the Aesthetic Education of Man,* "is an object to us because reflection is the condition of the feeling which we have of it; but it is also a state of our personality (our ego) because the feeling is the condition of the idea we conceive of it. In a word it is at once our state and our act. And precisely because it is at the same time both a state and an act, it triumphantly proves to us that the process does not exclude form, and that consequently the physical dependence to which man is devoted does not in any way destroy his moral beliefs."[24]

24. See *On the Aesthetic Education of Man,* trans. Reginald Snell (New Haven: Yale University Press, 1954), 25th letter, p. 122. The passage in the text is Cassirer's translation.—Ed.

In our aesthetic theories this polarity, which is an inherent condition of beauty, was expressed and explained in a twofold sense—and it seems to have led to diametrically opposed interpretations. On the one side we find spiritualistic theories that emphatically deny every connection between the beauty of art and the beauty of nature; they even deny that there is such a phenomenon as "natural beauty." According to Croce, who is one of the typical representatives of such an aesthetic speculation, it is mere rhetoric to speak of a beautiful tree or a beautiful river. All this is a mere metaphor, a figure of speech. Nature, says Croce, is stupid when compared with art; she is mute if man does not make her speak. On the other hand, the greatest artists have over and over again assured us that they felt unable to create beauty—they found it, they saw it in nature and they had only to elicit it from there. "Denn wahrhaftig die Kunst steckt in der Natur," said Albrecht Dürer, "wer sie heraus kann reißen, der hat sie" ("Art standeth firmly on Nature and who can rend her force hence, only he possesses her").[25]

I think, however, we can find a solution to this dilemma by making a distinction between what may be called "organic beauty" and "aesthetic beauty." If we define beauty in the sense of the classical formula as a "unity in the manifold," it is clear that we cannot restrict it to the field of art. It becomes a general predicate of organic nature. Kant was the first thinker who set himself the double task both to prove the communion between art and organic nature and to restrict it to its proper conditions. In his *Critique of Judgment* he treated the two problems side by side. Aesthetic judgment became a special case of the general function of teleological judgment. But the teleology of nature was, on the other hand, sharply distinguished from the teleology of the work of art. I cannot enter here into a historical interpretation of the Kantian thesis or into a systematic treatment of this interesting and intricate problem; that we can perhaps discuss later on. For the time being I content myself with a few general remarks.

25. See William Martin Conway, *Literary Remains of Albrecht Dürer* (Cambridge: Cambridge University Press, 1889), p. 182.—Ed.

"Nature" is a rather ambiguous term that is used in many and divergent senses. The "nature" of the scientist—that so-called physical world, the world of atoms and electrons, of general causal laws—is not the nature of our immediate experience. This scientific nature is no empirical datum—it is rather a theoretical construct the logical meaning and value of which has to be explained and clarified by an epistemological analysis, by a general theory of knowledge. What we first experience in nature are neither physical objects with definite qualities, nor mere sense-impressions. We live in a sphere of expressive qualities, each of which has a certain emotional line—of harshness, of loveliness, of smoothness, of roughness, of sternness and severity, or mildness and gentleness. The world of a child or a primitive man seems still, to a large degree, to consist of such emotional qualities, which, in the language of Dewey, may be described as tertiary qualities.[26] Even the work of art is filled out, so to speak, impregnated and saturated with these qualities. But here they are no longer the decisive feature; they are the material of the work of art, but they do not constitute its essence.

Let me attempt to make this clear by a concrete example. The natural beauty of a landscape is not the same as its aesthetic beauty. I may walk through a beautiful landscape and feel all its natural charms. I may enjoy the softness and mildness of the air; the brightness, the variety and cheerfulness of the colors, the gentle murmur of the brook or the fragrant odors of the flowers. All this gives me a very intense pleasure of a specific and characteristic kind. But this sort of pleasure is not yet an aesthetic experience. Aesthetic experience begins with a sudden change in my frame of mind. I begin to look at the landscape not with the eye of a mere spectator but with an artist's eye. I form, in my mind, a "picture" of the landscape. In this picture none of its former qualities is forgotten or effaced. Even the strongest and most powerful artistic imagination cannot create a new world—out of nothing. But when the artist approaches nature all its elements assume a new shape. Artistic imagination and contemplation does not give us the aspect of dead physical things or

26. See Cassirer's remarks on Dewey on this point in *An Essay on Man*, p. 78.—Ed.

of mute sense-qualities. It gives us a world of moving and living forms—a balance of lights and shadows, rhythms, and melodies, of lines and contours, of patterns and designs.

All this is not to be perceived or received in a passive way; we have to construct, to build up these forms, in order to be aware of them, to see and feel them. This dynamic aspect gives to the static material aspect a new tinge and a new significance. All our passive states are now turned into active energies: the forms that I behold are not only my states, but my acts. It is this character of aesthetic experience which to my mind gives to art its special place in human culture and makes it an essential and indispensable element in the system of liberal education. Art is a way to freedom, the process of the liberation of the human mind which is the real and ultimate aim of all education; it has to fulfill a task of its own, a task that cannot be replaced by any other function.

The Myth of the State

Philosophy and Politics

(1944)

Cassirer was invited to give this lecture to a class at Connecticut College, New London, Connecticut, on April 3, 1944 (MS #212). It exists in two copies: Cassirer's handwritten draft and a duplicated and stapled copy in typescript. The typed copy indicates that it was a lecture for the "29–30 lecture group." The typescript is different from the hand draft in some minor respects and the text here has been made by correcting the typescript with the hand draft.–Ed.

That philosophical thought is one of the necessary ingredients of theoretical and scientific culture in general is generally admitted.[1] Philosophy is the great effort of thought to embrace and unify all the different activities of man—to bring them into a common focus. In this regard its role and its mission is uncontested. But to speak of philosophy not only as a mainspring of human thought but also of human conduct seems to be an exaggerated view. In our practical life we are moved by quite different things. We are incited by emotions, not by thoughts; by the pressure and urgency of our immediate needs, not by general principles. Philosophy is too abstract, too far remote from this sphere of our immediate needs. It seems to consist of lofty speculations that have very little, if anything, to do with our actual world, with our political and social life. Such speculations

1. The text contains the following paragraph: "I must begin with expressing my cordial thanks to Professor Hafkesbrink for her kind invitation to address the members of this class. I have accepted this invitation with great pleasure, for the subject you are studying is of high importance, and to me it is not only interesting for general reasons, but also for many personal reasons. I am, however, perfectly aware of the fact that it is extremely difficult to speak about such a vast subject in the compass of a short hour. I must content myself here with a few general remarks and later on I shall try to specify these remarks by referring to the works of the German philosophers, Oswald Spengler and Martin Heidegger, who to a very great extent have influenced the development of German political thought in the period after the First World War."—Ed.

may arouse our intellectual curiosity but we are prone to forget and neglect them as soon as we are concerned with concrete practical problems. Philosophy is, to be sure, a great power of organization; but this power seems to stop short and to be paralyzed when we pass from the field of thought to the field of action.

Nevertheless the history of political and social thought shows us that this view of the role of philosophy is a rather short-sighted and inadequate one. Every great crisis in man's *thoughts* used to be accompanied by a deep crisis in his moral and social *conduct*. Let me illustrate this by a concrete historical example. If we pass from the eighteenth to the nineteenth century we find a profound change in the general orientation of philosophic thought. The eighteenth century was the period of Enlightenment. It was the triumph of rational thought. Rational thought had begun with conquering nature. Newton had found a universal law, the law of gravitation, that opened a new access to the interpretation of nature. He had given a very simple formula which seemed to contain the solution to the most complicated natural phenomena that hitherto had been regarded as inaccessible to human thought.

"Nature and Nature's law lay hid in night, God said, 'Let Newton be'—and all was light," said Alexander Pope in a famous verse. There remained, however, still a greater and more difficult task. The conquest of the physical world had to be complemented and completed by the conquest of the political and social world. It is not enough for man to discuss the laws of nature. As long as he does not know or does not understand the structure of the specifically human world, of the social and historical world, he is still living in a chaotic state of mind. To bring this chaos of the political world under the control of rational thought became the predominant and most serious problem of the period of Enlightenment. All the philosophers and all the great scientists of this period have cooperated in the solution of this great problem.[2] In England we find the political philosophy of

2. *The Philosophy of the Enlightenment*, trans. F. C. A. Koelln and J. P. Pettegrove (Princeton, N. J.: Princeton University Press, 1951; orig. German ed. 1932), ch. 6.—Ed.

Locke and his disciples and followers. In France we find the Encyclopaedists: the founders and contributors of the Great Encyclopaedia. In Germany we find Kant—the critic of theoretical and practical reason. There are strong differences between the various nations and the various philosophic schools. But all these differences are eclipsed by one and the same fundamental tendency of thought—by the common effort to find a philosophic, a rational answer to the most urgent problems of man's political and social life.

This effort was not restricted to a special country. It is a general feature that we find in the intellectual life of all civilized nations. In this respect all the boundary marks between different countries, even between different continents, are overthrown. We find the same fundamental political ideals and convictions spread over the whole cultured world. Perhaps their clearest and most characteristic expression is to be found in the American Bill of Rights—especially in the bill of rights of the state of Virginia. The same ideas were expressed in the American Declaration of Independence. All this was of the highest importance—even for the development of European political thought. "It is not enough," wrote one of the leading French philosophers, Condorcet, who also had an active part in the struggles of the French Revolution, "It is not enough that these original and imprescriptible rights live in the writings of the philosophers or in the hearts of all righteous men. We must read them in the example of a great nation. America has given us this example. The American Declaration of Independence is a simple and sublime expression of those sacred rights which for such a long time had been forgotten."[3]

The question of the historical origin of the Declaration of the Rights of Man and of Citizens by the French Constituent Assembly on August 26, 1789, is still much controverted. In a very interesting paper published in 1895, Georg Jellinek, a distinguished German scholar in constitutional law, has propounded the thesis that it is a mistake to regard this declaration

3. Condorcet, *De l'influence de la révolution d'Amérique sur l'Europe*, 1786, ch. 1.—Cassirer.

as the immediate outcome and the ripe fruit of the ideas of the French philosophers of the eighteenth century. According to Jellinek we have to seek the real source of the legal and political ideas of the French Revolution in the American Bill of Rights instead of in the writings of Montesquieu or Rousseau. Other authors have vividly attacked this view.[4]

We need not enter here into this highly debated problem. For the question of *priority* is here of little account. Both the champions of the French Revolution and "the fathers of American democracy" would scarcely have understood this question. Neither of them laid claim to any originality of their fundamental principles. They were convinced that these principles are in a sense as old as the world. The knowledge of the indefeasible rights of man was regarded as a "common notion," as something "that has been always, been everywhere, and been by all believed *(Quod semper, quod ubique et quod ab omnibus)*." As Jefferson wrote in one of his letters, "The object of the Declaration of Independence was not to find out new principles or new arguments, never before thought of, not merely to say things which had never been said before; but to place before mankind the common sense of the subject, in terms as plain and firm as to command their assent."[5]

This hope was not disappointed. The principles expressed in the American and French declarations won the whole civilized world. Everywhere they were hailed with the greatest enthusiasm. Germany was no exception. The greatest German thinker, Immanuel Kant, was a fervent admirer of the French Revolution. And it is significant for the strength of Kant's mind and character that he did not change his judgment when the cause of the French Revolution seemed to be lost. His belief in the

4. See V. Marcaggi, *Les origines de la déclaration des droits de l'homme de 1789* (Paris, 1904). For further details concerning the question, see Fritz Klövekron, *Die Entstehung der Erklärung der Menschen und Bürgerrechte* in *Hist. Stud.*, Heft XC (Berlin, 1911); and G. A. Salander, *Vom Werden der Menschenrechte* in *Leipziger rechtswissenschaftliche Studien*, Heft 19 (Leipzig, 1926).—Cassirer.

5. Letter of Jefferson to Lee in 1825; quoted by Carl Becker, *The Declaration of Independence: A Study in the History of Political Ideas*, 2d ed. (New York, 1942), pp. 25ff.—Cassirer.

ethical value of the thoughts expressed in the Declaration of the Rights of Man and of Citizens remained unshaken. "Such an event," he said, "does not consist in important deeds or misdeeds of men, whereby, what had been great, became little and old glorious political edifices were thrown down, whereas other ones grew out of the ground. No; nothing of the kind! The revolution of an ingenuous people which we have lived to see, may succeed or fail. It may be filled with such calamities and atrocities that a righteous man, even if he could be sure to carry it out luckily, never would decide to repeat the experiment at such a high price. In spite of all this such a revolution finds, in the minds of all spectators, a sympathy very near to enthusiasm. Such a phenomenon can never be forgotten; because it proves that in human nature there exists an inclination and disposition to the better which no politician ever could have been able to predict by summing up the course of former events."[6]

But this prophecy of Kant was not fulfilled. In Germany, at least, the principles of the French Revolution and of the American Declaration of Independence were not only forgotten; they were openly defied and attacked by almost all political and philosophical schools. Fichte was the only German thinker who, in his early writings, still spoke of the rights of man in the same vein as Kant. All the other Romantic writers, Schelling and Hegel, Friedrich Schlegel and Adam Müller, scorn the ideas of inborn imprescriptible natural rights. The first enthusiasm— even Hegel and Schelling had shared this enthusiasm—was followed by a deep disillusionment and mistrust. The political reasons for this attitude are obvious. The French Revolution had ended in the Reign of Terror and in the period of the Napoleonic wars. "I hope that this fire of freedom that gains the whole of Europe," wrote Benjamin Franklin in the beginning of the Revolution, in a letter from Paris, "will operate upon the invaluable rights of man in the same way as fire operates on gold; it

6. Kant, *Der Streit der Fakultäten* (1798), section II. *Works.* Edited by E. Cassirer, vol. VII, 391f.—Cassirer. See *Immanuel Kants Werke,* ed. Ernst Cassirer (Berlin: Bruno Cassirer, 1912).—Ed.

will purify without destroying."[7] But this hope seemed to be frustrated once and for all. The great promise of the French Revolution remained unfulfilled; the whole political and social order seemed to be threatened with a complete breakdown. Edmund Burke, one of the great authorities for the Romantic writers, called the French constitution of 1793 "a digest of anarchy," and the doctrine of inalienable rights was to him "an invitation to insurrection and a persistent cause of anarchy."[8]

The return to an absolute and firmly established authority seemed to be the only way of escape. To most of the Romantic thinkers, with the exception of Hegel, politics was not the first and principal concern. They lived much more in the world of "spirit," in the world of poetry, of art, of philosophy, than in the world of hard political facts. And in this world they had discovered a new province. Henceforth their whole attention was focused on this discovery which filled them with the greatest enthusiasm. In early Romanticism the interest in *history* overshadows all other interest. It is from this point of view that they denounce the natural-right theories of the state. The social compact is not an historical fact; it is fiction. All theories of the state which start from such presuppositions are built on sand. Law and the state have not been "made" by men. They are not products of individual wills, and they are, therefore, not under the jurisdiction of these wills; they are not bound to and restricted by our pretended individual rights. According to the principles of the historic right school, as they were expounded by Savigny, man could not make law any more than he could make language, myth, religion. Human culture is not an offspring of free and conscious human activities; it originates in a "higher necessity," in the national spirit which works and creates unconsciously.

If we accept these Romantic theories—the theories of the so-

7. *Correspondance de Benjamin Franklin,* traduite et annotée par Ed. Labouty, 2 vols. (Paris, 1866). Cf. Klövekorn, p. 60.—Cassirer.

8. See Charles Grove Haines, *The Revival of Natural Law Concepts* (Cambridge, 1930), p. 65.—Cassirer.

called historic right school—we must correct and even overthrow all those conceptions of the role of philosophy in man's
social and political life that were shared by all the great thinkers
of the eighteenth century. This change appears, in a most
characteristic way, in the system of the greatest philosophic
thinker of the nineteenth century—in the system of Hegel. To
be sure, Hegel never meant to sacrifice one of the inherent
rights of philosophic reason. He was, on the contrary, the most
resolute champion of rationalism that has ever appeared in the
history of philosophy. To him there exists no difference
between the real and the rational. All real is rational; all rational
is real. But the very term "reason" is no longer understood by
Hegel in the same sense as it was understood by Kant or the
other thinkers of the eighteenth century. According to Kant,
reason manifests itself in man's theoretical and practical life, in
science and in man's moral consciousness. "Nothing can possibly be conceived in the world, or even out of it," said Kant in
his *Fundamental Principles of the Metaphysics of Morals*, "which
can be called good, without qualification, except a Good
Will."[9]

But this ethical principle of Kant is constantly attacked by
Hegel. In his *Phenomenology of Mind* he declared that this so-
called good-will or, as he described it, that this "law of the
heart" is only a chimerical idea. Such a law may be regarded as
a rule for our private individual life but it has no power over the
true reality, over history and politics, over the life of the state.
We cannot measure the course of the world and great political
actions according to the petty standards of our moral consciousness. They have a reality and, therefore, a right of their own.
According to Hegel history is the incarnation of the "absolute
Idea"; it is "the development of Spirit in time." And the state is
defined as the same "divine Idea" as it exists on earth. Over
against this divine idea the individual as such has no right at
all. "The State," says Hegel, "is the ethical substance—the self-

9. See *Kant's Critique of Practical Reason and Other Works on the Theory of Ethics*, trans. T. K.
Abbott, 6th ed. (London: Longmans, Green, 1909), p. 9.—Ed.

certain absolute Mind which acknowledges no abstract rules of good and bad, shameful and mean, crass and deceptive."[10]

That means quite a new attitude of philosophic thought towards the political and historical world. For now philosophic thought gives up all claims to reform this world, to mold it into new shape. It becomes its highest and its only aim to understand and to interpret it—to describe the historical reality as it *is*, not as it ought to be. As Hegel declared, the philosopher must necessarily submit himself unto his present reality. He is the son of his time and he cannot jump over his time. He has to accept the given conditions of political and social life. We find the most characteristic and striking expression of this new attitude in the famous words of Hegel's preface to his *Philosophy of Right*. "One word more," says Hegel, "concerning the information of what the world ought to be; for that end philosophy always comes too late. As the thought of the world it first appears when reality has concluded its constructive process and brought itself to completion. What is thus taught by the notion history also shows to be necessary; only in the ripeness of reality does the ideal appear over against the actual and build up for itself that same world, apprehended in its substance, into an intellectual kingdom. When philosophy paints its grey in grey, some shape of life has become old, and by grey in grey it cannot be made young again but only known. The owl of Minerva spreads its wings only at the approach of twilight."[11]

Let us now, by one great jump, pass from Hegel's philosophy to contemporary German thought. In 1918, immediately after the end of the first world war, Oswald Spengler published his book, *Der Untergang des Abendlandes (The Decline of the West)*.[12] The book had at once a sensational success. It was read and studied, not only in Germany but also in all other countries,

10. Cf. Hegel, *Phänomenologie des Geistes* (Hamburg: Felix Meiner Verlag, 1952), pp. 355 ff.—Ed.

11. *Grundlinien der Philosophie des Rechts*, ed. Johannes Hoffmeister, 4th ed. (Hamburg: Felix Meiner Verlag, 1955), p. 17.—Ed.

12. Trans. C. F. Atkinson, 2 vols. (New York: Knopf, 1926 and 1928). Cf. *The Myth of the State* (New Haven: Yale University Press, 1946), pp. 289–92; and "The Technique of Our Modern Political Myths" and "Critical Idealism as a Philosophy of Culture" herein.—Ed.

and it was translated into almost all languages. What is Spengler's conception of man's cultural life? In his book a new step was made, a step that, in a certain sense, proved to be of much graver import and had more far-reaching political consequences than the system of Hegel. Spengler did not make the slightest attempt to change the given concrete historical situation. His only intention was to describe and interpret his situation, to make it clear to his readers. He described the decline and fall of all our cultural ideals as inevitable. His book is filled with the most somber prospects. No effort of thought or will, he declared, can change our destiny.

Even Hegel had glorified and even deified the historical process in which he saw the march of the absolute idea. Even to him the history of the world was the judgment of the world. Against the verdict of this highest court no appeal was possible. But Hegel believed in the unknown progress of history, and this progress meant to him the "progress in the consciousness of freedom." Such is the definition of history given by Hegel in his *Lectures on the Philosophy of History.*[13] Spengler's view is the very opposite. In his philosophy the idea of freedom is replaced by the idea of necessity and fatality. His system is a system of historical fatalism. And his judgment is that our cultural life is doomed once and for all. We cannot escape our fate and we cannot avert the danger. Nevertheless we must not despair. If we can no longer live up to our former ideals of civilization let us begin a new life! Let me describe it in Spengler's own words.

"We cannot revivify," he declares, "the dead body of human civilization. We cannot hope to think new thoughts or to create new great works of art. Of great painting or great music there can no longer be, for Western people, any question. . . . Only *extensive* possibilities are left to them. Yet for a sound and vigorous generation that is filled with unlimited hopes, I fail to see that it is any disadvantage to discover betimes that some of these hopes must come to nothing. . . . It is true that the issue may be a tragic one for some individuals who in their decisive years are overpowered by the conviction that in the spheres of architec-

13. Cf. Cassirer's discussion of "Hegel's Theory of the State" herein.—Ed.

ture, drama, painting, there is nothing left to *them* to conquer. What matter if they do go under! ... Now at last the work of centuries enables the West-European to view the disposition of his own life in relation to the general culture-scheme and to test his own powers and purposes. And I can only hope that men of the new generation may be moved by this book to devote themselves to technics instead of lyrics, the sea instead of the paintbrush, and politics instead of epistemology. Better they could not do."[14]

Technics instead of lyrics, politics instead of epistemology—this advice of a philosopher could easily be understood and was eagerly followed by the new generation that grew up in Germany. As a matter of fact, Spengler had not written a book on history—his mistakes in this respect are innumerable and conspicuous—but a book on divination. In the first sentence of his book Spengler boasted of having discovered a new art by which it became possible to predict the course of human civilization in an infallible way. "In this book," he said, "is attempted for the first time the venture of predetermining history, of following the still untraveled stages in the destiny of a Culture, and specifically of the only Culture of our time and on our planet which is actually in the phase of fulfillment—the West European–American."[15]

There is perhaps no older, no deeper, no more general mythical concept than the concept of fate. We find this concept, the concept of a mysterious, inscrutable, invincible power that governs all things in heaven and on earth, in the mythologies of all peoples, in Babylonian, Chinese, Egyptian, Greek, Iranian, German mythology. In the Homeric poems even the Olympian gods have to submit to the decree of Fate.

In Spengler's book and in other German writers of the same period this primeval mythical concept of fate was not only revivified; it was made the very center of the historical world. If we accept this system of Spengler we feel as if all our individual

14. *Decline of the West*, I, 40f.—Ed.

15. Ibid., introduction.—Ed.

mental powers were suddenly paralyzed. We are curbed under the yoke of a dire and inexorable fatality.

The same holds, although in a different sense, for Martin Heidegger's philosophy and for his book on *Sein und Zeit (Being and Time)*.[16] Heidegger was a pupil of Husserl. His book appeared in Husserl's *Annals of Philosophy and Phenomenological Research*.[17] For a long time he was thought to be one of the outstanding representatives of the German phenomenological school. But the general attitude of his book is entirely opposed to the spirit of Husserl's philosophy. Husserl had started from an analysis of the principles of logic. His whole philosophical work depends on the results of this analysis. His highest aim was to make philosophy an "exact science," to found it upon unshakable facts and indubitable principles. Such a tendency is entirely alien to Heidegger. He does not admit that there is something like "eternal" truth or a strict logical method of philosophic thought.

All this is declared to be elusive. In vain we try to build up a logical philosophy; we can only give an "existential philosophy" *(Existenzialphilosophie).* The philosopher cannot strive for an "objective," universally valid truth. He can only give the truth of his individual existence, and this existence has always a historical character. It is bound up with the historical conditions under which the individual lives. To change these conditions is impossible. In order to express his thought Heidegger had to coin a new term, a term that is scarcely translatable into the English language. He speaks of the *Geworfenheit* of man (the being-thrown of man). To be thrown into the stream of time is one of the fundamental and unalterable conditions of human life. Man cannot emerge from this stream, and he cannot change its course. He has to accept the historical conditions of his existence; he has to submit to his fate.

But I do not wish to be misunderstood. I do not mean to say

---

16. Trans. John Macquarrie and Edward Robinson (Oxford: Basil Blackwell, 1962). Cf. *The Myth of the State*, pp. 292–93; and "Critical Idealism as a Philosophy of Culture" herein. See the remarks on Cassirer and Heidegger in the fourth section of the introduction.—Ed.

17. *Jahrbuch für Phänomenologie und phänomenologische Forschung* (1927).—Ed.

that the cultural pessimism of Spengler or that works like Heidegger's *Sein und Zeit* were, to any large degree, responsible for the development of the political ideas in Germany. The ideology of National Socialism has not been made by philosophic thinkers. It has grown up from quite a different soil. But there is an indirect connection between that general course of ideas that we can study in the case of Spengler or Heidegger and German political and social life in the period after the First World War. As soon as philosophy no longer trusts its own power, as soon as it gives way to a merely passive attitude, it can no longer fulfill its most important educational task. It cannot teach man how to develop his active faculties in order to form his individual and social life. A philosophy that indulges in somber predictions about the decline and the inevitable destruction of human culture, a philosophy whose whole attention is focused on the *Geworfenheit,* the Being-thrown of man, can no longer do its duty.[18]

There was, however, one German thinker who very early felt this danger and constantly warned us against this danger. He was not a philosopher in the sense in which we commonly use this term. He never held a chair of philosophy and his life took a very unusual course. His personality is rich and so original that it is scarcely to be measured by our common standards. The man of whom I speak is Albert Schweitzer. If you study his autobiography, a most interesting and fascinating book, you will find that Schweitzer began as an historian of religion and as a theological critic. His first books are *The Quest of the Historical Jesus* and *St. Paul and His Interpreters.* From here Schweitzer passed to music and musicology. He is not only an excellent organist; he also gave one of the best interpretations of the work of Johann Sebastian Bach. But that is not all. Later on Schweitzer became a missionary and a physician. He became the founder and the leader of a great hospital for the Negroes in the French African colonies. Ever since, his whole life has been devoted to this task.

18. Although Cassirer's remarks on Spengler and Heidegger follow those in *The Myth of the State,* his conclusion here employs a more forceful style (cf. p. 293). His emphasis on "duty" is the language of Schweitzer's first chapter, "The Decay and the Restoration of Civilization." See Schweitzer, *The Philosophy of Civilization,* trans. C. T. Campion (New York: Macmillan, 1953), p. 8.—Ed.

He is still living as the administrator of this hospital in Lambaréné.

Schweitzer has told us of his experiences in a book: *On the Edge of the Primeval Forest: Experiences and Observations of a Doctor in Equatorial Africa.*[19] But here, "on the edge of the primeval forest," he began during the First World War, in 1917, more than twenty-five years ago, to form his first ideas about the decay and the restoration of civilization. Later on he expressed these ideas in lectures given at the University of Uppsala in Sweden. If you study these lectures, given in 1922—and I warmly recommend this study—you will be amazed to find here a perfect diagnosis of the present crisis of human culture.[20] There are two things which are thought by Schweitzer to be responsible for this crisis. The first is the predominance of nationalism; the second the overwhelming influence of what Schweitzer describes as the "collective spirit." Let me give you his own highly characteristic description. "What is nationalism?" asks Schweitzer. "It is an ignoble patriotism, exaggerated till it has lost all meaning, which bears the same relation to the noble and healthy kind as the fixed idea of an imbecile does to normal conviction."[21] And what is that "collective spirit" that we have to combat if we wish to develop the higher forms of our ethical life? "The modern man," says Schweitzer, "is lost in the mass in a way which is without precedent in history, and this is perhaps the most characteristic trait in him. His diminished concern about his own nature makes him as it is susceptible to an extent that is almost pathological, to the views which society and its organs of expression have put, ready made, into circulation. Since, over and above this, society, with its well-constructed organization, has become a power of as yet unknown strength in the spiritual life, man's want of independence in the face of it has become so serious that he is almost ceasing to claim a spiritual existence of his own. He is like a rubber ball which has lost its elasticity, and

19. Trans. C. T. Campion (New York: Macmillan, 1922).—Ed.

20. "The Decay and the Restoration of Civilization," part I of *The Philosophy of Civilization;* see note 18. See also "Critical Idealism as a Philosophy of Culture" herein.—Ed.

21. Ibid., p. 29.—Ed.

preserves indefinitely every impression that is made upon it. He is under the thumb of the mass, and he draws from it the opinions on which he lives, whether the question at issue is national or political or one of his own belief or unbelief."[22]

Can there be a better and more striking expression of the present state of mind in Germany and in other countries than these words spoken more than twenty years ago? And what did philosophy, asks Schweitzer, do to avert the danger? "In the eighteenth century and the early part of the nineteenth it was philosophy which led and guided thought in general. . . . Philosophy at that time included within herself an elementary philosophizing about man, society, race, humanity, and civilization which produced in a perfectly natural way a living popular philosophy that controlled the general thought and maintained the enthusiasm for civilization."[23] All this was lost during the second half of the nineteenth century. And philosophy did not even know this loss. It did not realize that the power of the ideas about civilization which had been entrusted to it was becoming a doubtful quantity. In spite of all its learning, philosophy had become a stranger to the world and the problems of life which occupied man and the whole thought of the age had no part in its activities. It philosophized about everything except civilization. "So little did philosophy philosophize about civilization that she did not even notice that she herself and the age along with her were losing more and more of it. In the hour of peril the watchman who ought to have kept us awake was himself asleep and the result was that we put up no fight at all on behalf of our civilization."[24]

That is one of the gravest and most serious charges made against our contemporary philosophy, but if we look at the development of our social and political life in these last decades we can hardly say that this charge was unjust.

22. Ibid., p. 17.—Ed.

23. Ibid., p. 3.—Ed.

24. Ibid., p. 8.—Ed.

Judaism and the Modern Political Myths

(1944)

This text is part of MS #162 and is marked "Jewish Record." It appears to be a draft of Cassirer's article "Judaism and the Modern Political Myths," Contemporary Jewish Record *7 (1944), 115–26. It generates the basic argument of this article, but in sharper focus and language, and directly overlaps with it at several points. This was very likely intended as the introduction or first section of the* Contemporary Jewish Record *article that was subsequently rewritten and expanded into the published form. The text is in English longhand.–Ed.*

If we ask for the reasons for the slow disintegration and the sudden collapse of our social and political life in the last decades it seems to be obvious that we are concerned with a practical, not with a theoretical or "philosophical" problem.[1] The device, *silent enim leges inter arma*, holds, first and foremost, for philosophy.[2] Its voice is too feeble to be heard in the tumult of arms. And there can be no doubt that these last thirty years have been a period of continuous war. We were suffering from a grave and perilous illusion when thinking that, in 1918, the World War had

---

1. Although these remarks have a principal relationship to Cassirer's "Judaism and the Modern Political Myths," *Contemporary Jewish Record* 7 (1944), 155–26, they also must be understood in relation to his larger project of the relationship of myth to the contemporary state. Cf. the summary of this project, "The Myth of the State," *Fortune*, vol. 29, no. 6 (June 1944), 165–67, 198, 201–02, 204, 206 (see Mrs. Cassirer's account of this in *Aus meinem Leben mit Ernst Cassirer*, New York: Privately issued, 1950, pp. 291–96); "The Techniques of Our Modern Political Myths" herein; and *The Myth of the State* (New Haven: Yale University Press, 1946), esp. pt. 3.—Ed.

2. "When arms speak, the laws are silent." The quotation is from Cicero's speech, *Pro Milone*, IV, 11.—Ed.

come to its end. The following years were, at best, a temporary appeasement, a sort of truce.

During this truce the arms were never laid down; they only changed their form. The nations were no longer fighting each other by machine guns or submarines. They had discovered and developed a much subtler and more sophisticated system of warfare. And it was here that philosophy began to play a new and unexpected role. It had, in a sense, to provide the "spiritual" weapons that were bound to complete and perfect the material weapons. Thereby the whole form of our public life underwent a profound change. New problems and new powers came to the fore. The struggle between political systems became a struggle of "ideas" and "ideologies."

In this combat the parts assigned to the different parties were very unequal. The Western democracies were, from the very beginning, on the defensive. They did not develop new forces; they stood for their old ideals, the ideals of the French Revolution. But these ideals had a long time ago lost their momentum and their original impulse. From revolutionary forces they had been turned into conservative forces. Accordingly they were not prepared for the new task they had to perform. The French Revolution had ended in the triumph and apotheosis of *reason*. Reason was regarded as the fundamental power in the organization of man's political and social life. All this was suddenly annulled and reversed. The new political systems began with opposing to reason its oldest and most dangerous adversary. The open and solemn enthronement of *myth* is the distinctive and most characteristic feature in the political thought of the twentieth century.

Henceforward an entirely new factor was introduced into the development of our political life. Of course it cannot be said that myth in itself was a new or unknown fact. Since the beginning of the nineteenth century we had a comparative mythology. In his last period Schelling produced his "philosophy of mythology."[3]

3. For Cassirer's discussion of Schelling's posthumously published *Philosophie der Mythologie* as a source for his own theory of myth see *The Philosophy of Symbolic Forms*, trans. Ralph Manheim, 3 vols. (New Haven: Yale University Press, 1953–57; orig. German ed. 1923–27), II, 3–16.—Ed.

The mythological elements of all the great religions of the world had been carefully studied. Later on anthropologists and ethnologists continued this work. An immense mass of facts was collected from all parts of the world and from all periods of history. And not only the facts, but also the *form* of mythical thought became an important problem that more and more attracted the general attention. This form was studied and analyzed by anthropologists, by psychologists, by psychoanalysts, by sociologists and philosophers.[4] But all the facts discovered by this analysis, although arousing our scientific curiosity, seemed to be very remote from our actual life. They were devoid of any practical interest. We were convinced that myth belonged to a cultural and mental stage that has passed once for all. That this "primitive" form would be revivified and that it was bound to play a decisive role in modern political life was a fact that was in strict opposition to our firmest theoretical convictions. The "myth of the twentieth century" was unparalled and unprecedented; it came as a reverse of all our principles of thought.

That myth is a necessary factor, a fundamental element in the development of human culture, was generally admitted. Romanticism had always insisted upon this fact; it had shown in which way and to what a high degree language, poetry, art, religion, even metaphysics and science are in their origin bound up with mythical elements and interpenetrated with mythical imagination. But the Romantic thinkers were very far from our modern political myths. They saw in myth an "unconscious" activity; they looked at it as a wild and exuberant stream springing forth from an unknown depth. In modern politics this stream was embanked and canalized. Myth was no longer a free and spontaneous play of imagination. It was regulated and organized; it was adjusted to political needs and used for concrete political ends.

What formerly appeared to be an ungovernable process was subject to a severe discipline. It was brought under control and trained to obedience and order. Our modern political myths are by no means the outgrowth of a dark or mythic power. They did not, slowly and unconsciously, grow up from the "national

4. See *The Myth of the State*, pt. 1.—Ed.

spirit." They were made deliberately and destined for special purposes. They were brought into being by the word of command of the political leaders. That was one of the greatest triumphs of modern political warfare. It became the very center in the new art of political tactics and strategy. From now on myth was no longer an incalculable and uncontrollable thing. It could be made at pleasure; it became an artificial compound manufactured in the great laboratory of politics.

What we find here is one of the greatest paradoxes in human history. It is a myth that in a sense is completely "rationalized." Myth remains irrational in its content, but it is very clear and conscious in its aims. The twentieth century is a technical century, and it applies technical methods to all fields of theoretical and practical activity. The invention and the skillful use of a new technical instrument—of the technique of political myths— decided the victory of the National Socialist movement in Germany. The opponents of National Socialism had lost their cause even before the battle began. For in the political struggle it is always a vital importance to *know* the adversary, to enter in his ways of thinking and acting. The political leaders of the Weimar Republic were not equal to this task. They completely failed to understand the character and the strength of the new weapon used against them.

In their sober, empirical, "matter of fact" way of thinking they had no eyes for the dangerous explosive force contained in the political myths. They could scarcely be prevailed on to take these things seriously. Most of them were determined Marxists. They thought and spoke in terms of economics; they were convinced that economy is the mainspring of political life and the solution of all social problems. Following this theory they missed the real point at issue; they did not understand what was really at stake. Undoubtedly economic conditions had a large share in the development and rapid growth of the National Socialist movement. But the deepest and most influential causes are not to be sought in the economic crisis which Germany had to endure. They belong to another field which in a sense was inaccessible to the socialistic leaders. When they began to see the danger, it was too late; the force of the political myths had become irresistible.

Did the makers of these myths act in good faith—did they believe in the "truth" of their own stories? We can hardly answer this question; we cannot even put it. For one of the first steps of the new political theory was to deny and destroy the very concept of "truth" which is implied in this question. What we call "objective" truth—we were told—is a mere illusion. To inquire into the "truth" of the political myths is, therefore, as meaningless and as ridiculous as to ask for the truth of a machine gun or a fighter plane. Both are weapons; and weapons prove their truth by their efficiency. If the political myths could stand this test they needed no other and no better proof. In this respect the theory was beyond attack and invulnerable. All it had to do was to put the political myths into action and to show their constructive or destructive power.

Even in its primitive, in its "naive" and unsophisticated form, myth does not serve as mere theoretical purpose. It does not give us a mere "representation" of the world. Its principal role is to arouse emotions and to prompt man to certain actions. "Myth as it exists in a savage community, that is, in its living primitive form," says Malinowski in his book, *Myth in Primitive Psychology*, "is not merely a story told but a reality lived. . . . As our sacred story lives in our ritual, in our morality, as it governs our faith and controls our conduct, even so does his myth for the savage. . . . Myth is thus a vital ingredient of human civilization; it is not an intellectual explanation or an artistic imagery, but a pragmatic charter of primitive faith and moral wisdom."[5] This view has given a new form to all researches in the field of ethnology and comparative mythology.

It seems now to be a generally admitted principle that *rite* is in a sense prior to myth; that in order to understand the nature of myth we must always begin with the studies of *rite*. Rite is always a social, not an individual, phenomenon. It is not an expression of thoughts or ideas; it is a collective set expressing some fundamental collective feelings and desires. A French scholar, E. Doutté, has given a short and striking definition of myth by saying that the demonic or divine powers we meet in primitive

5. London, 1926, p. 21.—Cassirer.

mythologies are not so much personifications of natural forces as personifications of social forces; they are "le désir collectif personifié."[6] This fundamental character is preserved in all our modern political myths. What we find here is not a system of "thoughts" but a turmoil of the most violent emotions.

The whole gamut of social passions, from the lowest to the highest notes, appeared and burst forth in the creation of the "myth of the twentieth century." And finally all these emotions were, as it were, focused in one point. They were personified and deified in the "Leader." The Leader became the fulfillment of all collective desires. To him point all hopes and all fears. One of the oldest and most widespread motifs in all the mythologies of the world is the idea of the "millennium"—of a period in which all hopes shall be fulfilled and all evils shall be removed. Such a millennium was promised to the German race by the modern political myths. But it was no longer, as in former times, a millennium of peace, but of war; for war was declared thè true ideal and the only permanent thing in man's social and political life.

We fail, however, to understand the true character and the full significance of myth if, according to its Greek name, we see in it a mere "narrative"—a recollection or recital of the memorable deeds of heroes or gods. This *epic* aspect is not the only one and not the decisive one. Myth has always a dramatic character. It conceives the world as a great drama—as a struggle between divine and demonic forces, between light and darkness, between the good and the evil. There is always a negative and a positive pole in mythical thought and imagination. Even the political myths were incomplete so long as they had not introduced a demonic power. The process of deification had to be completed by a process that we may describe as "devilization."

In the mythical pandemonium we always find maleficent spirits that are opposed to the beneficent spirits. There is always a secret or open revolt of Satan against God. In the German pandemonium this role was assigned to the Jew. What we find here is much more than what is usually described by the name

6. *Magie et religion dans l'Afrique du Nord* (Algiers: Typographie Adolphe Jourdan, 1909).—Ed.

"anti-Semitism." Anti-Semitism is not a new phenomenon; it has existed at all times and under various forms. But the German form of persecution was something that never had existed before. Its roots are to be sought at a different place; they are much deeper and much more poisonous. Anti-Semitism could have led to social discrimination, to all forms of oppression, to legal restrictions and exceptional laws. But it cannot account for the specific methods of the German anti-Jewish propaganda. What was proclaimed here was a mortal combat—a life-and-death struggle which could only end with the complete extermination of the Jews. I do not deny that all sorts of personal hatred or class hatred, that economic jealousy or race prejudices had their share in this combat. Yet all this could not have done its work and it would not have attained the desired end if it had not been supported by the force of a much more dangerous and powerful motive.

[*Cassirer's draft ends here. The opening and closing paragraphs of Cassirer's article, "Judaism and the Modern Political Myths,"* Contemporary Jewish Record *7 (1944), 115 and 126, are of particular interest for the point begun above. They are reprinted below.*—Ed.]

In order to understand the campaign against Judaism launched by the leaders of the new Germany it is not enough to consider the reasons usually given. In the beginning the National-Socialist propaganda often asserted that its only aim was to break the influence of the Jews in Germany's political and cultural life. But why did this propaganda persist and why did it assume a more and more violent character after this end was attained—in a period when no Jew could any longer speak or even breathe or live in Germany? For all this we must seek a deeper reason. In this struggle there is something more than meets the eye. To be sure, personal aversions and antipathies, deeply rooted prejudices, had their share in this campaign; but they cannot account for its specific character, its brutality and ferocity. We must try to understand the phenomenon not only from its emotional but also from its intellectual side.

However we may object to the German political system, we cannot say that it ever underrated the power of "ideas" in political and social life. From the beginning the National-Socialist leaders were convinced that the victory could not be gained by mere material weapons. They knew very well that their *ideology* was the strongest and, at the same time, the most vulnerable point in their whole political system. To deny or even to doubt this ideology was to them a mortal sin. It became a *crimen laesae majestatis*—a crime of high treason against the omnipotent and infallible totalitarian state. That the Jews were guilty of this crime was obvious. They had proved it by their whole history, by their tradition, by their cultural and religious life. In the history of mankind they had been the first to deny and to challenge those very conceptions upon which the new state was built; for it was Judaism which first made the decisive step that led from a *mythical* to an *ethical* religion. . . .[7]

When reading Hitler's last address marking the 11th anniversary of his National-Socialist regime, we meet with a strange phenomenon. Hitler has completely changed his tone: He is no longer promising the conquest of the world to the German race. He begins to see his defeat and he feels its consequences. But what does he say at this critical moment? Does he speak of the innumerable evils which his aggression has brought to the German people, to Europe, to the whole world? Does he think of the defeat of his armies, of the destruction of German cities? Nothing of the kind. His whole attention is still fixed on one point. He is obsessed and hypnotized by *one* thing alone. He speaks of—the Jews. If I am defeated—he says—Jewry could celebrate a second

7. Cassirer sees in the anti-Semitism of National Socialism a reenactment of the ancient struggle of the primitive "totem and taboo" system of human society and the arising of the ethical standpoint of religious consciousness. As he puts this at the end of his chapter, "Myth and Religion," in *An Essay on Man* (New Haven: Yale University Press, 1944): "All the higher ethical religions—the religion of the prophets of Israel, Zoroastrianism, Christianity—set themselves a common task. They relieve the intolerable burden of the taboo system; but they detect, on the other hand, a more profound sense of religious obligation that instead of being a restriction or compulsion is the expression of a new positive ideal of human freedom" (p. 108).—Ed.

triumphant Purim festival. What worries him is not the future destiny of Germany, but the "triumph" of the Jews.

By this utterance he proves once more how little he knows of Jewish life and Jewish feeling. In our life, in the life of a modern Jew, there is no room left for any sort of joy or complacency, let alone of exultation or triumph. All this has gone forever. No Jew whatsoever can and will ever overcome the terrible ordeal of these last years. The victims of this ordeal cannot be forgotten; the wounds inflicted upon us are incurable. Yet amidst all these horrors and miseries there is, at least, one relief. We may be firmly convinced that all these sacrifices have not been made in vain. What the modern Jew had to defend in this combat was not only his physical existence or the preservation of the Jewish race. Much more was at stake. We had to represent all those ethical ideals that had been brought into being by Judaism and found their way into general human culture, into the life of all civilized nations. And here we stand on firm ground. These ideals are not destroyed and cannot be destroyed. They have stood their ground in these critical days. If Judaism has contributed to break the power of the modern political myths, it has done its duty, having once more fulfilled its historical and religious mission.

The Technique of Our Modern Political Myths

(1945)

This is a lecture given at Princeton University on January 18, 1945, while Cassirer was teaching at Columbia University. Mrs. Cassirer, in Aus meinem Leben mit Ernst Cassirer *(New York: privately issued, 1950), reports that Cassirer prepared this as a summary of his work on* The Myth of the State *(New Haven: Yale University Press, 1946), which was then in preparation (see the foreword by Charles W. Hendel for details of its completion). Mrs. Cassirer reports that Cassirer's intention was to make his work on these problems known at various universities to provide a basis for understanding his theory when the book would appear (see* Aus meinem Leben, *p. 303). The text here is made from the typescript of MS #205, which also includes a longhand draft. The text is in English and its title is almost identical to the title of the final chapter of* The Myth of the State, *"The Technique of the Modern Political Myths." In its latter parts the lecture text corresponds to passages of this chapter.–Ed.*

The last decades, the period between the two world wars, have not only brought us a radical change in the forms of our political and social life but also a complete change in the forms of political thought.[1] In this field too we are confronted with entirely new problems that were unknown to the thinkers of the nine-

---

1. Although Cassirer's theory of the "myth of the state" and the relationship of technique to political life were central in the writings of the last two years of his life, his work on these questions are not his first writings on political questions nor on the nature of technique as a general dimension of the human world. See *Die Idee der Republikanischen Verfassung* (Hamburg: Friederichsen, De Gruyter and Co. M. B. H., 1929); "Vom Wesen und Werden des Naturrechts," *Zeitschrift für Rechtsphilosophie* 27 (1932), 1–27; and "Form und Technik," in *Kunst und Technik*, ed. Leo Kestenberg (Berlin: Wegweiser Verlag, 1930), pp. 15–61.—Ed.

teenth century. We are still very far from having found an adequate solution to these problems. When following our research methods of thought and of philosophical and scientific analysis, we have the greatest difficulties to see them in their true light and to understand their meaning and influence. Perhaps the most important and the most alarming feature in the development of our modern political life is the sudden rise of a new power, the power of mythical thought. The preponderance of mythical thought over rational and logical thought in the political theories of the twentieth century is obvious. After a short and violent struggle mythical thought seems to have won a clear and definitive victory. How was the victory possible—how can we account for the new phenomenon that suddenly appeared in our political horizon and proved to have such a tremendous practical influence?

It would not be correct to say that the phenomenon, as such, was new or unfamiliar to us. In a certain sense we were much better acquainted with the true character of mythical thought than previous centuries. The thinkers of the eighteenth century could find in myth nothing else than an uncouth mass of the crudest superstitions—a medley of the most obscure, absurd, and fantastic ideas. The opponents of the philosophers of the Enlightenment, the German romanticists, rejected and attacked this view. They saw in myth something entirely different—a great and indispensable constructive force—the basis of man's cultural life, poetry, art, religion, and history.

About one hundred years ago Schelling delivered his famous lectures on the philosophy of mythology and revelation at the University of Berlin.[2] This was the first time that myth was admitted in a system of philosophy and that, thereby, it won a full citizenship in the realm of thought. The metaphysical analysis of myth, contained in the work of Schelling, was superseded by other attempts of a more critical and empirical character. Myth was studied as a "symbolic form" like language, art, religion, and science, or it was studied from a genetic point of view.

2. See *Philosophie der Mythologie*, 2 vols. (Darmstadt: Wissenschaftliche Buchgesellschaft, 1957).—Ed.

Ethnologists, sociologists, anthropologists, and psychologists have an equal share in these studies. They have amassed an immense and highly interesting material from all the parts of the world; they have shown that myth is a common element in human life that appears, in a similar shape, under the most various and divergent conditions.

But all these studies were based on one presupposition. Philosophers, ethnologists, and sociologists agreed that human culture had long ago outgrown its mythical age. This age has gone forever; for it represented a type of thought entirely different from our own ways of thinking and arguing. According to the well known theory of Lévy-Bruhl there is a deep gulf, an insurmountable barrier between the primitive mind and our own mind. They do not belong to the same genus; they are incomparable and incompatible.[3]

I do not deny the interest and the merits of this theory of Lévy-Bruhl. However, if we accept this theory we are confronted with an almost hopeless problem. If myth is a typical outcome of the primitive, that is to say the prelogical and mystical mind, how can we account for its sudden reappearance under the conditions of our own highly sophisticated culture? The men who became the authors of our modern political myths, who created and propagated them, were by no means "primitive." They were quite the contrary. They were very good and very cool calculators. They knew their ends and their means. Nor were the people for whom these myths were destined primitive. They were highly educated. Many of them were scholars, scientists, and philosophers. How was it that these people could be so deeply impressed by the modern myths that they seemed to forget all they had learned before? Many have described myth as a sort of atavism. But this too does not answer our question. An atavism is an exception, it is not the rule. An atavism of whole nations would be a very paradoxical and almost inexplicable thing. Myth

3. The manuscript here has a space indicating that Cassirer intended to quote a passage from Lévy-Bruhl. Cassirer apparently has in mind a passage explaining Lévy-Bruhl's distinction between "prelogical" and logical mentality such as is presented in part I of *How Natives Think*, auth. trans. Lilian A. Clare (London and New York: George Allen and Unwin, 1926).—Ed.

is indeed a sort of remnant—a ghost that returned from another world. But if our political myths belong to the same family they do not resemble their brothers. They are of a peculiar type. Other ghosts appear, to use the words of Hamlet, "Thou com'st in such a questionable shape ... making night hideous." It is quite different with our political myths. They appear in broad daylight, they do not fear the light of the sun and cannot be expelled or exorcized; they stand their ground firmly and stoutly.

All this would be impossible to understand if myth were nothing but a mere relic—the remains of a dead past. It is however much more. It is not an outgrowth of primitive mentality; it still has its place in the most advanced stages of human culture. To banish myth, to eradicate it root and branch, would mean an impoverishment. What would become of poetry and art if we would no longer be able to understand the language of myth; if this language were to us no more than a dead language which we can reconstruct in its grammatical rules but which we cannot feel any longer? Then we would have no access to the world of our great poets, painters, and sculptors—to the works of Aeschylus, Pindar, or Pheidias, to the works of Dante, Shakespeare, Milton, or Michelangelo. Yet there is no danger that mankind ever will forget or renounce the language of myth. For this language is not restricted to a special field; it pervades the whole of man's life and existence.

In Molière's comedy, *Le bourgeois gentilhomme*, the hero of the play, M. Jourdain, is very much surprised when he first learns from his philosophical teacher that he has spoken prose for more than fifty years without even knowing it. We are exactly in the same position; we are speaking myth without being aware of the fact. Human speech is full of metaphors of which the origin is to be sought in the same tendency to personify things and events, which is one of the principal sources of mythical thought. If we should succeed in eliminating from human speech all its metaphorical and figurative elements, language would have lost all its plastic expressive power; it would have been changed to an abstract symbolism, like the symbolism of a mathematical formula.

Myth is, in fact, not only a transient but a permanent element in human culture. Man is not exclusively a rational animal, he is and remains a mythical animal. Myth is part and parcel of human nature. We may apply to it the saying of Horace: *Naturam expellas furca, tamen usque recurret.*[4] We cannot entirely suppress or expell it; it always recurs in a new shape. If we wish to express this fact in a philosophical language, we could say, with Hegel, that in all fields of human culture and human activity, in language, religion, poetry, and art, myth always is present as *aufgehobenes Moment*. It is not destroyed or annihilated; it has only changed its form. But this very change is of paramount importance. The organism of human culture does not eliminate the mythical elements root and branch, but it learns to control them. It develops new constructive powers of logical and scientific thought, new ethical forces and new creative energies of artistic imagination. By the appearance of these new forces myth is not entirely vanquished, but it is counter-balanced and brought under control. It is true that this equilibrium is rather a labile than a static equilibrium; it is not firmly established but liable to all sorts of disturbances.

The character of these disturbances becomes particularly clear in the field of political life. From the first beginnings of a political philosophy, from the times of Plato and Aristotle, we find a continuous struggle between logos and mythos; between a rational and a mythical conception of the state. But finally the end seems to be attained. The rational character of politics seems to be firmly established. But this victory remains always doubtful and precarious. In politics we are never living on a firm and stable ground. In quiet and peaceful times, in periods of relative stability and security, it is easy to maintain a rational order of things. But we are always standing on a volcanic soil and must be prepared for sudden convulsions and eruptions. In the critical moments of man's political and social life myth regains its old strength. It was always lurking in the background, waiting for its hour and its opportunity. This hour comes if the other binding forces of our social life, for one reason or another, lose their

4. *Epistles,* I, x, 24.—Ed.

influence; if they can no longer counterbalance the demonic power of myth.[5]

All these conflicts between logos and mythos, between rational and mythical motives, were unknown in primitive society. Here myth was still the only ruler; its sovereignty was unlimited and uncontradicted. And its rule was absolute; it did not admit of any exception or exemption. From a certain point of view this state of affairs may be regarded as one of the great privileges of primitive social life. More advanced and sophisticated stages of human culture were often apt to look back to this condition with a certain envy. In contradistinction to the civil state, the *status naturalis,* the state of nature, was described as a real paradise, a paradise of simplicity, harmony, and innocence. The progress of ethnological research has, unfortunately, completely destroyed this philosophical idyll of the thinkers of the eighteenth century. Modern anthropology has turned Rousseau's famous description of the state of nature into its very contrary. The savage pictured by Rousseau was thought to live in complete isolation and to be free to follow his natural impulses and instincts.

Now we have learned that social pressure is nowhere so strong, so implacable and irresistible as in primitive societies. The savage cannot make a single step without the constant fear of violating a special taboo. Every such violation means misery and death, however, not only to the individual but to all the members of the community. There is no act, however trivial and insignificant, that is not regulated by fixed collective rules. These rules, the social rules, are universal, eternal, and unchangeable, whereas the so-called laws of nature, if there are any laws of nature, are always changeable and flexible because they are subject to the influence of the magic word and are pliable to our human wishes. All social life and all natural life depends on the strict performance of religious and magical rites. If these rites are not performed in due time, at the right place, and in the right moment; if the words of a spell or a prayer do not follow the same inviolable order; if they are not spoken in the same rhythmical sequence, the whole life of the society and the whole

5. Cf. *The Myth of the State* (New Haven: Yale University Press, 1946), p. 280.—Ed.

life of nature are at stake. The rain will not fall, the corn will not ripen, the soil will not bear its fruit without the steady help of man. This help is never thought to be a technical, but always a magic help.

That explains the fundamental and indispensable role of myth in primitive society. Myth is not an independent or separate element in man's social and cultural life; it is only the correlate and counterpart of rite. It has an explanatory function, but its principal task is not to explain physical phenomena but human actions. Every important step in man's individual and social life is accompanied by a special rite. There are rites of birth, death, and initiation. The primitive man is not in need of a historical or genetic explanation of these rites. He is not primarily interested in their origin; for, strictly speaking, all these things have no origin. They have existed forever; they have been performed in the same regular and unchangeable way from immemorial times. They are the great inheritance from the mythical ancestors, and it is the highest religious duty of man to keep this inheritance intact. The words of a magic formula, of a spell or incantation, the single phases of a sacrifice or a prayer—all this must be repeated in one and the same invariable order. The slightest change would immediately destroy the force and efficiency of the magical world or religious rites.

But man cannot over and over again repeat these acts without feeling a desire to *understand* them. He does not perform them in a mere mechanical way; he does not act like an automaton. He asks for the reasons for his act; he wishes to grasp their meaning and purport. All men, says Aristotle, by nature desire to know. This saying holds just as much for the lowest stages of human culture as for the higher stages. The desire to know is no privilege of the civilized man; it is a common goal. But it is clear that, under the conditions of primitive society, this desire cannot be satisfied in the same way as in the more advanced stages. A theoretical or scientific answer to all these first questions of mankind is neither possible nor would it be intelligible to the primitive man. It is here that myth steps in. Man may act very unreasonably; but even in his most irrational acts he cannot refrain from asking for the motives of his acts. Myth alone can supply such a motive. It becomes the interpreter of rite; it enables man to understand what he does. From our point of view its answers may seem to be absurd and fantastic; but the strangest and most extravagant motivation is better than no motivation at all. This general formation of myth in primitive society has become very clear through recent anthropological research.

Bronislaw Malinowski, who had lived for many years among the natives of the Trobriand Islands in the South Pacific, has given a detailed account and a searching analysis of the customs, mythical beliefs, and magic rites of these natives. In his description we find still another point which is of special interest for the point of view of our present problem. Malinowski's observations are not apt to support the thesis of Lévy-Bruhl, that between our own mentality and the mentality of the primitive men there is no point of contact; that the primitive man always acts according to "mythical" principles which are contrary to all our principles of rational and empirical thought. As Malinowski pointed out, we find, even in the life of the primitive man, a certain sphere of action which may be described as the profane or secular sphere. As long as man is moving in this sphere he is seldom influenced by mythical motives, nor does he take refuge in magic rites. All this begins only in a later stage, when a problem becomes too difficult to be handled by ordinary means.

> When the native has to produce an implement he does not refer to magic. He is strictly empirical, that is, scientific, in the choice of his material, in the manner in which he strikes, cuts, and polishes the blade. He relies completely on his skill, on his reason and his endurance. There is no exaggeration in saying that in all matters where knowledge is sufficient the native relies on it exclusively. . . . The Central Australian possesses genuine science or knowledge, that is, tradition completely controlled by experience and reason, and completely unaffected by any mystical elements. . . .
>
> There is a body of rules, handed from one generation to another, which refers to the manner in which people live in their little shelters, make their fire by friction, collect their food and cook it, make love to each other, and quarrel. . . .

> That this secular tradition is plastic, selective, and intelligent, and also well founded, can be seen from the fact that the native always adopts any new and suitable material.[6]

The belief in magic is not a mere theoretical act; it is an emotional act. It needs a special emotional stress to produce this belief. As long as man is still confined within the narrow limits of his everyday experience; as long as he has to do with a comparatively easy situation which he can handle and master himself, he is not likely to take recourse to magic. He acts empirically and technically as we do; he uses his simple implements for answering simple and commonplace questions. But if it comes to more serious and difficult tasks which seem to be far beyond his individual powers, man inevitably gropes after higher and more potent means. He must go to extremes in order to cope with an extreme situation.

Psychologically speaking, the belief in magic always shows us a double face. It is a combination of despair and overconfidence. Man feels a deep mistrust in himself and in his individual abilities. But on the other hand he has an extravagant trust in the power of collective wishes and actions. What gives to the magician, to the wizard and sorcerer his real force is that he does not act as an individual, but that in him the power of the whole tribe is condensed and concentrated. In totemistic societies the different clans that are distinguished by their totemistic ancestors are in possession of special magic rites which are kept as a secret and are inherited from one generation to another. Every professional group, such as the hunters, fishermen, and farmers, have their own magic ritual which is only used if the situation needs a special effort, if the tribe is engaged in a difficult and dangerous enterprise. But to these magic rites nothing can resist. There is no natural force that does not yield to the collective wishes of man. *Carmina vel caelo possunt deducere lunam*, says Medea in

---

6. *The Foundations of Faith and Morals* (London: Oxford University Press, 1936), pp. 32ff. Cassirer's text indicates a quote from Malinowski's *Foundations of Faith and Morals* is to be inserted here. The passage here is taken from Cassirer's discussion of this point in *The Myth of the State,* p. 278.—Ed.

Ovid's *Metamorphoses*, the magic charm and incantation have the power to drag along the moon from the heavens.[7]

We needed this long general introduction in order to understand the true character of our modern political myths. At first sight these political myths are highly complicated and sophisticated products which cannot be put on the same level as those myths which we find in primitive societies. There are, however, two elements which these two widely different phenomena have in common. They are expressions of collective wishes, and they could only arise after these wishes had won an unprecedented and overwhelming strength. Even in our modern political myths we find the same strange mixture between conflicting tendencies. They are just as much an outgrowth of despair as of confidence. It was indeed a desperate situation which led to the development of our political myths. All rational means to handle this situation seemed to have been exhausted. They had to be thrown away; they were declared to be idle and futile.

But if all ordinary technical means have failed, there still remains the *ultima ratio*, the final argument, which consists in a negation and reversal of all our usual modes of ratiocination and argumentation. We cannot solve the Gordian knot, but we can cut it. The magic word has not lost its power. But it must be used in the right way, at the right moment, and by the right man. All our efforts would be in vain if it were not possible to concentrate them to one point—in the same way in which in primitive society the collective power of the tribe is condensed and embodied in the person of the sorcerer, who commands the powers of nature, and who, as a medical man, knows the remedies for all evils.

The French scholar E. Doutté has written a very interesting book, *Magie et religion dans l'Afrique du Nord*, in which he deals with the religious rites and ceremonies of some savage tribes in North Africa.[8] In this book he tries to give a short and clearcut definition of the origin of myth. He calls the mythical gods and demons "le désir collectif personifié." The divine and demonic powers that we find in mythical thought are nothing but the per-

7. Cf. Bk. VII, lines 207–09.—Ed.

8. Algiers: Typographie Adolphe Jourdan, 1909.—Ed.

sonifications of collective desires. This definition was given about thirty-five years ago, and, of course, the author did not think of our political problems. Nevertheless there is perhaps no better and no more laconic and trenchant description of the modern principle of leadership than this formula of Doutté. The desire for leadership always originates in an intense collective wish. But it is not enough that the wish exists; it must be personified; it must assume a concrete, plastic, and individual shape. At this moment the decisive step takes place. We live no longer in a rational world; we live in a mythical world. We have no longer to do with laws or statutes, with constitutions or political charters. All this has vanished; it has resolved itself into thin air. Law, justice, constitutions, and bills of rights have lost their meaning and their validity. What alone remains and what alone matters is the power and authority of the mythical god: "the Leader's will is supreme law."

But how could this new principle be enforced on a whole nation? How could it become efficient and break all resistance? Here the modern political myth had to stand its most difficult test. Obviously a great civilized nation cannot be ruled according to the same very simple and rudimentary principles which were possible and sufficient in a primitive society. The problem is immensely complicated, and to solve it it was necessary to find an entirely new way, to develop a technique of rulership which had been unknown to previous ages. That became one of the first tasks of the new men. But from a logical point of view this task was, in a sense, very much alike to the quadrature of the circle.

The historians of civilization have told us that mankind in its history had to pass through two different stages. Man began as *homo magus* or *homo divinans*, he tried to enforce his will on nature by the use of magic formulas. But his hopes were constantly disappointed and frustrated. He had to break through the magic circle in which he had enclosed himself, and had to force his way out. The *homo magus* became a *homo faber*. The technical age followed and superseded the magic age.[9] If we

9. Cf. Cassirer, "Form und Technik," p. 28.—Ed.

admit this distinction the modern political myths become a very strange and paradoxical thing. For what we find here is the blending together and even the complete fusion of two contradictory and incompatible elements: of the elements of magical and technical thought. The modern politician had to combine in himself two entirely different functions. He had to be a *homo magus* and a *homo faber* at the same time. He was the spokesman for and the priest of a new and entirely irrational and mysterious religion. But if he and his collaborators had to defend and propagate this irrational religion, they were by no means irrational. They were sharp and cool thinkers and very good calculators. They proceeded very thoroughly and methodically. Nothing was left to chance; every step was premeditated and well prepared.

This strange combination is one of the most striking features in the development of the modern political myths. Myth had always been described as the result of an unconscious social activity. But here were men who acted very deliberately and "according to plan." They knew their way very well and watched every step. From now on myth was no longer allowed to grow up freely and indifferently. The new political myths were by no means wild fruits of an exuberant imagination. They were artificial things made by very skillful and cunning artisans. To put it bluntly we may say that what we see here before our very eyes is a new type of a completely rationalized myth. The twentieth century developed a *technique* of mythical thought which had no equal in previous history. Henceforth myths were invented and manufactured in the same sense and according to the same methods as machine guns or airplanes. And they were used for the same purpose, for internal and external warfare. This was an altogether unprecedented fact, a fact which has changed the whole face of our modern political life.

Within the narrow compass of this lecture I cannot hope to give a full impression of the very refined and complicated technique of the modern political myths. All I can do is to illustrate the point by a few examples. The first step that had to be taken was a change in the function of language. In ordinary speech our words have a double function: a descriptive and an emotional function. They express human feelings, or they describe objects or relations of objects. Under normal circumstances both functions are in a harmonious equilibrium; they complete each other and each cooperates with the other. "Subjective" and "objective," emotional and propositional language are used as means which lead to the same end, to the end of social communication and mutual understanding. In the language introduced by the political myths, however, this equipoise was greatly disturbed. The whole emphasis was laid on the emotional side; the descriptive and logical word was transformed into the magic word. New words were coined, and the old ones underwent a deep change of meaning. All this was done in a few decades, and it had a tremendous effect. If nowadays I happen to read a German book published in the last ten years, which deals with a theoretical subject such as problems of philosophy, history, politics, or economics, I find to my amazement that I no longer understand the German language. I find many terms which I have never heard before, and the old and familiar terms have won a different and strange connotation. The ordinary words are charged with feelings and violent emotions.

In 1944 there was published a very interesting book in New York by the Frederick Ungar Publishing company. Its title is *Nazi-Deutsch. A Glossary of Contemporary German Usage.*[10] The name of the author is Heinz Paechter. This book contains a list of all those terms which, in the last two decades, were introduced into German language by the representatives and followers of the Nazi regime. The author of the book tried to translate these terms into English, but in this attempt he was not very successful. What he gives is only a circumlocution, a paraphrase of the German words and phrases, not a real translation. For unfortunately, or perhaps fortunately, it was impossible to render these words adequately into English. What characterizes these parvenus, these new-fangled terms, is not their objective meaning— in many cases they seem to have no meaning at all—but the emotional atmosphere which surrounds and envelops them. This atmosphere may be felt, but it cannot be translated. Let me give you at least one characteristic and striking example.

10. Cf. *The Myth of the State*, pp. 283–84.—Ed.

I have learned from Paechter's book that in contemporary German usage there is a sharp difference between the two terms *Siegfriede* and *Siegerfriede*. Even for a German ear it is not easy to grasp the difference. The two words seem to mean exactly the same. *Sieg* means victory, *Friede* means peace; a *Siegfriede* or *Siegerfriede* would, therefore, be a peace which follows a victory. Nevertheless, we are told that the connotation of both terms is by no means the same. A *Siegfriede* is the very opposite to a *Siegerfriede*, for, as the glossary tells us, a *Siegfriede* means a peace through German victory, whereas a *Siegerfriede* is a peace which would be dictated by the allied conquerors. Between the two terms there is, therefore, all the difference in the world. But what is the reason for this strange terminology? The glossary does not give this reason, but for anyone who is acquainted with the language and ideology of the National-Socialistic system it is not difficult to find out this reason. The only palpable difference between the two terms is a grammatical or morphological difference. In the word *Siegfriede* the term *Sieg* (victory) appears in the singular form; in *Siegerfriede*, however, it appears in the plural form. Now the singular can only apply to the German people. The German people is not a *mixtum compositum*, a mere aggregate of many millions of men and women. It is a homogeneous whole, a *corpus mysticum*, a deep and mysterious unity. But in the case of the adversaries and enemies of Germany we cannot speak of such a unity. They call themselves the "allied nations," but they are not at all allied, they are divided and rifted. What we find here is only a confused medley, a heterogeneous mixture of various races, various political aims, and various and diametrically opposed ideologies. All this is expressed in the two words *Siegfriede* and *Siegerfriede*. Certainly the man who coined these words was a master in his art, in the art of political propaganda. He has attained his end by the slightest and most insignificant means. He was able to compress in one syllable the whole gamut of human passions and a whole scale of hatred, anger, and fury, of haughtiness and contempt, of arrogance and disdain.

But the skillful use of magic words is not all. As we pointed out, even in primitive society the magic word never stands alone. It is only a corollary and accessory of another force, it accompanies and interprets the magic rite. If the new political myths were to have their full effect, they had to be supported by new rites. Even in this respect the National Socialistic leaders proceeded very thoroughly and very methodically. In this respect, too, German social life was radically changed in the last decades, in the period between the First and the Second World Wars. There was no political action that had not its special ritual. In addition, since, in the totalitarian state, there was no longer any separation between private and public life, even private life was suddenly inundated by a high tide of new rituals. They were as regular, as rigorous, and inexorable as any primitive ritual. Every class, every sex, and every age had a rite of its own. No one could walk in the street or greet his neighbor or friend without performing a ritual act. To neglect one of the prescribed rites became a very dangerous thing. Even in children this was not regarded as a mere sin of omission; it was a *crimen laesae maiestatis*—a crime against the majesty of the leader and the totalitarian state.

What was the purpose of all these new words and rites? Obviously they were not fabricated for their own sake; they had a very definite and deliberate aim. It is easy to understand this aim if we think of the function of rites in primitive society. Rites are not individual acts; they are always performed by a community and, in most cases, by all the members of the tribe. It is their principal effect that the men and women who are performing these rites lose every sense of their individuality. They are melted together; they act, think, and feel as a whole. "The savage," says E. Sidney Hartland in his book on *Primitive Law,* "is far from being the free and unfettered creature of Rousseau's imagination. On the contrary, he is hemmed in on every side by the customs of his people; he is bound in the chains of immemorial tradition. . . . These fetters are accepted as a matter of course; he never seeks to break forth. . . . To the civilized man the same observations may very often apply, but the civilized man is too restless, too desirous of change, too eager to question his environment, to remain long in the attitude of acquiescence."[11]

11. London: Methuen and Co., 1924, p. 138.—Ed.

These words were written in 1924; how much the situation has changed in these last two decades! In spite of their restlessness— and perhaps precisely by virtue of their restlessness—great nations seem to have lost every desire and every impulse of questioning their environments. They live in an attitude of complete acquiescence; they have an implicit faith in the new god, the god of the totalitarian state. How could free nations ever be induced to accept this intolerable pressure? To answer this question we must begin with an analysis of the term *freedom*. Freedom is one of the most ambiguous and ill-defined terms. By the interminable discussion of the opposite metaphysical schools and by the struggle of political parties the *ethical* concept of freedom has been so very much obscured that it has become almost unrecognizable. Here I cannot enter into a discussion of this great problem, of the problem of ethical freedom. I think, however, that the best and, in a sense, the classical definition of this concept has been given by Kant. As Kant pointed out in his *Critique of Practical Reason,* freedom is not an exemption from binding rules; it is, on the contrary, a rule which the moral will gives to itself. It means "autonomy," that is to say, it means self-control and individual responsibility. As Kant says, freedom is not *gegeben,* but *aufgegeben.* It is not a gift, but a task, and perhaps the hardest task that we can impose upon ourselves. To fulfill this task became so much the more difficult in times like ours, in times of severe social crises and violent political agitations.

At these times the individual begins to feel a deep mistrust in his own formative and creative powers. It is liable to all influences from without; it becomes an easy prey to those political parties that exploit the situation for their own purpose, especially if those parties have provided themselves with such powerful weapons as myths and rites are. Nothing is more apt to suppress our critical judgment and to break every resistance on the part of the individual than the steady repetition of the same magic formulas or the incessant performance of the same rites. In primitive societies, the whole life of which is governed by magic and ritual, we find, indeed, no clear concept of individual obligation or self-responsibility. Not the individual but the group is the real "moral subject." The whole tribe, the clan, and the family are responsible for the actions of all their members. If a crime is committed, it is not imputed to an individual person. By a sort of miasma and social contagion the whole group becomes infected with the crime. Also revenge and punishment are directed to the group as a whole. In those societies in which the blood-feud is regarded as one of the highest religious and moral obligations it is by no means necessary to take revenge on the murderer himself. It is quite enough to kill a member of his family or clan. In some cases as, for instance, in New Guinea or among the African Somalis, it is the oldest brother of the offender rather than the offender himself who is killed.

All this returns in our modern political life. Here it appears, however, according to the much more complicated forms of this life, on a much larger scale. It is no longer the tribe or the family which is accountable for individual actions; it is the whole nation or the whole race. It is clear that such a perversion of all moral standards, such a complete elimination of individual judgment and self-responsibility, required the most extraordinary means; but the political myths provided for these means by going back to the most rudimentary forms of man's social life.

In our description of the political myths, however, one more feature must be discussed, unless the picture is to remain incomplete. As we pointed out, in the totalitarian states the political leaders had to take charge of all those functions which in primitive societies were put into the hands of the magician. They claimed to be the political rulers, the medicine men who could cure all social evils, the technicians who pulled the strings of the whole social organization. In primitive society, however, the sorcerer has still another and even more important task. He is the *homo divinans;* he reveals the will of the gods and foretells the future. Hope and fear are perhaps the most general and deepest human emotions. To live in hope and fear, to anticipate the future in thought and feeling is one of those characteristics which, profoundly and radically, discriminate human life from animal life. Myth is the first attempt to organize this feeling. The soothsayer has his firm place and his indispensable role in primitive social life, and even in highly developed stages of political culture we find him still in full possession of his rights and privileges. In Rome no important political decision was ever made, no difficult enterprise was undertaken, no battle was fought without the advice of the augurs and haruspices. When a Roman army was sent out it was always accompanied by its haruspices. The book of Appius Claudius Pulcher, *De disciplina augurali*, was dedicated to Cicero, and Cicero himself, in the course of his political career, performed the office of augur.

In this respect, too, our modern political life abruptly returned to forms which seemed to have been entirely forgotten. It is true that we have a much more refined and elaborate technique of divination. We have no longer the primitive kind of sortilege, the divination by lot; we no longer observe the flight of birds, nor do we inspect the entrails of slain animals. These things seem to us to be absurd and ludicrous. But even if the modern methods have changed, the thing itself has by no means vanished. The modern politicians knew very well that great masses can be moved much easier by the force of imagination then by sheer physical forces. Accordingly they played this instrument with the greatest skill and virtuosity. The modern politician became the *vates publicus*. Prophecy was an essential part in the new technique of politics. It is not necessary to enter here into a detailed description of these political prophecies; we know them only too well. The millennium was predicted over and over again. This time, however, it was no longer the millennium of mankind, but the millennium of a special nation and a special race.[12]

Curiously enough, this new art of divination made its first appearance not in German politics but in German philosophy. In 1918 there appeared Oswald Spengler's book *Der Untergang des Abendlandes (The Decline of the West).*[13] Perhaps never before had a philosophical book had such a sensational success. It was translated into all languages and read by all sorts of readers: by philosophers and scientists, historians and politicians, students and

12. Cf. *The Myth of the State*, p. 289.—Ed.

13. Trans. C. F. Atkinson, 2 vols. (New York: Knopf, 1926 and 1928). Regarding Spengler, cf. "Critical Idealism as a Philosophy of Culture" and "Philosophy and Politics" herein.—Ed.

tradesmen, scholars and the man in the street. What was the reason for this unprecedented success; what was the magic spell
which this book exerted upon its readers? To my mind the cause
of this success is to be sought rather in the *title* of the book than
in its contents. The title *Der Untergang des Abendlandes* was the
electric spark which set the imagination of Spengler's readers
afire. The book was published in July 1918, that means at the
end of the First World War. At this time many, if not most, of us
had realized that something was rotten in the state of our highly
praised Western civilization. Spengler gave a sharp and trenchant expression to this general uneasiness; his thesis seemed to
explain it and to justify it. He spoke by no means as a scientist.
He despised and openly challenged all scientific methods. "Geschichte wissenschaftlich behandeln wollen," says Spengler, "ist
im letzten Grunde immer etwas Widerspruchsvolles. Natur soll
man wissenschaftlich traktieren, über Geschichte soll man dich-
ten." "Nature is to be handled scientifically, history poetically."

But even this does not express the real meaning of Spengler's
book. A poet lives in the world of his imagination, and if he is a
great religious poet like Dante or Milton he may also live in a
world of prophetic vision. But he does not take these visions for
realities and does not make of them a philosophy of history.
That was, however, precisely the case of Spengler. He boasted of
having found a new method by which the future course of
human culture could be predicted in the same sense as an
astronomer predicts an eclipse of the sun or the moon. "In this
book," said Spengler, "is attempted for the first time the venture
of predetermining history, of following the still unraveled stages
in the destiny of a Culture, and specifically of the only Culture of
our time and on our planet which is actually in the phase of
fulfilment—the West European-American."[14]

Here, I think, we have found the clue to Spengler's book and
to its enormous influence. If it was possible not only to tell the
history of human civilization but to predetermine it, to show its
future fate and to prove that this fate was inevitable and inexorable, this was indeed a great step in advance. Other philosophers

14. *Decline of the West*, introduction.—Ed.

of history, as for instance Hegel, had tried to reveal the march of the world-spirit. They had started from the presupposition that there must be a definite plan in human history, and that without such a plan history would become a meaningless thing. All this is rejected by Spengler. Mankind has no aim, he declares, no idea, no plan any more than the family of butterflies or orchids. Nor has the course of history a "cause"—if we understand the terms "cause" and "effect" in an empirical sense. The rise, the decline, and fall of civilizations are determined by a rule much higher and much more sublime than all our so-called laws of nature. This rule is the rule of destiny. Destiny, not causality, is the true moving force in history. The birth and death of a cultural soul is always a mystical act; it cannot be accounted for by our poor, abstract, scientific or philosophical concepts. "Eine Kultur wird in dem Augenblick geboren, wo eine grosse Seele aus dem urseelenhaften Zustande ewig-kindlichen Menschentums erwacht."[15] I make no attempt to translate this mystical language of Spengler into commonplace idiomatic English; such an attempt would take away their special flavor and spoil the whole effect.

I think that in Spengler's idea of destiny we have found the clue to his whole book and to the success of the book. When I first read it, I was engrossed in studies of the philosophy of the Italian Renaissance. What struck me most at this time was the close analogy between Spengler's book and some astrological treatises of the fourteenth and fifteenth centuries which I had studied quite recently. Of course Spengler does not make an attempt to read the future of cultures in the stars. Nevertheless his prognostics are of the same type and express exactly the same mentality as the prognostics of the astrologers. The astrologers of the Renaissance did not content themselves with exploring the destiny of individual men; they applied their methods also to the great historical and cultural phenomena. One of them was condemned by the church and burnt at the stake because he had cast the horoscope of Christ and from Christ's nativity had deduced that the time of Christian religion was over, and that

15. See *Der Untergang des Abendlandes*, 2d ed. (C. H. Beck'sche Verlagsbuchhandlung, Oskar Beck: München, 1923), I, 144.—Ed.

Christianity was near its decline and fall. In fact Spengler's book was neither a scientific book, nor was it a poem or a philosophy of history. It was an astrology of history and the work of a fortune-teller of human culture who unfolded his somber apocalyptic vision.

Here an important question must be raised. Can we really connect the divination of Spengler with those of the later prophets? Can we put the two phenomena on the same level? At first sight this seems to be impossible. Spengler's myth of the cultural souls is, in a certain sense, in strict opposition to the myth of the twentieth century, as it is described in the notorious book of Alfred Rosenberg. Spengler was a prophet of evil; the political leaders of nazism, however, tried to evoke in their adherents and believers the most extravagant hopes. Spengler spoke of the decline of the West, while the others spoke of the conquest of the world by the German race. He was a conservative, an admirer and eulogist of Prussian militarism, but he seems to have had a dislike and contempt of the ideas propagated by the new men. Nevertheless there was one point in which his book could exert a great political influence. What was the conclusion which Spengler drew from his deep cultural pessimism? He declared that the modern man cannot avert his fate; he has to accept it. No effort of the human will can revivify a dead body. Let us, therefore, no longer persevere in vain attempts; let us not construct philosophical systems or create works of art.

"Of great painting or great music," declared Spengler,

> there can no longer be, for Western people, any question. . . . Only *extensive* possibilities are left to them. Yet, for a sound and vigorous generation that is filled with unlimited hopes, J fail to see that it is any disadvantage to discover betimes that some of these hopes must come to nothing. . . . It is true that the issue may be a tragic one for some individuals who in their decisive years are overpowered by the conviction that in the spheres of architecture, drama, painting, there is nothing left to *them* to conquer. What matter if they go under! . . . Now at last the work of centuries enables the West-European to view the disposition of his own life in

relation to the general culture-scheme and to test his own powers and purposes. And I can only hope that men of the new generation may be moved by this book to devote themselves to technics instead of lyrics, the sea instead of the paint-brush, and politics instead of epistemology. Better they could not do.[16]

If we have to die, let us die heroically. If our science, our art, our philosophy are doomed, let us make a fresh start; let us become the rulers of the world. Technic instead of lyric; politics instead of epistemology—this slogan could easily be understood by the new generation of politicians which grew up in Germany, and it was rapidly and eagerly put into action.

From this strange analogy and this parallelism between astrological and modern political thought we can draw still another inference. We are proud of our modern natural science; but we should never forget that natural science is, after all, very young. Even in the seventeenth century, in the great century of Descartes and Newton, of Galileo and Kepler, the victory of natural science was by no means assured. In the Renaissance the so-called occult sciences—magic, alchemy, and astrology—were still in full possession of the intellectual world. Kepler was the first great empirical astronomer; the first who succeeded in discovering exact laws of the movements of celestial bodies. But if we look at Kepler's biography and at his scientific work, we find that he had continually to struggle against astrological conceptions. He had been appointed as an astrologer at the Imperial Court of Prague, and in his last years he became the astrologer of Wallenstein.

We can follow the way in which Kepler freed himself, in which he became one of the founders of modern natural science, step by step. The study of this intellectual process makes one of the most important and most fascinating chapters in the history of science. Kepler himself declared astrology to be the mother of astronomy, and he said that it would be unfair if the daughter would neglect and despise her mother. It was the same with

16. *Decline of the West,* I, pp. 40ff.—Ed.

alchemy. If we study Lynn Thorndike's monumental *History of Magic and Experimental Science,* we shall receive a striking impression of the fact that, for thousands and thousands of years, there was no strict line of demarcation between empirical and mythical thought.[17] A scientific chemistry in the modern sense of this term did not appear until the seventeenth and eighteenth centuries, until the times of Robert Boyle and Antoine Laurent Lavoisier.

How could this state of affairs be changed? What was the first principle that led to our modern conception of the true character of empirical and exact science? This principle has found one of its best and most trenchant expressions in a formula of Bacon, who was one of the pioneers of modern empirical thought. *Natura non vincitur nisi parendo*—nature can be ruled only by obedience. It was the great ambition of Bacon's theory to found the *regnum hominis* on earth. Man was to cease being the slave of nature; he had to become its master. But this technical mastery over the powers of nature must be understood in the right way. We cannot enforce on nature our own wishes; we must learn to think *ex analogia universi,* not *ex analogia hominis.* We must respect and obey the laws of nature if we wish to control nature. For this purpose the first and most important step is to free ourselves from all sort of illusions, fallacies, and prejudices and from our human freaks and fancies. In his *Novum Organum* Bacon tried to give a systematic survey of these human prejudices. He has given a list of the different kinds of idols: the *idola tribus,* the *idola specus,* the *idola fori,* and the *idola theatri,* and he tried to teach how to overcome them in order to clear the way which at last will lead to a true empirical science.

Of all these idols the *idola fori* are the most dangerous and tenacious ones. It is clear that these idols, the idols of the marketplace, have, so to speak, their natural place in politics. When compared with other branches of human knowledge political science will always remain *instabilis tellus, innabilis unda.* Since the time of Plato it was one of the highest tasks of philosophy to find

17. 8 vols. (New York: Macmillan and Columbia University Press, 1923–58). Cf. "Critical Idealism as a Philosophy of Culture," herein.—Ed.

a rational method of politics. The thinkers of the nineteenth century were convinced that, after innumerable vain attempts, they had at last found the right way. In 1830 Auguste Comte began to publish his *Cours de philosophie positive*, in which he tried to build up the world of science in a definite hierarchic order. He began with analyzing the structure of mathematical and natural sciences and went from astronomy to physics, from physics to chemistry, and from chemistry to biology. But to him natural science was only the first step that was to lead to a higher end. "Theological and metaphysical methods," wrote Comte in the introduction to his work, "exploded in other departments, are as yet exclusively applied, both in the way of inquiry and discussion, in all treatment of Social subjects. . . . This is the great, while it is evidently the only gap which has to be filled, to constitute, solid and entire, the Positive Philosophy. Now that the human mind has grasped celestial and terrestrial physics,— mechanical and chemical; organic physics, both vegetable and animal,—there remains one science, to fill up the series of Sciences of observation,—Social physics. That is what men have now most need of: and this is the principal aim of the present work to establish."[18]

The sudden rise of the political myths in the twentieth century has shown that these hopes of Comte and the positivists of the nineteenth century were premature. Politics is very far from being a positive science, let alone an exact science. It is in many respects still an occult science. I do not doubt that later generations will look at many of our political theories with the same feeling with which a modern astronomer looks at astrology or a modern chemist at alchemy. In the science of politics we have not yet found a firm ground. We are building up high and proud edifices, but we forget to secure their basis. The belief that man, by the skillful use of magic rites and magic formulas, is able to change the course of nature has prevailed for many thousands of years in human history. In spite of all the obvious and inevitable frustrations and disappointments mankind clung stub-

18. *The Positive Philosophy*, trans. Harriet Martineau, 3 vols. (London: George Bell, 1896), I, 7–8.—Ed.

bornly, forcibly, and desperately to this belief. It is, therefore, not to be wondered at that myth and magic have still such an overwhelming influence in political thought and action. Small groups try to enforce their wishes and fantastic ideas on whole nations and the whole of the body politic. They may succeed for a while; they may even achieve great triumphs. But their triumph will always be ephemeral. There is, after all, a logic of the social world just as much as there is a logic of the physical world. There are certain laws of a social statics and dynamics which cannot be violated with impunity. Even in this sphere we must follow the maxim of Bacon. We must learn how to obey the laws of the social world before we can undertake to rule the social world.

What can *philosophy* do in this struggle against the political myths? It is clear that the role of the individual thinker is a very modest one. As an individual the philosopher has long ago given up all hopes to reform the political world. He feels like Faust:

> Bilde mir nicht ein, ich könnte was lehren,
> Die Menschen zu bessern und zu bekehren.

But philosophy as a whole is not allowed to yield to this feeling. It is true that its contribution to the solution of the problem will always remain rather an indirect than a direct contribution. Myth cannot be overcome by logical and rational arguments; it is in a sense impenetrable by and invulnerable to these arguments. But if philosophy cannot overcome myth by a direct frontal attack, it can do us another service. It can make us understand the adversary. This is a point of vital importance. In order to fight an enemy one must know him. And to know him means not only to know his defects but also his strength. To all of us it has become clear that we have greatly underrated the strength of the political myths. We should not repeat this error. We should see the adversary face to face; we should try to understand his true character, and we should study his methods. To be sure that is no very attractive task.

As an individual the philosopher would widely prefer to be engaged in quite different fields of study, in studies of a more abstract and theoretical nature. But if he happens to be a Kantian he has at least one relief. According to Kant's principles it is not enough that our actions conform to duty. In order to give them an ethical value we must be sure that they are done *from* duty. This remains always questionable when the action accords with duty and the subject has besides a direct inclination to it. In this case we never know how much in our actions was due to obligation, how much to inclination. When dealing with the modern political myths we have at least a clear case. We are pretty sure that we are not following our personal inclinations, and so we may cherish the hope to fulfill our duty, that is to say, to fulfill the function which philosophy has to perform in the whole of our social life.[19]

19. Cf. Cassirer's view in "Philosophy and Politics," herein, that the philosophies of Spengler and Heidegger put philosophy in a position where it "can no longer do its duty."—Ed.

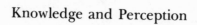

Knowledge and Perception

Reflections on
the Concept of Group and
the Theory of Perception

(1945)

*This lecture is marked "Concept of Group, Philosophy Club, April 1945"
and constitutes summary comments and reflections on his article on this
subject prepared by Cassirer while visiting professor at Columbia University (1944–45). This manuscript, MS #214, has a connection with MS
#163. MS #163 consists of several pages of notes on the same subject,
indicated as a Philosophy Club lecture for the spring of 1944, while
Cassirer was at Yale University. Mrs. Cassirer reports, in* Aus meinem
Leben mit Ernst Cassirer *(New York: Privately issued, 1950), p.
308, that the introduction to MS #214 was written on the morning of
Cassirer's death (April 13, 1945). The envelope containing it has this
date written at the bottom.–Ed.*

Before entering into the subject matter of this paper I hope
you will allow me to say a few personal words. First of all, a word
of cordial thanks to the Philosophy Club that invited me for this
lecture. When I received your kind invitation I immediately
accepted it with great gratitude,.and I decided to avail myself of
this opportunity to speak, in a circle of philosophers, about a
problem that had occupied my thoughts for a very long time. As
a matter of fact the subject of this paper was one of the first to
arouse my philosophical interest; I began to ponder on it when
still an undergraduate in philosophy. It took, however, a very
long time before I found the courage to publish the results to
which I had been led. I always feared lest my conclusions should
not yet be ripe for publication. And I must frankly confess that
even now, after many years of labor spent on this problem, I
have by no means overcome these scruples.

Nevertheless, I tried, some years ago, to give a first and preliminary description of my results. I wrote an article, that was
published in French, in 1938, in the *Journal de Psychologie*[1]; later
on the same article also appeared in an English version, made on
the request of some of my English and American friends. You
will find this article in the journal of *Philosophy and Phenomenological Research,* in the September issue of last year.[2] Here I
shall not repeat all the facts and arguments that I have alleged in
this article in support for my general thesis. I can only give you a
very condensed and concise "statement" in order to have sufficient room for the following discussion. I am quite aware of the
dangers and disadvantages of such a brief and sketchy treatment
of a difficult and highly involved problem. Within the compass
of this short lecture I cannot offer a definitive solution.

Instead of answering the question I can only pose the question. For a more detailed and comprehensive analysis you must
allow me to refer to the article mentioned before. What I can
give in the following remarks is not an exhaustive treatment of
the subject itself; it is rather a chapter of my intellectual autobiography—a short report of the way in which I myself became
engaged in the study of this problem and of the trend of
thought by which I reached my conclusion. Such a procedure
would be out of place in a paper destined for publication in a
philosophical journal.[3] But in a meeting like this it is perhaps
admissible and excusable. If I understand the character and the
purpose of this club in the right way I should say that the
members of this club, when exchanging their thoughts, are not
only engaged in discussing philosophical problems in an imper-
sonal way. They are also bound together by a personal interest,
by a sort of intellectual sympathy and comradeship. They wish to

1. "Le concept de groupe et la théorie de la perception," *Journal de Psychologie* (July–
Dec. 1938), 368–414.—Ed.

2. "The Concept of Group and the Theory of Perception," trans. Aron Gurwitsch, *Philosophy and Phenomenological Research* 5 (1944), 1–35.—Ed.

3. The published version of "The Concept of Group and the Theory of Perception" is
much longer and develops its points in greater historical and technical detail. All of its
points are developed from quite an "objective" stance and it contains none of the elements of intellectual autobiography that Cassirer employs here.—Ed.

understand each other—to enter into their ways of thought, which, objectively speaking, may often be widely divergent.

As for myself, I found it always very instructive and stimulating not only to read the books of contemporary philosophers but also to learn something about the intellectual motives that had induced them to study certain problems and to accept certain theories. It is this personal approach to the problem about which I shall speak here and for which I ask your friendly interest.

The concept of group that I intend to discuss in this paper is in the focus of modern mathematical thought. It has played an important role in the history of mathematics in the nineteenth and twentieth centuries. It seems to be one of the most abstract concepts of modern mathematics and, at first sight, it seems to be far remote from the problems we are studying in empirical science—in experimental physics and in empirical psychology. As Hermann Weyl says in his "Philosophy of Mathematics and Natural Science," the theory of group is the most striking example of "pure intellectual mathematics."[4] What I should like to emphasize in this paper is the fact that in spite of this abstract character—or perhaps just *because of* this abstract character—the concept of group is able to elucidate some problems that are of general interest and of great import for a theory of empirical knowledge. Yet in this field of inquiry the concept of group has, to my mind, been unduly neglected. That the concept has not only a mathematical or physical but a universal *epistemological* interest is a fact that, as yet, has not been fully recognized.

So far as I know no modern philosopher has discussed and analyzed the concept and used it for the solution of epistemological problems. As for myself, I am convinced that, in the present state of our mathematical and empirical knowledge, such a discussion is highly desirable and even necessary, and that it will prove to be pregnant with very important consequences for the philosophy of science.

Before entering into this subject itself let me begin with a few

4. "Philosophie der Mathematik und Naturwissenschaft," in *Handbuch der Philosophie* (Munich and Berlin, 1926), II A, p. 23.—Cassirer.

preliminary historical remarks. At the beginning of the nineteenth century Cauchy had introduced the concept of group into
the study of combinations and algebra. The concept immediately
proved to be eminently fruitful; in the hands of the young
French mathematician Galois—who died at an age of twenty-one
years—it led to a new and very original theory of algebraic
equations.

Yet in these first beginnings the concept was still confined
within comparatively narrow limits and restricted to a special
field of investigation. It was not before the second half of the
nineteenth century that the theory of groups was established as a
new and universal branch of mathematical knowledge. It led to a
general reorientation not only of algebra but also of geometry.
Later on it found its way into physics; in the development of
modern quantum mechanics the theory of groups has played an
important role. There must be a reason for this universal applicability of the concept to so many fields of inquiry that, at first
sight, seem to have little in common, or even to deal with quite
disparate subjects.

In order to find this reason we must begin with a definition of
what a "group of transformations" is. The first clear and adequate definition was given in the work of the Norwegian mathe-
matican Sophus Lie and the German mathematician Felix Klein.
It is not necessary and it is not possible to enter here into the
technical details of this definition; it will be enough to insist on
those points that are of special logical and epistemological interest. As Sophus Lie and Felix Klein pointed out, it is indicative of
the theories of group, but what we are studying here are not
certain types of mathematical *objects* or *elements*—let us say
numbers or geometrical figures. We are not inquiring into the
nature or properties of these elements but into the *operations* to
which these elements are *subject*. A group is defined by Klein and
Lie as the totality of unique operations $a, b, c, \ldots$ so that from
the combination of any two operations a and b there results an
operation c which also belongs to the totality.

In other words, a group is a set of operations having the property that when two operations are carried out in succession the
result is one that would be reached by a single operation of the

set. Such a set of operations is called a *closed* set and the property of closure is called the "group property." The combination—or, as it is usually called, the product—of any two elements *a* and *b* of this set, whether *a* and *b* are here distinct elements or the same element, is a *unique* element *c* which is an element of the set *ab* = *c*. There are some formal laws which a group has to fulfill; for instance:

The associative law for multiplication holds $(ab) \cdot c = a \cdot (bc) = abc$.

The *commutative* law of multiplication does not hold for *all* groups, but it holds for certain *kinds* of groups—for so-called. Abel-groups—called by the name of Abel, the famous Norwegian mathematician.

But instead of entering into any mathematical technicalities let us begin with one of the most general questions of the theory of knowledge, with the question, What is space? The great thinkers of the past—mathematicians, philosophers, natural scientists— have given us their answers to this question. But these answers are widely divergent, and the problem is still highly controversial. In the seventeenth century we find the famous discussion between Newton and Leibniz, a discussion I have recently dealt with in a paper published in the *Philosophical Review*.[5] This discussion had, however, not led to a definite result. Philosophers and mathematicians approached the problem from quite different angles and they were very much divided on their theories of the nature, the logical and ontological character of space. And this problem has become even more involved and perplexing since the beginning of the nineteenth century. For here philosophers and mathematicians were suddenly encountered with a new difficulty. Lobachevsky, Bolyai, Riemann began to develop their systems of non-Euclidean geometries. Before the times of Lobachevsky, Bolyai, or Riemann the philosophical question "what is space?" could be answered in a very simple way. If you wish to know the makeup of space—it could be said—study geometry.

5. "Newton and Leibniz," *Philosophical Review* 52 (1943), 366–91.—Cassirer.

The axioms of geometry describe, in the most exact manner, the nature and essence of space. But through the discovery of non-Euclidean geometries the situation had completely changed. Space could no longer be regarded as a unique object, endowed with a definite structure. There seemed to be as many types of space as there were different geometries. Which of these different geometrical spaces—the space of Euclid, of Bolyai, of Lobachevsky, of Riemann—is the "real" space, the space to which we may ascribe an ontological, not only a formal or mathematical, truth? Which of the different geometries that logically are equally possible and equally valid conforms to reality? Mathematicians were always inclined to reject these questions. They continued their analytical work, regardless of all metaphysical problems and of all ontological consequences. But to the philosophers such an attitude was inadmissible. To most of them—if not to all of them—the very fact of the non-Euclidean geometries came as a real shock. For a long time the fact remained a stumbling block for all the philosophical systems of the nineteenth century.

Let me illustrate this by a very characteristic example. In 1878 Hermann Lotze published his system of philosophy. In the second volume of this book he discussed, very thoroughly and explicitly, the problem of *space*.[6] At this time Lotze was one of the great thinkers of Germany. He was generally regarded as one of the foremost living philosophers, as one of the great representatives and the last heir of German idealism. But what was Lotze's judgment about the systems of non-Euclidean geometry? He did not only think they were devoid of any philosophical— that is to say, of any *metaphysical*—interest. He went much farther—he spoke of them as if they were meaningless or nonsensical. Philosophers, declared Lotze, should not be afraid of these new mathematical speculations; they should openly challenge them and show their inherent contradictions and absurdities. A whole chapter in Lotze's metaphysics is devoted to this purpose. "I trust," said Lotze (and I quote), "that in this point

6. See Hermann Lotze, *Metaphysic,* trans. Bernard Bosanquet, 2d ed., 2 vols. (Oxford: Clarendon Press, 1887), I, bk. 2. ch. 2.—Ed.

philosophy will not allow itself to be imposed upon by mathetics. I begin my task with a very frank confession. I am quite unable to persuade myself that all those among my fellow-students of philosophy, who accept the new theories with applause, can really understand with such ease what is quite imcomprehensible to me; I fear, that from over-modesty they do not discharge their office, and fail on this borderland between mathematics and philosophy, to vindicate their full weight for the grave doubts which they should have raised in the name of the latter against many mathematical speculations of the present day. I shall not imitate this procedure; but while on the contrary I plainly say that the whole of this speculation seems to me one huge coherent error."[7]

This attitude of the first philosophers who dealt with the problem of non-Euclidean geometry is easily understandable. There were two different theories of space that prevailed in the philosophy of the nineteenth century. The one was a realistic, the other an idealistic theory. In the first case, space was regarded as a real thing—or even as an absolute thing—in the sense of Newton. This absolute thing had some absolute qualities—homogeneity, infinity, infinite divisibility, and so on. Kant had denied this absolute Newtonian space as an *Unding*—as an eternal, infinite and self-subsisting nonentity. To the conception of space as a self-subsisting, absolute entity he opposed his own critical theory. Space, he declared, is not a thing; it is neither an empirical nor a metaphysical object. It is an a priori condition of all experience, a form of pure intuition. But even in his case it seemed to be obvious such an a priori form must have a definite *structure*. If this structure—as Kant took for granted—is expressed in the axioms and postulates of Euclidean geometry, then this geometry is the only one to which we can ascribe an objective validity. If there are many and different systems of geometry one of them must be true, the others must be false, or at least devoid of any empirical meaning—of any applicability to the problems of our empirical world.

How was this puzzle to be solved? For the sake of clearness

7. See ibid., I, p. 276.—Ed.

and brevity, I begin here with a personal reminiscence. I remember very well the great difficulties I felt, when I began to study the different systems of non-Euclidean geometry. At this time I was a student of Kantian philosophy. I had read *Critique of Pure Reason* with the deepest interest and a real enthusiasm. I had no doubts that the Kantian thesis—the thesis of the empirical reality and the transcendental ideality of space—contained the clue to the solution of this problem. But how was this thesis to be reconciled with the progress of geometrical thought, made in the nineteenth century? As for myself, I was quite unable to find any flaw, any vulnerable point in the new geometrical systems. Even from a philosophical and epistemological point of view they opened a much larger perspective; they were pregnant with new problems and new promises. To follow the advice of Lotze seemed to me very precarious. I think we can hardly adopt the maxim that philosophers should not allow themselves to be imposed upon by mathematical speculations. As for myself, I was very much imposed upon by thinkers like Gauss, like Riemann and Helmholtz. I could not understand that a philosopher of the rank of Lotze could speak with such a disdain of the work of these great mathematicians and scientists—but he regarded their work as one huge coherent error.

I found the escape from this dilemma when I happened to study a short article of Felix Klein titled "Vergleichende Betrachtungen über neuere geometrische Forschungen" ("Comparative Studies into Recent Geometrical Investigations")—an article that, later on, was usually quoted as the so-called *Erlanger Programm* [1872] because it was the inaugural address of Klein when he took his chair as a professor of mathematics in Erlangen.[8] Curiously enough, I had never met with the name of Felix Klein in the philosophical literature of this period. The article was by no means new; it had been published as early as in 1872. But it was written in a highly technical style; it refrained from all general metaphysical or epistemological discussions about the nature of space—and it had, therefore, failed to arouse the interest of philosophers.

8. *Gesammelte mathematische Abhandlungen* (Berlin, 1921), vol. 1. See "The Concept of Group and the Theory of Perception," 6–8.—Ed.

After having studied Klein's *Erlanger Programm* I began to see this problem in an entirely new light. What we have learned from the non-Euclidean geometries, said Klein, is that geometry is not as simple a thing as it was supposed to be in former times. We must give up our traditional view of geometry; we must seek for a new and deeper insight into the method and character of geometrical thought. This new insight was won, in this article of Klein, by the introduction of a new concept: the concept of group. The generalization of geometry, he said, leads to the following problem: "Given a multiplicity *(Mannigfaltigkeit)* and a group of transformations referring to the former; the problem is to study the elements of the multiplicity with regard to those properties which are not affected by the transformations of the group."[9]

In order to understand this definition let us begin with the simplest case. What are we studying in Euclidean geometry? The obvious answer seems to be that we are concerned with the properties of a certain thing—called "space." But this answer is not satisfactory. There are many ways to deal with spatial objects and spatial relations that have nothing to do with geometry. An artist or a natural scientist may be engaged in a study of spatial forms without, for this reason, becoming a geometer. A painter, a sculptor, or an architect may express his intentions by spatial forms—an anatomist may describe the structure of the human body, a geographer may give us his descriptions of certain parts of the earth, an astronomer a description of the solar system. But all this is not geometry. We must find a new criterion in order to define the subject matter of geometry. Not every apprehension and description of a spatial object is, by this token, a geometrical characterization. If we consider the object simply in its *hic et nunc*, looking merely at its individuality, the latter does not reveal its geometrical character and significance. By describing a spatial form as such in its particularity and concreteness, we attain, at the utmost, to its geographical or "topographical" but not to its geometrical concept.

What makes the distinction, asks Klein, between this "topographical" and a truly geometrical description? The answer is given

9. *Gesammelte mathematische Abhandlungen,* vol. 1, p. 461.—.Ed.

by the group concept. We consider as geometrical only such properties as remain unaffected by certain spatial transformations. Hence a new definition of geometry: "Geometry is distinguished from topography by the fact that only such properties of space are called geometrical as remain unchanged in a certain group of operations." In each geometry a manifold is studied with regard to a certain transformation group; the general problem is to develop the invariant theory applicable to the group. So far as Euclidean geometry is concerned, it is characterized and distinguished from other geometries, which logically are equally possible and equally justified, by the fact that it considers a special group of spatial relationships and investigates the invariant properties with respect to this group. The group in question was called by Klein the *Hauptgruppe*—the principal group. It consists of a sextuple infinity of movements, a unidimensional infinity of transformations by similarity, and the transformation by reflection in the plane. Euclidean geometry deals only with those properties of spatial figures which are independent of the location of the figures and also of their absolute magnitude; it does not distinguish between the properties of a body and those of its image produced by a mirror.

If we accept this theory of geometrical knowledge—the fact that, besides the classical geometry, the geometry of Euclid, there are other entirely consistent geometrical systems, becomes not only understandable—it becomes even necessary. In fact, What *is* a geometry? It is not a description of a certain metaphysical or empirical thing called "space." It has no *ontological,* but an *epistemological* meaning and purport; it is a mode of thinking and arguing by which we organize our experience—of spatial forms.[10] In this process of organization our mind is completely free—it has only to study its own inherent logical laws, it does not imitate or copy an outward reality. In Euclidean geometry we are studying a manifold with regard to a certain transformation group, and we are developing the invariant theory appli-

10. See also Cassirer's discussion of Euclidean and non-Euclidean geometry in *Einstein's Theory of Relativity,* trans. W. C. Swabey and M. C. Swabey, pub. with *Substance and Function* (Chicago: Open Court Publishing Co., 1923; orig. German ed. 1921), ch. 6.—Ed.

cable to this group. But it is clear that *with the choice of the group itself* we are entirely free. We may be induced by some practical reasons, or by reasons of simplicity, to choose this group rather than another. But, logically speaking, we are at liberty to pass from one group to another—and to develop the invariant theory corresponding to the latter.

In this case we have introduced a new frame of reference—and to this new frame of reference, to the new transformation group, there corresponds a new invariant theory, that is to say, a new geometry. Yet here we have to add a new determination that, epistemologically speaking, is of high importance. No geometrical system can be said to be "truer" than another. Nevertheless the different systems are not all on the same level. When comparing two systems we may find that one of them is more *general* than the other—that it includes the other as a special case. From the point of view of mathematics this generality is obviously a great advantage. Let us clarify this point by comparing the system of ordinary metrical geometry—that all of us have learned in school—with those systems of *projective geometry* that since the eighteenth and nineteenth centuries have been developed by great mathematicians, as, for instance, Poncelet, Cayley, Staudt, Möbius.

When Cayley introduced his system of descriptive geometry he claimed for it a real logical superiority. Of course he never meant to deny the truth of our ordinary metrical geometry—that would have been an absurdity—he simply meant to say that his system was more comprehensive, more universal. "Metrical geometry," Cayley said, "is a part of descriptive geometry, and descriptive geometry is all geometry and reciprocally."[11] This result is not only easily understandable, it is even necessary for the new standpoint—the standpoint of group theory. For the group at the base of projective geometry is wider than that underlying metrical Euclidean geometry. When passing from the latter to the former we must enlarge the *Hauptgruppe*, the "principal group" that characterizes Euclidean geometry. To the transformations by similarity in the usual sense there are six

11. See "Concept of Group," p. 7.—Ed.

adjoined parallel and central projections and all transformations derived from the latter.[12]

Says Klein: "Projective geometry developed only when one began to consider the original form and all those forms resulting from the latter by projection as essentially identical and to formulate the properties transferred by projection so as to make appear their independence from the alteration connected with projection."[13] Thus, what in the geometrical sense must be taken as "identical" and what as "different" is by no means predetermined at the outset. On the contrary, it is decided by the nature of the geometrical investigation, viz., the choice of a determinate group of transformations.

The progress achieved in the construction of the universe of geometrical concepts may be illustrated from another side. The transition from mere "topographical" to genuinely geometrical properties may be characterized as a progress from merely *local* to truly *spatial* determinations. All those determinations, that can be given only by "pointing," a τόδε τι, in Aristotle's sense, are "local." These determinations refer to a simple *hic et nunc* which can only be pointed at; their meaning derives from a concrete intuitive situation. From the viewpoint of ordinary sense perception, all individual differences between figures are equal in value and importance. Every particular triangle, every particular circle is to be considered as something in and by itself. Its location in space, the lengths of the sides of the triangle or of the radii, etc., belong to its "nature," which latter cannot be defined except with reference to particular local circumstances. Our geometrical concepts ignore these individual differences—or, as we usually say, they abstract from them. But the term "abstraction" itself is not very clear; it needs a sharper and more precise determination.

This determination is easily to be found if we look at Klein's theory of geometry, based on his conception of transformation group. There we find immediately that there are various *degrees* of abstraction that lead us to a higher and higher universality. From a first act of abstraction as contained in Euclidean geome-

12. H. Weyl, p. 59.—Cassirer.
13. See "Concept of Group," p. 7.—Ed.

try, we may ascend to freer, to larger and more comprehensive perspectives. The introduction of a new group of transformations always involves a completely new orientation and interpretation of the relations of spatial forms—and these various modes of interpretation are expressed by the different types of geometry. Thus modern group theory is far from denying the truth of any geometrical system; but it declares that no single system has a claim to definitiveness. Only the *totality* of possible geometrical systems is really definitive.

Each geometry is to be considered as a theory of invariants of a certain group; and these groups themselves may be classified in the order of increasing generality. The principal group of transformations which underlies Euclidean geometry permits us to establish a number of properties that are invariant with respect to the transformations in question. But when we pass from this principal group to another, by including, for example, affinitive and projective transformations, all that we had established thus far and which, from the point of view of Euclidean geometry, looked like a definitive result and a consolidated achievement, becomes fluctuating again. With every extension of the principal group some of the properties that we had taken for invariant are lost. We come to other properties that may be hierarchically arranged. Many differences that are considered as essential within ordinary metrical geometry may lose this privilege. With reference to the new group principle they appear as incidental modifications. Thus when we pass from ordinary to affinitive geometry the difference between circle and ellipse vanishes. Circle and ellipse are taken as *one* figure, since by affinitive transformations circles are transformed into ellipses.

Going a step further, when we pass to projective geometry, we meet with a still further restriction on what may be considered as an "essential" geometrical property. Now even the difference between the circle and all other conics must be abandoned. In projective geometry there is but one single conic, for any two conics are transformable into a circle and hence also into each other. From this point of view the difference between ellipse, parabola, hyperbola is no longer absolute; it concerns but the accidental position with respect to some line considered as "infinite." In another geometry, the so-called geometry of reciprocal radii, the concepts of a line or a plane, which are fundamental for Euclidean geometry, have no more independent meaning; the line is subordinated to the circle, the plane to the sphere as special cases. The same fact appears, in an even more drastic way, in one of the most universal forms of geometry, in the so-called *Analysis situs* that was first introduced by Leibniz and Euler. For *Analysis situs* there is no such thing as what is usually meant by "identity of shape." A given shape is here regarded as the "same" in spite of all sorts of distortions it may undergo—provided that these distortions are continuous. The question is no longer raised whether a given line is "straight" or "curved," whether a given length is equal to or the double of another length. The nature of a given geometry is, then, defined by the reference to a determinate group.

"The progressive separation of affinitive and projective geometry from metrical geometry," thus Klein comments on this procedure, "may be compared to the procedure of the chemist who, by applying more and more powerful decomposers, isolates more and more valuable elements from a substance; our decomposers are first the affinitive, then the projective transformation."[14] What is separated out by the latter kind of transformations is more "valuable" insofar as it proves invariant with respect to a wider group of possible changes. In affinitive and projective geometries, parallel and central projection is superadded to the principal group of transformations admitted in Euclidean geometry. *Analysis situs* leads us still farther in this direction. Considered from the modern point of view, *Analysis situs* is the most general kind of geometry, the theory of purely topological relations, entirely independent of metrical relations. In Klein's phrase, it "results, so to speak, from the most powerful corrosion"; it considers the "totality of properties that are invariant with respect to all possible one-to-one continuous transformations."

From the point of view of modern geometrical systematization, geometrical judgments, however "true" in themselves, are never-

14. Ibid., p. 30.—Ed.

theless not all equally "essential" and necessary. Modern geometry endeavors to attain progressively to more and more
fundamental strata of spatial determination. The depth of these
strata depends on the comprehensiveness of the concept of
group; it is proportional to the strictness of the conditions that
must be satisfied by the invariance that is a universal postulate
with respect to geometrical entities. Thus the objective truth and
structure of space cannot be apprehended at a single glance, but
have to be *progressively* discovered and established. If geometrical
thought is to achieve this discovery, the conceptual means that it
employs must become more and more universal.

But now let us proceed to our second problem that, at first
sight, seems to belong to quite a different field of inquiry—to the
problem of sense perception. Not only our theories of geometry
but also our theories of sense perception have, in these last
decades, undergone an essential change. Is there any connection
between the two phenomena? Psychologists were, as a rule, not
especially interested in mathematical speculations; mathematicians did not care about psychological problems. That may be
regarded as a sound division of labor; but, from the point of
view of a theory of knowledge, such a separation is of questionable value. Of course we cannot mix up the two fields of investigation; we must make a sharp distinction between the
mathematical and the psychological problem of space. But that
ought not to prevent us from looking for a connecting link
between the two problems; and I think that the concept of group
may be regarded as such a connecting link. What is sense perception; and what does it mean in the general process of human
knowledge?

All of us know the answer to this question that had been given
by the English empirical schools, and that, since the time of Berkeley and Hume, had dominated the whole psychology of the
nineteenth century. Sense perception is nothing but an aggregate or conglomerate of isolated sense data—colors, sounds, tactile, kinaesthetic data held together by the laws of
association—association of similarity or contiguity in space and
time. Such was, for instance, the thesis that had been developed
by a great physicist of the nineteenth century, by Ernst Mach, in

his book *Die Analyse der Empfindungen* [*The Analysis of Sensations*], published in 1886.[15] But this whole thesis was suddenly called into question and openly challenged by the rise of a new tendency of thought that we nowadays call Gestalt psychology. Historically, Gestalt psychology started from a simple fact. In order to make clear his concept of *Gestaltqualitäten,* Christian von Ehrenfels, in one of his first publications, referred to melodies and to the similarity of spatial figures. "A melody is not substantially altered, when all of its notes are subjected to the same relative displacement; an optical spatial figure remains approximately the same when it is presented in a different place or in a different scale, but in the same proportions."[16]

This was a very simple, we may even say a trivial observation, but it was pregnant with important consequences; it led to a fundamental change in the *method* of psychology. I need not enter here into these well-known methodological problems; they have been eagerly and thoroughly discussed in the psychological literature of the last decades. To connect the observation of Ehrenfels with the problems I have treated in the first part of this paper, we may say that a melody is a certain invariant. It remains the same, even if we change all its elements. It cannot, therefore, be described as a mere aggregate of those elements; or—as Wertheimer used to say—as a mere *Und-Verbindung.* But long before the development of Gestalt psychology—before the work of Wertheimer, Köhler, Bühler, Koffka—psychologists had been confronted with another problem that, from the point of view of our present question, is still more important and interesting. It was the problem that was termed *Wahrnehmungskonstanz*—perceptual constancy.

What does perceptual constancy mean? It means that we perceive the objects of our surroundings in approximately the same size, the same shape, the same color, even if we change, to a considerable extent, the physical conditions. If I see an object at

---

15. Cassirer is here referring to the first edition of Mach's work: *Beiträge zur Analyse der Empfindungen* (Jena, 1886), but uses the later title: *Die Analyse der Empfindungen,* 5th ed. enlarged (Jena, 1906).—Ed.

16. See "Concept of Group," p. 25.—Ed.

a certain distance *a* and, at a later moment, in a double distance *b*, the physiological conditions of the act of seeing are altered. The image on the retina is considerably reduced in size—it is not only two times but four times as small. But I scarcely notice this difference; under usual conditions I ascribe to the object the same size as I did before. The same holds for the perception of colors. Very interesting observations and experiments in this respect have been made by the distinguished physiologist Ewald Hering.[17] As Hering pointed out, even in elementary sense perception the human mind does not simply act as a *tabula rasa* or as a photographic camera which simply receives or reproduces an outward stimulus. The process is a much more complicated one; and the metaphor of the "empty table" fails to see this complexity.

To the objects of our environment we ascribe certain comparatively consistent qualities. We *attribute* to them a certain size, a certain shape, a certain color. And we continue to speak of the same shape, the same size, the same color, even when the physical conditions on which the act of sense perception depends have been considerably changed. When a sheet of paper appears "white" in ordinary daylight, we do not hesitate to recognize it as "white" in very dim light as well; for instance, in the light of the full moon. And a piece of coal which looks "black" under a cloudy sky looks also black to us in full sunshine. Considerable changes of the intensity of illumination, and, within certain limits, also of the color of illumination do not, in any appreciable degree, influence our ordinary vision of colors. A sheet of paper appears white also in the greenish shadow of foliage or in the rays of one or the other of the usual artificial sources of light, all of which emit more or less chromatic light. A piece of paper, for instance, which looks blue in daylight looks blue also in the reddish-yellow light of the gas flame.

Physicists like Helmholtz, physiologists like Hering and Johannes von Kries, psychologists like Bühler, Katz, James, etc., have developed various theories to account for this phenomenon; but the question seems still to be highly controversial, and

17. See ibid., pp. 10–12, 15–16, and 34–35.—Ed.

all these theories are open to doubt. But what is clear and what had been emphasized by almost all scholars who were engaged in the study of the phenomenon is the fact that these observations have not only a psychological, but also a great epistemological interest.

Hering, for instance, declared that the fact of perceptual constancy is one of the most important and, indeed, indispensable elements in our conception of an "objective world." Without this fact it would be impossible to segregate "things" or "properties" from the stream of becoming. To use Heraclitus' metaphor, we would be unable "to step twice in the same river." As Hering pointed out, a piece of chalk would, on a cloudy day, present the same color as a piece of coal on a sunny day; and in the course of one day it would display all possible colors intermediate between black and white. "A white flower seen under green foliage would display the same color as a green leaf in the open air, and a ball of thread, white in daylight must, in gas light, have the color of an orange."

Even ordinary sense perception could, indeed, not fulfill its task—the task of building up an objective world—if it were not able to comprehend the isolated sense data under certain group concepts and if it could not determine the "invariants" in reference to this group. In this respect sense perception is a first and elementary stage of a general process that comes to its climax and its perfection in science, in geometrical knowledge. In both cases we find, on a different scale, the same characteristic operations.

As Helmholtz pointed out, in his great work, *Physiological Optics,* we have the capacity of correcting colors that are presented in unusual illumination. We "see," we perceive them as though they appeared under normal conditions of illumination. The same holds for the perception of space. Impressions received by peripheral parts of the retina are translated into those that would result from direct perception of the object by means of the center of the retina. It is on such translations and transformations that the awareness of an "objective" world depends. Reference to typical configurations is one of the essential conditions of the process of spatial objectification. As William

James puts it in his felicitous manner: "in our dealings with objects we always do pick out one of the visual images they yield, to constitute the real form or size."[18]

James expressed the same idea in speaking of "the choice of the visual reality." The free choice of a certain transformation group proved to be one of the outstanding features of modern geometrical thought—and this free choice accounted for the possibility of different systems of geometry. But the same free choice appears already—although much less distinctly—in the act of sense perception. Even here we constantly make selections from among the vast manifold of utterly heterogeneous sense data. We give preference to certain phenomena which hence assume a privileged position. These phenomena—for example, the spatial forms that appear in orthoscopic vision by means of the central part of the retina—receive a typical value. They become centers of reference, and these centers define a kind of norm, a standard which determines the "objective" meaning and truth of our sense impressions. Sense perception, true, is not merely passive or receptive; it is an active, a selective and constructive process.

Before concluding I must, at least, mention another problem that could not be treated within the narrow compass of this short paper. In the foregoing considerations I spoke only of the importance of the concept of group in the field of mathematical and psychological investigations. It is, however, obvious that the influence of this concept extends over a much wider field. In these last decades the concept of group has become more and more prevalent in the development of modern physics. When Max Planck, in 1900, first introduced those ideas that became the cornerstone of quantum mechanics, he based his theory on a searching analysis of some experimental data that could not be accounted for by the classical theory. Neither Planck nor Niels Bohr tried to connect their views with the general theory of groups. As far as I know this step was first made in Hermann Weyl's book *Gruppentheorie und Quantenmechanik*. The first Ger-

18. *The Principles of Psychology*, 2 vols. (New York: Henry Holt, 1890), II, 238.—Cassirer.

man edition of this book was published in 1928; an English edition appeared three years later.[19]

I have followed this new development with keen interest. For here I found a new confirmation of my general conviction that the concept of group is of universal applicability and extends over the whole field of human knowledge. It is perhaps not by chance that this synthesis between the mathematical theory of group and quantum mechanics—two branches of knowledge that hitherto had been regarded as so widely separated—was made by a man who was not only one of the most distinguished mathematicians of our time but who also had a deep understanding of philosophical problems—a man who in the *Handbuch der Philosophie* had published a philosophy of mathematics and natural science.[20]

Nowadays the close connection between the mathematical theory of groups and the problems of quantum mechanics seems to be a generally acknowledged and firmly established fact. To quote only one example I mention that Eddington, in one of his last books, *The Philosophy of Physical Science,* published in 1939, declared that the conception of structure which he thinks to be the basic concept of modern physics has been made much more precise by the connection between the foundations of physics and the mathematical theory of groups. "Our knowledge of structure," says Eddington, "is communicable whereas much of our knowledge is incommunicable. Physical science consists of purely structural knowledge. . . . This is not a conjecture as to the nature of physical knowledge, it is precisely what physical knowledge as formulated in present-day theory states itself to be. In fundamental investigations the conception of group-structure appears quite explicitly as the starting point; and nowhere in the subsequent development do we admit material not derived from group-structure."[21] Here we have another striking example of the fundamental role that the group concept plays in our knowledge of the physical universe.

19. Trans. H. P. Robertson, *The Theory of Groups and Quantum Mechanics* (New York, 1932).—Ed.

20. See note 4.—Ed.

21. Cambridge: Cambridge University Press, 1939, pp. 142–43.—Cassirer.

In the foregoing remarks I could not confine myself within the limits of a special field of investigation. I had to move in the boundary region between different sciences—between mathematics, physics, psychology, epistemology. I am quite aware of the fact that in these boundary regions we cannot move forward with the same certainty as in other fields. At every new step we encounter new difficulties. We cannot follow a trodden path; we have, in a sense, to grope our way in the dark and we are liable to make many mistakes. I do not assume for a moment that I have escaped this danger. But if the journey through such a boundary region is perilous, it is, on the other hand, highly interesting and fascinating from the point of view of the philosophy of science. For all the difficulties and uncertainties we have to face we are richly compensated by the wide horizon opened to us. We find new problems; we find a broader perspective that gives us a clearer scientific and philosophic outlook. The definitive solution of this problem is beyond the powers of an individual thinker; maybe it is beyond the powers of philosophical and epistemological research in general; it will only be found by a close cooperation between various fields of investigation: mathematics, physics, psychology, philosophy.

APPENDIX: *A Description of Cassirer's Papers*

These remarks are intended to provide a broad view of Cassirer's unpublished papers considered as a whole. Scholars interested in the papers must of course examine them for themselves.

The manuscript numbers used throughout this volume are those of a card-file list which Yale University Press had prepared, after it acquired the papers, for the purpose of initially surveying their nature and contents. The papers are thus not catalogued in the usual sense of the term. This working list is not without error, but it is basically useful when used with judgment and with a knowledge of Cassirer's published works and biography. The list shows 219 items. There is a typescript of an essay on Giovanni Pico della Mirandola, which is related to a longhand draft of MS #79, which is not entered on the working list; thus the number might better be thought of as 220. Many numbers on this working list, however, designate more than one manuscript under a single number. If each manuscript were numbered separately, the list would be considerably increased.

The manuscripts are held in the Beinecke Rare Book and Manuscript Library. They are the property of Yale University Press and do not appear in the card catalogue of Beinecke Library. However, one manuscript of Cassirer is the property of the Beinecke Library and is listed in the card catalogue. This is a German longhand draft of *The Philosophy of the Enlightenment*. It does not appear on the working list prepared by Yale University Press.

Most of the manuscripts are in large manila envelopes, many of which previously have been used for mailing. Many of the envelopes are marked as to their contents. These identifications were apparently done by Mrs. Cassirer, or perhaps in some cases by Cassirer himself. The numbers on the working list give no indication of chronological order or grouping by subject, but present the manuscripts in a random sequence, perhaps as they were originally taken from their storage boxes. For example, parts of the drafts and materials relating to both *An Essay on Man* and *The Myth of the State* are dispersed throughout a wide range of manuscript numbers. Most of the manuscripts are in German longhand rather than typescript. Cassirer wrote in a good clear Latin hand. A significant number of manuscripts are in English, as Cassirer wrote in English during his stay in Oxford and in his years in the United States.

I have not approached the manuscripts as a cataloguer but I have had the opportunity over several visits to familiarize myself with them and I have gone through them systematically and examined each one while making notes. As my interest led me to specific manuscripts, I did not give equal attention to all. Thus the following estimations are not exact bibliographic analyses but are intended as observations which may answer some preliminary questions on the general character of the papers.

A major division within the papers can be made between those which are drafts of published works and those which are without specific relation to published materials.

1. Approximately two-thirds of the manuscripts are drafts, partial drafts, or notes relating to published essays and books. These are in typescript and longhand and they cover the whole range of Cassirer's career. There are manuscripts of many of Cassirer's essays and there are longhand manuscripts of many major works, such as the three volumes of the *Erkenntnisproblem,* the second and third volumes of *The Philosophy of Symbolic Forms, Kants Leben und Lehre, Freiheit und Form, Substance and Function, An Essay on Man, The Myth of the State,* and others. The drafts relating to *An Essay on Man* show that it went through one or more earlier versions.

2. The remaining one-third of the papers constitute the second major category, that of papers not clearly related to specific published works. (a) Approximately half the items in this category are course lectures and notes. (b) The other half are materi-

als of more independent status: manuscripts, partial manuscripts, or schematic notes of essays, lectures, and works. (c) In addition there are a few items classifiable as miscellaneous, including, for example, notes from Cassirer's student days, some corrected page proofs, probably from Cassirer's edition of Leibniz, odd sheets of notes, several lists of book titles written in examination blue books, and several letters written to Cassirer on routine matters.

a. The course lectures and notes range across Cassirer's entire teaching career. There are some lectures from Cassirer's Berlin years, marked for various summer and winter semesters between 1908 and 1911 (MS #101), concerning such topics as *Erkenntnistheorie, Naturphilosophie,* and *Grundfragen der Logik.* There is also a long manuscript of a course in Greek philosophy (MS #112). There is some material written out, marked *"Grundprobleme der Kulturphilosophie,"* and dated for the summer semesters of 1927 and 1929, from Cassirer's Hamburg period (MS #131). From Cassirer's stay in England, there is a first lecture for a seminar on Leibniz, marked "1933–34" (MS #45), written out in English, although the course was taught in German. There is a written-out course of lectures on Hegel, marked "Oxford 1934" (MS #46), and a long manuscript of a lecture on Plato marked "Oxford 1935" (MS #50).

There are systematic notes for a course of lectures, *Geschichte der philosophischen Anthropologie,* dated September 1, 1939, to January 15, 1940 (MS #139), from Cassirer's years in Sweden. There are lectures for courses or parts of courses for most of the seminars that Cassirer taught at Yale, which have been discussed in the introduction to this volume, and parts of which appear herein. There is also a large set of lectures for what was probably an undergraduate course in Greek philosophy taught at Yale (MS #8) and some material from Cassirer's teaching at Columbia, relating probably to his course for the winter semester of 1944–45 on the origin and nature of political myth (e.g., MS #171). The above are some representative items from the category of course material.

b. Among those manuscripts which are not part of course

material, and which do not appear in this volume, are two items
of particular note: Cassirer's notes from his lectures at the Second Davos University Courses, which he participated in with
Heidegger in 1929 (MS #94); and a partial draft and notes (MS
#184) for the volume which Cassirer mentions in the preface to
volume 3 of *The Philosophy of Symbolic Forms,* for which he
advances the title of *"Leben" und "Geist"—zur Kritik der Philosophie
der Gegenwart.* Cassirer's notes for the Davos meeting are not
very long—forty-three pages of copybook size and ten pages on
some additional folded sheets. They match generally with the
subject matter of the problems of space, language, and death,
particularly space and death, that are described in the *Davoser
Revue* as constituting Cassirer's three course lectures at the conference, which I have discussed in the introduction.

MS #184 is identified as *The Philosophy of Symbolic Forms,* vol.
4. It seems clearly to be Cassirer's draft of that study which he
indicated would follow the third volume and would critically
relate the philosophical position of the philosophy of symbolic
forms as a philosophy of *Geist* to other philosophies, principally
"philosophies of life." The first part of this manuscript is a draft
of 284 pages, in longhand, of booklet-sized pages, with a date of
June 16, 1928. It has the title "Toward the Metaphysics of the
Symbolic Forms," and has two chapters, the first concerning
"spirit" and "life" and the second on the problem of the symbol
as the fundamental problem of philosophical anthropology. This
is followed by a packet of notes indicating that Cassirer intended
to trace out historically the distinction between "spirit" and "life"
from the Greeks forward. There is also some material indicating
a critique of Bergson, whom Cassirer associated with his general
category of "life-philosophy," and some notes marked "Material:
Scheler-Vortrag, Wien 1928" (probably related to the lecture
which Cassirer gave on Scheler at Davos and later published as
an essay in 1930; see the introduction to this volume). There is a
sheet where Heidegger's name is listed along with Klages,
Scheler, Pascal, Hegel, and Kierkegaard. Following this is material titled "Historical Part," indicating that Cassirer intended to
trace the problem of "spirit" and "life" from Descartes through
modern idealism. The problems with which Cassirer is dealing in

this material can be found in Cassirer's article, dealing mostly with Scheler, but titled " 'Geist' and 'Leben' in der Philosophie der Gegenwart," which appeared in *Die Neue Rundschau* in 1930 (translated in the Library of Living Philosophers volume on Cassirer), but the manuscript bears examination.

One question is why Cassirer never published this material or, for that matter, never really finished writing the volume. One answer may be that he felt that his single article of almost the same title as the publication which he promised in volume 3 of *The Philosophy of Symbolic Forms* was sufficient. Another may be that he decided that *The Philosophy of Symbolic Forms* constituted a work of constructive philosophy and that a volume of criticism, when he actually worked it out, did not appear to be a proper part of this work.

The other writings and manuscripts that fall into this category of material not related to Cassirer's courses are diverse and in various states of order. They involve, for example, some special lectures and writings on historical figures and topics, some small political addresses, and some discussions of epistemological subjects.

c. The papers contain no correspondence. There is an occasional miscellaneous letter; for example, a letter to Cassirer from Hanna Hafkesbrink, concerning the typing of Cassirer's lecture at Connecticut College in 1944, and a letter from Ake Petzält, editor of *Theoria*. The main sources of Cassirer's correspondence are those letters and portions of letters quoted by Toni Cassirer (1883–1961) in *Aus meinem Leben mit Ernst Cassirer* (1950), and Cassirer's letters to Paul Schilpp, regarding the planning of the Library of Living Philosophers series volume on his thought, which are in the special collections section of the library at Southern Illinois University, Carbondale.

Although not related to the character of the papers as such, it may be of interest to scholars concerned with Cassirer's thought to know that Cassirer's personal library, which for a period of years following his death was housed in a seminar room in Sterling Memorial Library at Yale University, was purchased by the University of Illinois at Chicago Circle, in the spring of 1966. At that time Cassirer's library was approximately 2,500 volumes.

Volumes of first and rare editions from Cassirer's library, of which there are a significant number, and some with marginalia, are held in the special collections and rare book section of the Circle Campus library; others were dispersed throughout the general collection.

Index

Absolute idealism. *See* Hegel, idealism of

Aesthetics: form of, 211–14; Kant's approach to, 86, 87; role of symbolic form in, 24–25, 28, 30–31. *See also* Art

Alchemy, 263–65

Analysis situs, 284

Animals: experience of, 168–69, 171, 172; language of, 150–51, 179–80

Anti-Semitism, 238–41

Anxiety, 176

Aphasia, 149

A priori knowledge, Kant's theory of, 52, 53

Aristotle: definition of matter, 75; Goethe's characterization of, 50–51; on imitation, 204; theory of catharsis, 198–99, 211

Art: cathartic effect of, 198–99, 211; contemplation of, 212; correlation with symbolic forms, 24–25, 29, 31–32; creative expression through, 208–09; educational value of, 201–02, 204, 210, 215; emotionalism of, 192, 207–08; interpretation of reality through, 193; intuition in, 186, 187, 188–89; Kant's approach to, 86, 87–88; language of, 76–77, 86; lyricism in, 210; passion in, 163–64; perceptual approach of, 186; place in culture, 145–46, 162–63, 165; Plato's opinion of, 147, 163, 196–98, 201; purpose of, 200–01; relation to language, 158–59, 191; relation to morality, 87–88; relation to myth, 188, 191; value of, 154–57, 160, 199–200, 211

Astrology, 261–65

Ausdruck, 77n

Ausdrucksfunktion, 3–4, 5, 31

Autonomy of reason, 84–85

Bacon, Francis, 153–54, 184, 264

Batteaux, Charles, 205

Beauty: in art and nature, 212–14; as intuitive approach to reality, 155; Kantian definition of, 186, 191

Bedeutung, 77n

Being, as process, 194

Berkeley, George, 67–68

Bible, Spinoza's study of, 99

Bill of Rights, American, 221–22

Bing, Gertrude, 78

Biogenesis, 125

Biology: expression of processes of, 158, 208; logical structure of, 124–25

Bohr, Niels, 76

Burke, Edmund, 224

Cassirer, Ernst: biography of, 16–24; emigration from Germany of, 4, 7, 20; Kant's influence on, 3, 4, 6, 9, 15, 17; method of, 7–9, 10; neo-Kantian origins of, 4–5, 15

Cassirer, H. W., 20

Catharsis, 198–99, 211

Cauchy, Augustin Louis, 274

Causality, historical, 83, 128–29, 131–34

Cayley, Arthur, 281

Christina, Queen of Sweden, 11, 97

Cicero, 259

Civilization, Vico's philosophy of, 103–07

Cohen, Hermann, 2, 4–5, 6

Collective spirit, 231, 252, 257–58

Collingwood, R. G., 157, 192, 208–09

Columbia University, Cassirer as professor at, 23

Comte, Auguste, 127–28, 265

Conceptus cosmicus, 9, 58–59

Condorcet, Marquis de (M. de Caritat), 221

Consciousness, 3–4, 32

Contemplation of art, 212

Correspondence, principle of, 76

Critical idealism, 70–71, 80–81, 89–90

Croce, Benedetto, 156–57, 158, 160–61, 190, 206–07, 213

Culture: aim of, 72–73; Cassirer's theory of, 9–10; causality in study of, 83, 128–29, 131–34; conditions determining, 127–28, 132–33, 168; correspondence to language, 73–74, 106–07; dependence on symbols, 12–13; dynamic nature of, 107n, 137–38; ethics in study of, 81, 82, 83–85; idealism as philosophy for, 64–65, 70–71, 80–81; morality as basis of, 84–85; mythical thought in, 86–87, 235, 243–46; as objectification of experience, 167; philosophy of history applied to, 82–83; relation to freedom, 10–13, 83–84, 88–90; relation of philosophy to, 10–12, 32; Schweitzer's view of, 59–60; significance of, 57–58, 72; symbolic nature of, 137

Darstellungsfunktion, 3–4, 5, 77n
Darwin, Charles, 173, 208
Dasein, Cassirer-Heidegger debates on, 35–38, 40
Declaration of the Rights of Man and of Citizens, 221–22, 223
Decline of the West, The (Spengler), 259–63
DeLaguna, Grace, 177
Descartes (Cassirer), 11
Descartes, René: approach to history of, 96–98; Cassirer's study of, 6, 11, 20–21, 43; definition of matter by, 75; monism of science, 121–22
Determinism: Spengler's, 260–62; in study of culture, 83
Determinism and Indeterminism in Modern Physics (Cassirer), 5
Dialectic method, 146
Diderot, Denis, 123–24
Dilthey, Wilhelm, 17
Doutté, E., 237–38, 250–51

Eddington, Arthur Stanley, 290
Ehrenfels, Christian von, 286
Einstein's Theory of Relativity (Cassirer), 27
Erkenntnisproblem in der Philosophie und Wissenschaft der neueren Zeit, Das (Cassirer), 2–3, 16–17, 21
Essay on Man, An (Cassirer), 4, 12, 13

Ethics: dependence on symbols, 12–13; Fichte's subjective approach to, 112; Greek classification of, 70; religious, 76–77; Schweitzer's view of, 59–60; in study of culture, 81, 82, 83–85
Euthymia, 199
Existence: problem of defining, 81–82; as a process, 194
Expression: art as, 157–61; in biological processes, 158, 208

Fatalism: of Heidegger, 229–30; of Spengler, 227–29, 262–63
Fichte, Johann Gottlieb, 112, 223
Fixation, 152, 181–82
Form and content, Cassirer's interpretation of, 7
Franklin, Benjamin, 223
Freedom: as aim of history, 84–85; as aim of philosophy, 10, 88; Cassirer's views on, 10, 39, 40–41; ethical character of, 257; Hegelian idealism and, 114, 227; Heidegger's views on, 39–40; relation to culture, 10–13, 83–84, 88–90; in systems of natural right, 111–12
Freiheit und Form (Cassirer), 17
French Revolution, 221, 222, 223–24; Hegel's criticism of, 116
Function-concepts, 3–4, 5

Galois, Évariste, 274
Gardiner, A. H., 150, 179–80
Geisteswissenschaften, Vico as founder of, 43
Genius, 191
Geometries: group concept applied to, 279–84; problem of defining space in, 275–77, 279
Gestalt psychology, 286
Geworfenheit, 229
Goethe, Johann Wolfgang von: on classical philosophers, 50–51; influence on Cassirer, 18, 26; as lyric poet, 209–10
Government, correspondence of, to development of culture, 106
Group, concept of: applied to perceptual constancy, 288–89; applied to theory of knowledge, 273, 275, 285–90; in mathematics, 273–75, 279–85

Haeckel, Ernst Heinrich, 125
Hägerström, Axel, 21
Hamann, Georg, 102, 107, 184
Haym, Rudolph, 115
Hedonism, aesthetic, 201–04
Hegel, Georg Wilhelm Friedrich: on art, 155–56; Cassirer's assessment of, 43–44; on freedom, 114; idealism of, 79–80, 88, 89, 109–10, 113, 227; influence on Cassirer, 6; on reason, 62; theory of the state of, 111–20, 225–26, 227
Heidegger, Martin: debates with Cassirer, 36–38; fatalism of, 229–30; influence on Cassirer's view of culture, 4, 32–33, 36–37; review of The Philosophy of Symbolic Forms by, 34–35; on freedom, 229–30
Heller, Hermann, 115
Hendel, Charles, 22
Heraclitus, 72, 192
Herder, Johann Gottfried von, 102, 107, 171
Hering, Ewald, 287, 288
Hertz, Henrich, 28
History, philosophy of: Cassirer's approach to, 10, 22; causality in, 83, 128–29, 131–34; Descartes's approach to, 96–98; determinism in, 260–62; interpretation of, 129–30, 135–39; Kant's approach to, 84–86; Leibniz's approach to, 100–02; relation to science, 122–23, 126–28, 130–31, 138–39; sense of time in, 80; in study of culture, 82–83; Vico's approach to, 103–07
Hitler, Adolf, 238, 240–41
Humboldt, Wilhelm von, 56, 73, 189, 288
Husserl, Edmund, 33, 229

Idealism: of Berkeley, 67–68; critical, 89–90, in ethics, 13; growth of, 43–44; Hegelian, 79–80, 88, 89, 109–10, 113, 227; in human activities, 3; Kantian, 68, 69, 86–88; as philosophy of culture, 64–65; Platonic, 52, 53, 65–67; relation to realism, 51
Ideas, Platonic doctrine of, 65–67
Individual and the Cosmos in Renaissance Philosophy, The (Cassirer), 4
Imagination, Spinoza's definition of, 99
Infinity, 38–39

Interjectional theory of language, 177
Intuition: in art, 186, 187, 188–89; Spinoza's definition of, 99

Jackson, John H., 149, 180–81
James, William, 172, 288–89
Jellinek, Georg, 221–22
Jespersen, Otto, 177–79
Judgment, Kant's approach to art through faculty of, 86, 87
Judaism, German campaign against, 238–41

Kant, Immanuel: on art, 86, 87–88; on freedom, 257; idealism of, 68, 69, 86–88; influence on Cassirer, 3, 4, 6, 9, 15, 17; on moral law, 58–59, 222–23; opposition to Berkeley, 68–69; philosophical method of, 50–55; philosophy of history of, 84–86; on religion, 86–87; on science, 123; on space, 277
Kants Leben und Lehre (Cassirer), 3
Kepler, Johannes, 263
Kierkegaard, Søren, 176
Kirchoff, Gustav Robert, 125–26
Klein, Felix, 274, 278–80, 284
Klibansky, Raymond, 20
Knowledge: concept of group applied to, 273, 275, 285–90; consciousness as basis for, 3–4; continuity of scientific, 123–24; culture as, 10; Descartes's approach to, 96, 98; historical form of, 130–31; objectification in, 166–67; philosophy applied to, 27; relation to reality, 67; Spinoza's theory of, 99
Kroner, Richard, 109

Language(s): aim of, 182, 183, 185; animal, 150–51, 179–80; comparison of different, 182–83; correspondence to cultural development, 73–74, 106–07; Descartes's view of, 98; disciplinary nature of, 76–77; evolution of, 153; fixation through, 152, 181–82; Herder on origin of, 171; Kant's theories applied to, 147–48; lyricism in, 190; of National Socialists, 254–55; necessity of, 145, 148, 152–53, 165; Plato's views on, 146–47; poetic, 188–89; propositional vs. emo-

Language(s) (continued)
  tional, 149–50, 181; relation to art, 158–
  59, 161–63; relation to myth, 176–77,
  245; religious, 76–77; scientific, 75–76,
  154, 184–85; symbolic function of, 179–
  80, 183, 185; theoretical origins of, 171,
  177–79
Lamprecht, Karl, 133–34
Langer, Susanne, 25
Leadership, totalitarian, 252–53, 258
Leibniz, Gottfried Wilhelm von, 6, 100,
  171
Lévy-Bruhl, Lucien, 244
Lie, Sophus, 274
Linguistics, Humboldt's study of, 56
Locke, John, 169–70
Logic: Greek classification of, 70; of his-
  tory, 130–31; in language, 190; Leibniz's
  view of, 100
Lotze, Rudolf Hermann, 11, 276–77
Lyricism, 190, 205, 206n, 210; Croce's
  theory of, 206–07

Mach, Ernst, 285–86
Machiavelli, Niccolò, 113–14
Magical thought, 176, 250–51, 265–66
Malebranche, Nicolas de, 98
Malinowski, Bronislaw, 249
Marburg School of Neo-Kantianism, 2, 4–6
Marx, Karl, 115, 127, 132
Mathematics: concept of group in, 273–75,
  279, 281–85, 290; Vico's opinion of,
  103–04
Matter, 74, 75–76
Metaphysics, 54, 99
Montesquieu, Baron de (Secondat), 127
Millennium, idea of, 238, 259
Monad, Leibniz's theory of the, 101
Morality: as basis of culture, 84–85; Kant-
  ian view of, 85–86; relation to art, 87–
  88; relation to philosophy, 57–59, 60–61
Motion, symbolic nature of, 74
Müller, Max, 177
Myth: Cassirer's approach to, 10, 13–14;
  collective spirit of, 257–58; danger of,
  234–38, 244–47, 265–66; effect on politics, 265–66; in evolution of science, 87;
  in human cultural activities, 86–87, 235,
  243–46; organization in, 172–75, 187;

  phenomenological issues of, 33–35; purpose of, 237; relation to art, 188, 191;
  relation to language, 176–77, 245; relation to philosophy, 266–67; role in
  primitive society, 247–51. See also Political myth
Myth of the State, The (Cassirer), 4, 10,
  13–14

Nationalism: Montesquieu's physical presuppositions for, 127; Schweitzer's opinion of, 231
National Socialist movement (Germany),
  230; anti-Semitism of, 236–41; language
  of, 254–55
Natorp, Paul, 5
Neo-Kantianism, 2–5, 9
Newton, Isaac, 220

Objectification, 166–67, 172, 189; in mythical thought, 172–75; in speech, 180
Onomatopoetic theory of language, 177
Oxford University, Cassirer's appointment
  to, 20

Paton, H. J., 20
Pearson, Karl, 74
Perception, 285–86; as approach to art,
  186; as basis for truth, 67; concept of
  group allied to, 288–89; constancy of,
  286–88; underlying symbolic forms,
  29–31
Philosophy: Cassirer's view of, 9, 19, 27,
  43, 53–54, 57, of culture, 64–65, 70–73,
  80–83; ethical dimensions of, 32, 40, 41–
  42, 84–85; Greek classification of, 70;
  Heidegger's and Schweitzer's differing
  views of, 32–33; importance to society
  of, 10–12; Kantian, 52–55; moral
  responsibility of, 231–32; opposite elements in, 50–52; relation to culture, 57–
  62; relation to freedom, 39, 40–41;
  relation to myth, 266–67; role of, 219–
  20, 226, 230; scholastic conception of,
  58; as study of forms, 81
Philosophy of the Enlightenment, The (Cassirer), 4
Philosophy of Symbolic Forms, The (Cassirer),
  3–4, 27–29, 30, 34–36

Physics: classification of knowledge in, 125–26; Greek classification of, 70

Planck, Max, 289

Plato: on art, 147, 163, 196–98, 201; Cassirer's view of, 53; Goethe's characterization of, 50–51; on language, 146–47; on religion, 176

Plotinus, 160

Poetry, 161–63, 184; educational value of, 197–98; language of, 188–89

Political myth; 234–38; 246–47, 258–59; collective spirit of, 257–58; danger of, 234–38, 244–47, 265–66; ideological struggles through, 234, 252; magical element of, 265–66; passion of, 238; philosophy in relation to, 264–67

Polytheism, 175

Power, in Hegel's theory of the state, 117–18

Primitive society, role of myth in, 247–51

Problem of Knowledge, The (Cassirer), 21–22

Psychopathology, 149

Quantum mechanics: concept of group applied to, 289–90; effect on physical concepts, 75–76

Rationalism, 100, 103–04, 220–21, 225

Realism, 51

Reality: art's approach to, 154–55; as process, 194; identity with knowledge, 67

Reason: as aim of history, 169–71; autonomy of, 84–85; dynamic nature of, 62; Spinoza's definition of, 99; as substance, 110

Relativity, theory of, 75

Religion: ethical advancement of, 240, 240n; language of, 76–77; Kant's approach to, 86–87; organization of mythical thought in, 175

Rights of man, 221–25; Hegelian state in relation to, 225–26; as necessity of philosophy, 57–58

Rites, 256, 257–58

Roman culture, magic practice in, 259

Rosenberg, Alfred, 262

Rousseau, Jean-Jacques, 57–58, 205–06

Santayana, George, 202

Saussure, Ferdinand de, 152, 183, 189

Saxl, Fritz, 90, 91n

Schelling, Friedrich von, 13, 155, 234, 243

Schleiermacher, Friedrich Ernst, 175–76

Schopenhauer, Arthur, 68

Schulbegriff ("scholastic" conception of philosophy), 9

Schweitzer, Albert, 32–33, 59–60, 230–31

Science: Cassirer's philosophy of, 19–20; classification of, 70, 121, 124–26; Descartes's approach to, 121–22; Kant's view of, 55, 123; language of, 75–76, 154, 184–85; mythical thought in evolution of, 87; occult science in relation to, 263–64; relation to history, 122–23, 126–28, 130–31, 138–39; symbolization of, 28, 29, 32, 74–76

Sensationalism, 159–60

Sense perception. See Perception

Set theory, 274–75

Shaftesbury, Anthony Ashley, 102n

Sophists, 146, 147

Space: concept of group applied to, 288–89; problem of defining, 275–77, 280, 285

Spengler, Oswald: Cassirer's rejection of, 32, 41–42, 61; view of history, 226–29, 230, 259–63

Spinoza, Baruch, 99, 101

State: dialectic process of, 120; Hegel's theory of the, 44–45, 111–20, 225–26, 227; myth of the, 45; naturalistic, 117; natural-right theories of the, 221–25; Plato's theory of the, 197–98. See also Political myth

Substance and Function (Cassirer), 3, 5, 17

Substance-concepts, 3–4, 5, 101, 110

Symbolic forms: Cassirer's development of, 17, 26–30; distinction of man by, 12–13; influence on art, 24–25, 29, 31; of language, 73–74, 154, 185; perception as basis for, 29–31; in science, 28, 29, 32, 74–75, 154, 185; unity of, 71

Symbolic pregnance, 30–31

Taine, H. A., 132–33, 134, 139–41

Thorndike, Lynn, 87, 264

Time, 80, 101–02

Tolstoi, Leo, 163, 199, 200–01
Tragedy, Aristotle's theory of, 198–99, 211
Transcendental idealism, 69–71, 80–81, 89–90
Transcendental method, Kant's use of the, 54–55
Transformation groups, 274–75, 280–83, 289
Truth: Descartes's approach to, 96, 100; Hegelian idealism applied to, 110; Leibniz's approach to, 100; perception as basis for, 67; Platonic theory of, 67; political myth in relation to, 237

Uexküll, Johannes von, 12, 168
Usener, Hermann, 174

Vico, Giambattista influence on Cassirer, 6, 13, 43; philosophy of civilization, 103–07

Vischer, Friedrich Theodor, 26–27
Vitalism, modern, 124
Vossler, Karl, 190

Warburg, Aby, 77n, 78–79
Warburg Institute Library: classification of books in, 77n; influence on Cassirer, 18, 78–79, 90–91, 91n
Weimar Republic, 236
Weltbegriff (concept of philosophy as related to the world), 9, 11
Weyl, Hermann, 273, 289–90
Windelband, Wilhelm, 122
Wordsworth, William, 188, 193

Yale University, Cassirer's professorship at, 22
Young, Edward, 164